A THEORY OF PHRASE MARKERS AND THE EXTENDED BASE

SUNY Series in Linguistics
Mark Aronoff, editor

A THEORY OF PHRASE MARKERS AND THE EXTENDED BASE

Robert A. Chametzky

State University of New York Press

Published by
State University of New York Press, Albany

Printed in the United States of America

For information, address State University of New York Press, State University Plaza, Albany, NY 12246

Production by Dana Foote
Marketing by Fran Keneston

Library of Congress Cataloging-in-Publication Data

Chametzky, Robert A.
A theory of phrase markers and the extended base / Robert Chametzky.
p. cm. — (SUNY series in linguistics)
Includes bibliographical references (p.) and index.
ISBN 0-7914-2971-7. — ISBN 0-7914-2972-5 (pbk.)
1. Phrase structure grammar. 2. Grammar, Comparative and general—Syntax. 3. Generative grammar. I. Title. II. Series.
P158.3.C48 1996
415—dc20 95-26184
CIP

10 9 8 7 6 5 4 3 2 1

For Ann,

. . . Nothing but blue skies from now on . . .

It is the business of the theorist to inspect the tools and to ask that they be cleaner.

—Rudolf Arnheim,
Film as Art

CONTENTS

ACKNOWLEDGMENTS

I had to do this one pretty much by myself. My erstwhile Iowa colleagues Bill Davies, Alice Davison, and Chris Culy read and commented on various drafts of this book, much to its benefit. The time and mental energy they spent on a project that, after all, had very little to do with their own syntactic work or interests is a tribute to both their generosity and their professionalism. John Richardson had—and shared—the original insight into C-command, and my response to not getting versions of chapter 2 into print was to write this book. John has also been willing to continue discussing matters of linguistic theory over the years and over the Net. Teun Hoekstra is unique among journal editors: willing to listen, to argue, and, *mirabile dictu,* to even admit having made a mistake—I am grateful nearly as much for the argument as for the admission. I wish I could thank the linguists to whom I sent versions (or pieces) of this work, the editors and readers for the journals to which I submitted parts of it, and the audiences that heard me deliver talks based on it; unfortunately, such response as I have received has been depressingly uniform in its combination of the idiotic with the irrelevant, so there is no one to thank. It is no doubt likely that the work is a poorer thing thereby; I take some consolation in that it is also thereby more mine own.

The College of Liberal Arts at the University of Iowa supported this work with an Old Gold Summer Stipend in 1989 and with a semester's leave in autumn 1991. I am grateful for the time and the money.

I spent that leave in New York City, writing the first draft of this book. I lived there with my old friend Ben DeMott, in his apartment on Claremont Avenue. I also wrote the second draft there, the next summer. My thanks to Ben for sharing that too rare a possession, a place to write and think seriously—that we wrote on such different subjects (and even on different computers) probably did not hurt. My thanks, too, to my college teacher the late Robert Austerlitz, who got me visiting scholar status at Columbia that fall.

My parents, Jules and Anne (Halley) Chametzky, apparently gave me such unstinting and unearned love and support as a child that I seem not to require a lot in the way of external approval as an adult. This has proven most helpful in seeing this project to completion.

Were it not for the gentle reproofs of my wife, Ann Fennell, the manuscript would be in a box in a file drawer somewhere—indeed, had she been any less gentle, or any more reproving, it probably would be there still. Somehow, she got it just right, which is typical of her, and which is why this book is dedicated to her.

Material in Chapter 1 is reprinted with permission from Robert Chametzky, "Dominance, Precedence, and Parameterization," *Lingua* 96, nos. 2-3 (1995): 163-78, Elsevier Science B.V., Amsterdam, The Netherlands.

Material in Chapter 4 is reprinted with permission from Robert Chametzky, "Chomsky-Adjunction," *Lingua* 93, no. 4 (1994): 245-64, Elsevier Science B.V., Amsterdam, The Netherlands.

INTRODUCTION

0.0

When syntax is done, it typically looks something like the following. A set of sentences is presented and a proposal is given for how and why such sentences are licensed by the syntactic theory employed. Then, or perhaps simultaneously, a set of nonsentences is presented, and it is argued that the account of the sentences also accounts for why these examples are not sentences. Finally, some more sentences and nonsentences are introduced, and it is shown that the account either extends to these immediately or that these examples require some adjustment in the original proposal, which adjustment is natural and easy.

There is very little of this in the essay that follows.

0.1

Instead, the essay that follows is a theoretical work. Because the sort of work just described is usually called "*theoretical syntax,*" I suppose this requires some discussion.

0.2

There are three sorts of work that can generally be distinguished in empirical inquiry. One is metatheoretical, a second is theoretical, and the third is analytic. As is often the case, the boundaries are not sharp, and so the types shade off one into the other, but the distinctions are real enough for the core cases. I take up each in turn.

Metatheoretical work is theory of theory, and divides into two sorts: general and (domain) specific. *General* metatheoretical work is concerned with developing and investigating adequacy conditions for any theory in any domain. So, for example, it is generally agreed that theories should be (1) consistent and coherent, both internally and with other well-established theories; (2) explicit; and (3) simple. This sort of work is philosophical in nature (see, e.g., Sober 1975). *Specific* metatheoretical work is concerned with adequacy conditions for theory in a particular domain. So, for example, in linguistics we have Chomsky's (1964; 1965) familiar distinctions among observational, descriptive, and explanatory adequacy. Whether such work is "philosophy" or, in this case, "linguistics" seems to me a pointless question.

Theoretical work is concerned with developing and investigating primitives, derived concepts, and architecture within a particular domain of inquiry. This work will also deploy and test concepts developed in metatheoretical work against the results of actual theory construction in a domain, allowing for both evaluation of the domain theory and sharpening of the metatheoretical concepts. Note this well: **deployment** of metatheoretical concepts is *not* metatheoretical work; it is theoretical work.

Analytic work is concerned with investigating the (phenomena of the) domain in question. It deploys and tests concepts and architecture developed in theoretical work, allowing for both understanding of the domain and sharpening of the theoretical concepts. Note this well: **deployment** of theoretical concepts is *not* theoretical work, it is analytic work. Analytic work is what overwhelmingly most linguists do overwhelmingly most of the time. This is as it should, and indeed must, be: an empirical discipline only exists insofar as there is a community of scientists investigating the domain. For linguistics to be the science of language, this must be where linguists do their work.

Linguists tend to confuse analytic work with theoretical work, and theoretical work with metatheoretical work. Thus, as noted, the type of work described in the opening paragraph, which is essentially analytic, is called "theoretical," and work such as in this essay, which is essentially theoretical, when done at all is called "metatheoretical," if anything.

Linguists typically distinguish not among the three sorts of work described above, but rather between "theoretical" and "descriptive" work, where both of these are better understood as analytic work with, respectively, more or less explicit reliance on and reference to a specific framework and its concepts and architecture. Therefore, it will be true that such "theoretical" work will, in general, be more likely than "descriptive" work to impinge on purely theoretical issues and concerns. This distinction between "theoretical" and "descriptive" is not only ill-conceived, but also, for reasons I do not fully understand, invidious. The tripartite distinction discussed above involves no evaluative component for or ranking of the three sorts of work, other than the noted priority of analytic work in constituting any empirical discipline.

With these general considerations out of the way, I return to the the main discussion.

0.3

Mostly, syntax as described in Section 0.0 is about possible sentences. The theory proposed and developed here is a theory about possible base phrase structures. The claim to be advanced is that the theory will limit the range of possible structures (for sentences) in ways that are linguistically significant. The theory of structures, then, is the motor for analysis.

This should be contrasted with the usual approach, which is concerned with structures only derivatively. That is, in general, structures are the result of an analysis in terms of other principles, rather than being either the result of a theory of structure or a basis for analysis. So, for example, an analysis might be done in terms of Conditions A and B of the Binding Theory, which require that a certain structural relation (e.g., C-command or M-command) holds between positions in a phrase marker. So, typically, it is concluded that the structure is therefore whatever it has to be for the analysis in terms of Binding Theory to go through. In this approach, structure is not the motor of the analysis; it is, so to say, an effect, not a cause. I have no principled objection to this style of inquiry. But it is a style, and not the one I employ here. Instead, I propose to directly theorize about and work with structure.

This work is, then, generally at one remove from the data that ordinarily engage working syntacticians, even "theorists."

One more observation is in order before outlining the chapters. An inquiry of this sort presupposes a great deal of the sort that it is not: in order to take as given the structural facts I do, much analysis has to have been done (by others) in order to "give" those facts. Theoretical work that ignores the findings of analytic work is not merely intellectually irresponsible, it is also likely to be entirely irrelevant.

1.0

The essay is organized as follows. Chapter 1 introduces the phrase structure theory. The theory is developed first in its formal aspect, with a discussion of definitions for phrase markers (PMs). PMs are understood to be collocations of nodes and labels. The theory of the base is the theory of (well-formed) PMs. A particular, minimal proposal is adopted for defining PMs—one that has no formal primitive of *precedence,* but only a formal primitive of *dominance.* A new argument against precedence as a primitive is developed, and the exclusion of precedence as a formal primitive also serves to explain a previously unnoticed asymmetry with respect to parameterization of dominance versus precedence mediated relations and predicates.

Next the substantive ("X-Bar") aspect of the theory is elaborated. Again, a particular, minimal proposal is adopted (basically, that of Speas (1990)). The two aspects are independent but, it is argued, reinforce one another. I call the result the *Minimal Phrase Structure Theory* (MPST).

1.1

Chapter 2 pursues the formal vector of the MPST. An account of C-command (and other command relations) is developed which flows from the bases of the MPST. I argue that PMs of the form the MPST licenses naturally lead one to C-command as it is herein explicated. That conception of C-command is non-standard but well-motivated. Crucial to the argument are (1) the fact that the MPST has no primitive precedence relation, and (2) reorienting our view of C-command to ask, "what set of nodes C-command node A?" rather than "does Node B C-command Node A?." The core insight is that C-command has no specifically linguistic content. Other approaches to (C-)command are examined in some detail, as the argument is that the nonstandard assumptions of the present work allow for insight into understanding (C-)command that the standard assumptions do not.

1.2

Chapters 3 & 4 largely follow the substantive vector and develop what I call the "extended base." The central idea here is that not all base structures are licensed by the MPST as characterized in Chapter 1. Instead, some base structures are "derived structures." This may strike a few as paradoxical, so some comment may be in order.

First, it should be recalled that, at least in early versions of transformational grammar, what we call base structures were derived, if we mean by "base structures" the output of the phrase structure rules. Until McCawley (1968) suggested interpreting phrase structure rules as node admissibilty conditions—well-formedness conditions on representations—these rules were understood to be string-to-string rewrite rules which applied in a derivation. And even earlier, in Chomsky (1955/1985), a PM is understood as the set of all the lines that occur in the equivalent phrase structure derivations of a sentence. So, the idea that all "derived structures" are **transformationally** derived is not one that is constant in the history of generative syntax.

Second, it is not exactly clear why anyone would object *in principle* to the notion of "derived base structures." It is not as though anyone much accepts, say, the theory of Chomsky (1965), in which a theory of the base is explored at some length. Since then, however, there has been little in the way of a consensus on what a "base component" is, or might be. We are as free here as anywhere to make a proposal for specifying the "base component." So, I do.

Returning to the extended base, then, the crucial proposal is that the set of PMs can be extended by rules (generalized transformations). The output of the rules, however, is subject to the conditions on representations of the MPST. This is so for a simple reason: because the outputs are in the set of PMs, they must themselves be PMs, and the MPST defines the set of PMs. It might now seem that, therefore, the rules that extend the base are otiose, as the outputs are PMs. It is shown, however, that this is not so, due to the derivational nature of the extensions proposed.

The areas analyzed are coordination in Chapter 3 and adjuncts & adjunction in Chapter 4. The basic argument is that if we want to accept the restrictive MPST, then we cannot have base PMs for these phenomena. But, these phenomena must have base PMs. Therefore, there must somehow be an **extended** base. Remarkably, the formal primitives of our theory—nodes and labels—provide us with exactly two means to expand the base, and these two correspond to our problem phenomena.

1.3

Chapter 5 also develops the substantive portion of the theory. In it, a proposal is made for understanding syntactic Islands. The idea is that Subjects, Adjuncts, and Complex NPs (CNPs) are all members of the set of extended base structures either adumbrated in the previous two chapters or elaborated on in this one. This membership can be used to (1) group these structures together and (2) explain **why** they are Islands, and not something else. Learnability considerations are crucial to the proposal, as is an analysis of the concepts Core and Periphery in syntactic theory. In addition to the generalized transformations discussed in the previous two chapters, explicit phrase structure rules are (re)introduced into the theory. Islands, it is argued, are *rule-licensed base structures,* where this last concept serves to explicate both the notion *Periphery* in the Core versus Periphery distinction and the concept *characteristic structure* from the Learnability Theory of Wexler & Culicover (1980). Thus, disparate areas from syntactic research are brought together for the first time. Bounding theory plays no role in the proposal.

The Coordinate Structure Constraint and WH-Islands are discussed in an appendix to the chapter, because they present certain problems for the proposal.

1.4

The conclusion does three things. First, some residual conceptual questions concerning the relations of coordinate structures, adjunct(ion)s, and their respective operations are cleared up. The questions concern, for example, why the operations line up with the constructions they do, and what the domains of the operations are. Second, there is a relatively lengthy discussion of Chomsky's (1993) "A minimalist program for linguistic theory" because the architecture there proposed denies one of the crucial assumptions of this work—viz., the existence of D-structure.[1] Finally, the findings are reviewed and the contents of each chapter are related to the theory as a whole, stressing overall interconnections.

2.0

As noted, there is relatively little syntactic argument of the usual sort in this work (most of what there is is in Chapter 3). Sets of sentences rarely occur, and when they do they are primarily illustrative, rather than evidential, and often from other sources.

This is a work of theory construction with explanatory pretensions. I hope to make plausible—indeed, attractive—a particular theory of phrase markers and the base component. I paint with relatively broad strokes, usually going more for breadth and insight than depth and detail. This is not because I devalue the latter; on the contrary, it is because I do value them. Better, I believe, not to do them at all than to do them badly, for that only hurts the general argument, because the general argument must—eventually—stand or fall on the basis of the details. But before such an "eventually" can be reached, there need to be reasons to proceed. If, as they say, god is in the details, then, so we can say, the promised land is envisioned in the theory.

1

Minimal Phrase Structure Theory

0.0

The two basic **concepts** of the theory of syntax are *category* and *structure.*[1] A particular syntactic theory consists largely of elaboration (and defense) of specific **conceptions** of these concepts by means of (1) a theory of category (2) a theory of structure, and (3) a theory of the relation between (1) and (2). This chapter develops my versions of (1), (2), & (3). Most of the novelty inheres to (2), as seen in Sections 1 and 2. With respect to (1), I largely adopt the position defended in Speas (1990). It then develops that these theories mutually support one another in such a way that an approach to (3) virtually falls out. My primary finding, then, is that these independently justified theories of category and of structure find further justification in their interaction.[2]

A further finding is an explanation for a hitherto unremarked on theoretical problem: why are *dominance*-mediated predicates and relations not parameterized. That is, why is it not suggested that grammars differ with respect to, say, the hierarchical position of complements or of specifiers?[3] The theoretical problem becomes clearer when we contrast this situation with *precedence*-mediated relations and predicates. Grammars do differ, it is often claimed, with respect to linear position of, say, heads and complements, heads and specifiers, or governors and governees. We can, then, sharpen the original problem: why should there be this asymmetry with respect to parameterization of relations and predicates mediated by dominance and precedence, respectively? Essentially as a by-product, our theory solves this problem.

It is worth pointing out that our theory of structure is *formal* and our theory of category is *substantive,* in senses that will become clear below. A recurrent theme of this book is that formal and substantive issues can and should be separated from one another, given independent theoretical elaboration, and that once this is done, convergences between the two may be discoverable. Finding such convergence supports the independent theoretical inquiries; correspondingly, lack of such convergence should lead us to question one or the other theory.

I turn now to a preview of the chapter.

0.1

Sections 1 and 2 deal with (the theory of) the conception of structure by way of an investigation of formalization of phrase markers (hereafter, PMs) and trees. In Section 1, some conventional ideas are canvassed; in Section 2, some alternatives are discussed and my own position is presented. The point of the investigation is to argue that PMs have only one basic formal relation, viz., *dominance*, not two—dominance and *precedence*. The argument hinges on a problem within those formalizations which both (1) take account of the empirical possibility of "discontinuous constituents" and (2) assume and include a (putatively) basic precedence relation. The problem is that such formalizations can use precedence only insofar as they (1) incorporate elements not founded in their conceptions of the basic syntactic concepts of category and structure for basic precedence relations and (2) mediate other precedence relations by means of the dominance relation.[4] This is in contrast to the dominance relation, which is internally well-founded, and this contrast supports our conclusion that precedence is not formally primitive.

Note that the claims to be advanced are neither that there are no precedence relations nor that no syntactic phenomena can be sensitive to precedence facts. Rather, the claim is that there is—and will be—no general theory based on a primitive, formal precedence relation in syntax in the sense that X-Bar theory is a general theory in syntax based on the primitive, formal relation of dominance. And this is because there is no primitive, formal relation of precedence for syntax.

Section 3 turns to the substantive area: the theory of category and Speas's (1990) approach to X-Bar theory. Speas has "reduced the content" of X-Bar theory, following and completing the research program initiated by Stowell (1981). Familiar notions from earlier X-Bar theory such as "bar-level," "rule-schemata," or "cross-categorial harmony" play no role in the current view. There is now but "one rule [or principle—RC] of the base" (Speas 1990: 43).

The Stowellian program of "X-Bar reduction" has not been

without detractors, notably Pullum (1985) and Kornai & Pullum (1990). To clear the decks for what follows, in Section 3.3 I discuss Kornai & Pullum's objections. I argue that their positive findings are in many cases the same as Speas's and that one of their apparently most telling objections is based on a misunderstanding. Therefore, we need not (yet) give up our "reduced X-Bar" theory.

Section 4 summarizes the argument and shows how the theory explains the asymmetry with respect to parameterization of dominance-versus precedence-mediated relations and predicates.

The theory I develop consists of a reduced formal conception of PMs and a reduced substantive conception of X-Bar relations which, I show, dovetail with each other. Indeed, a major point of this book is that, if you work with what I propose, you can get rather a lot out of some apparently meager resources.[5] We move now to PM formalization.

1.0

There is a standard view of the formal nature of PMs. On this view, PMs are trees, in a sense that is close, though not identical, to the conception of tree employed in graph theory. A standard linguistic axiomatization for trees is given by Partee, ter Meulen, & Wall (1990: 443-44).

(1) Definition 16.6 A (*constituent structure*) *tree* is a mathematical configuration ⟨N, Q, D, P, L⟩, where

N is a finite set, the set of *nodes*

Q is a finite set, the set of *labels*

D is a weak partial order [i.e., it is transitive, reflexive, and antisymmetric—RC] in N × N, the *dominance* relation

P is a strict partial order [i.e., it is transitive, irreflexive, and asymmetric—RC] in N × N, the *precedence* relation

L is a function from N into Q, the *labeling function*

and such that the following conditions hold

(2) $(\exists x \in N)(\forall y \in N) \langle x,y \rangle \in D$ (*Single Root Condition*)

(3) $(\forall x, y \in N)((\langle x, y\rangle \in P \vee \langle y, x\rangle \in P) \leftrightarrow (\langle x, y\rangle \notin D \,\&\, \langle y, x\rangle \notin D))$ (*Exclusivity Condition*)

(4) $(\forall w, x, y, z \in N)((\langle w, x\rangle \in P \,\&\, \langle w, y\rangle \in D \,\&\, \langle x, z\rangle \in D) \rightarrow \langle y, z\rangle \in P)$ (*Nontangling Condition*)

A number of assumptions—empirical assumptions—are embodied in these formal statements. First, there are two primitive relations that are, formally, on a par: dominance and precedence. Second, no node can bear more than one label; this is incorporated into the specification of the relation between the sets N and Q as a **function from N to Q.** Third, any two nodes are related either by dominance or by precedence, but not by both (Exclusivity). Finally, ancestor and descendant nodes maintain constant precedence relations; that is, if two nodes in a precedence relation each have descendants, then those descendants are also in a precedence relation, and the descendant of the preceding ancestor is the preceding descendant (Nontangling).

I will argue against and reject each of these assumptions in Sections 2.2-2.4.

1.1

Although (1) defines a tree as a (complex) 5-tuple, it can be useful to think of a PM—as Ojeda (1987) does—as a set of ordered pairs, where the members of the pairs are themselves pairs of a node and a label. In Chapter 3's analysis of the syntax of coordinate structures, we shall return to this idea, making it more precise. More generally, the idea can be helpful because it reminds us that the usual ways of representing trees, with *tree diagrams* or labelled bracketings, are just that, ways of representing. We turn to an example, adapted from Ojeda (1987: 258); we use a label alone to stand for a node-label pair.

(5) a. $[_{VP}\ [_{V[PRT]}\ [_{V}\text{look}]\ [_{PRT}\text{up}]\ ]\ [_{NP}\text{something}]\ ]$
b. D = {(VP, VP), (V[PRT], V[PRT]), (V, V), (PRT, PRT), (NP, NP), (V[PRT], V), (V[PRT], PRT), (VP, NP), (VP, V[PRT]), (VP, V), (VP, PRT)}
c. P = {(V[PRT], NP), (V, PRT), (V, NP), (PRT, NP)}

In (5), V[PRT] is a nonce label for the verb and particle, similarly, PRT for the particle; D is the set of dominance pairs, and P is the set of precedence pairs. The union of these two can be understood as a representation of the (constituent structure) tree for the phrase *look up something.* This union totally orders the labelled nodes, since as well as being transitive, reflexive, and antisymmetric, this set is also connected.

1.2

It may be noted that in (5b) and (5c) the lexical items do not appear. This is counter to the standard / traditional approach to trees, in which lexical items (referred to as *terminal elements*) are included as distinct syntactic nodes. This traditional view is incorrect, although, historically, it is understandable.[6] Within the pre-Chomsky (1965) theory—that found in Chomsky (1957)—lexical items were introduced by means of phrase structure rules, just as the (rest of the) constituent structure tree was also licensed by phrase structure rules. Given this formal similiarity, it was natural (though, perhaps, not inevitable) that it would be presumed that there is also a substantive similarity. That is, the presumption was encouraged, and encoded in the representation, that the relation between two labelled nodes in a dominance pair is the same relation as that between a lexical item and a node labelled with a lexical category name. But the former is the part-whole relation of constituency, whereas the latter is not; it is rather an exemplification relation that, following Richardson (1982), we can call **instantiation** (analyzed and formalized in Chametzky 1987a: 51f.).

Post Chomsky (1965) and the introduction of a separate lexicon and lexical insertion, there is no reason at all to continue conflating these distinct relations. Some recognition of this can be found in the literature (e.g., Higginbotham 1985, McCawley 1988). Indeed, this conflation should be theoretically and formally costly. This is because it no longer follows simply from the interpretation of phrase structure rules that both labelled node-labelled node relations and lexical item-labelled node relations are immediately accounted for. Because lexical items no longer are introduced by phrase structure rules, one would have to stipulate that the result of lexical insertion is identical to the result of (the interpretation of) phrase structure rules. This should be kept in mind should it seem that instantiation carries extra costs. In any event, lexical items do not constitute syntactic nodes distinct from those they instantiate. This will be of some signficance to the argument against precedence in Section 2. This concludes the exposition of the standard formalization.

2.0

In this section, we turn to some alternatives to the standard approach to PMs that have been suggested in the literature. The compass here is fairly narrow, as I only consider alternatives that share basic assumptions about PMs; thus, I do not discuss, for example, Lasnik & Kupin (1977).[7] The alternatives focus on the the issue of discontinuous constituents and their import for syntactic theory and the formalization of PMs.

The point of what follows is this: whether or not the evidence and argument for discontinuous constituency is overwhelming, the very existence of the evidence and argument is what is important. They strongly suggest that discontinuity is in fact an empirical issue. But, the standard formalization rules out discontinuity, and thus it cannot be correct if the issue is an empirical one. Rather, some formalization that allows for discontinuity is required—if there is no discontinuity, it is not on account of formal stipulation but because substantive, linguistic analysis shows it to be unnecessary (or impossible).

2.1

McCawley (1982: 94) suggests that Parenthetical Placement, Scrambling, Relative Clause Extraposition, Heavy NP Shift, and Right Node Raising are "*order-changing transformations*" which involve "no change in constituency." This means that the structure of, for example, (6a), should be represented by something like (6b) (McCawley 1982: 98 (10b)).

(6) a. A man entered who was wearing a black suit.

b.

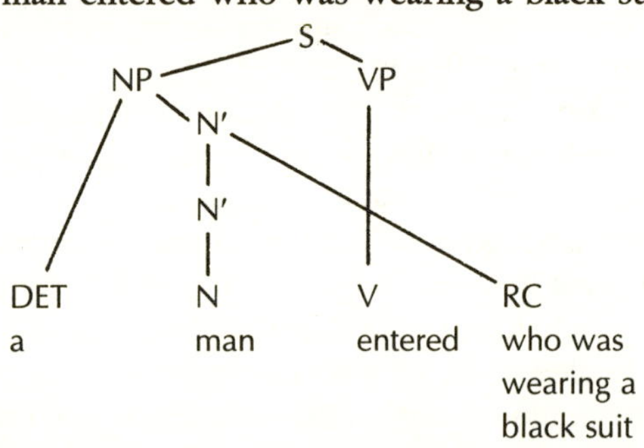

The traditional formalization (1) for PMs does not license structures of the sort represented by (6b) on account of the Nontangling

Condition (see (2) above). McCawley (1982: 93 (3)) therefore offers (7), an alternative set of axioms for a well formed tree, which, as we shall see, does license (6). (The otherwise similar axioms in McCawley 1968 do not allow for objects such as (6).)

N is a set of nodes with two binary relations "directly dominates" (= immediately dominates) and "is to the left of".[8]

(7) a. There is an $x_0 \in N$ such that for every $x \in N$, x_0 dominates x (that is, the tree has a root; "dominates" is the minimal reflexive and transitive relation containing "directly dominates").
b. For every $x \in N$, x_0 dominates x (that is, the tree is connected).
c. For every $x_1 \in N$, there is at most one $x_2 \in N$ such that x_2 directly dominates x_1 (that is, the tree has no loops).
d. "is to the left of" is transitive and antisymmetric (that is, "is to the left of" is a partial order).
e. If x_1 and x_2 are two distinct terminal nodes (a node x is terminal if there is no $y \in N$ such that x directly dominates y), then either x_1 is to the left of x_2 or x_2 is to the left of x_1 (that is, the terminal nodes are totally ordered).
f. For any $x_1,x_2 \in N$, if x_1 dominates x_2, then neither x_1 is to the left of x_2 nor x_2 is to the left of x_1 (that is, a node has no order relationship to nodes that it dominates).
g. For any $x_1,x_2 \in N$, x_1 is to the left of x_2 if and only if for all terminal x'_1,x'_2 such that x_1 dominates x'_1 and x_2 dominates x'_2, x'_1, is to the left of x'_2 (that is, nonterminal nodes stand in an ordering relationship if and only if all their descendents stand in the same relationship).

Unlike the earlier formalization, these axioms allow two nodes to have neither relation (dominates, precedes) to each other—this is ruled out by the Exclusivity Condition (3) of the standard axiomatization. Notice that (7f) states only that nodes do not precede or are not preceded by nodes they dominate; unlike Exclusivity, it is not a biconditional. In our example (6), the node labelled VP and that labelled NP stand in neither a dominance nor a precedence relation to each other, which is allowed by (7f) but not by Exclusivity.

On account of axiom (7g) that the precedence relation does not hold here. It does not hold because NP dominates both the terminal N and every terminal node (that is, node labelled by a lexical category) dominated by the node bearing the nonce label RC (for relative clause). The N bearing node is to the left of the node labelled V, while this latter is to the left of every terminal dominated by the node labelled RC; and the VP labelled node dominates the V bearing node. Thus, it is neither the case that all terminals dominated by NP precede all terminals dominated by VP nor is it the case that all terminals dominated by VP precede all terminals dominated by NP. But if neither of these is the case, then the nodes labelled NP and VP do not satisfy axiom (7g), hence they stand in no precedence relation to one another. This does not mean the structure is ill-formed—it is precisely the point of the revision (replacing Exclusivity with (7f)) that it licenses (6) as well-formed.

McCawley's work has aroused response. I turn now to some responses which enable us to see that once we try both to allow for discontinuous constituents and to maintain a formal primitive of precedence, we run into problems.

2.2

Huck (1985: 93 (11)) points out that in a structure such as that represented in (8)—his more abstract representation for a structure such as that in (6)—both the Nontangling Condition and, if precedence is transitive, the Exclusivity Condition are violated, and that McCawley (1982) has substituted (7f) and (7g) for Exclusivity and Nontangling, respectively, while adding (7e), thus licensing (8), as described above.

(8)

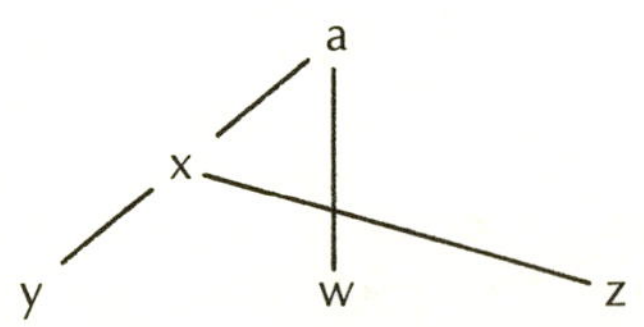

Huck makes two further points about McCawley's axioms. First, the union of dominance and precedence does not totally order an object such as that represented in (8), because the pair (x, w) is not a member of either relation, as (9) illustrates (see Huck 1985: 93 (12), (13)) (compare (5) in Section 1.1).

(9) Dominance in (8) = {(a, a), (a, x), (a, w), (a, y), (a, z), (x, x), (x, y), (x, z), (y, y), (w, w), (z, z)}

Precedence in (8) = {(y, w), (y, z), (w, z)}

Second, according to Huck, "no phrase structure grammar, or grammar strongly equivalent to one, can be constructed which will generate [(8)] as determined by McCawley's axioms, since, . . . phrase structure grammars do not permit rules whose right hand sides are not linearly ordered." (Huck 1985: 93–94)

Huck (1985: 94 (A5″)) goes on to formulate what he calls the *Inclusivity Condition* (10), which has the effect of requiring every pair of nodes to be related by either dominance (D in (10) and (11)) or precedence (P in (10) and (11)), or both.

(10) (∀ x)(∀ y) ((D(x, y) v D(y, x)) v (P(x, y) v P(y, x)))

However, as Huck (1985: 94) further argues, it is unclear "that in [(8)] x precedes w in any sense so far made precise, since one daughter of x precedes w and another follows it." To remedy this, Huck (1985: 94 (A6")) proposes the Head Order Condition (HOC), (11).

(11) (∀ x)(∀ y) (P(x, y) ↔ P(Hx, Hy)), where Hw = head of w

Given this, and the assumptions that y is the head of x and x is the head of a, then the structure represented in (8) is fully ordered, and a phrase structure grammar can be given that generates (8) (see Huck 1985: 94 (14)).

Huck's HOC, although it is not discussed in this way, appears to represent a radical change in the approach to PMs. One of the fundamental ideas seemingly codified in both the standard axioms and McCawley's revision is that there are two primitive formal relations, dominance and precedence. The HOC implicitly denies that precedence is such a formal primitive. This is so because there is no notion of "head of" independent of some version of syntactic theory. Huck (1985: 94) offers one possible way to "define 'head of w' categorially as the daughter w/X of w, where X = w, or as the daughter w if X = w." But, of course, should this definition not pan out empirically, it would naturally be modified or eliminated, as is proper for any substantive linguistic notion. In other words, unlike dominance, this notion of precedence depends on syntactic theory and analysis. More concretely, without the stipulations that y is the head of x and x is the head of a, there is no way to interpret (8) in terms of the HOC. Until the "head of" relations are determined, there literally is no object under Huck's proposal. That is, a representation such as (8) can be determined to be a well-formed PM under McCawley's axioms, an ill-formed (or non-)PM under the standard axioms, but, under Huck's HOC, no determination can be made at all until "head of" relations are discovered or stipulated.[9]

I do not intend this as a criticism of Huck; indeed, I shall argue that only the standard formalization actually treats dominance and precedence as on a par. And, I think Huck's shift—moving the status of precedence from that of formally primitive to substantively analytic—is essentially correct. However, this shift is due to the HOC, and Huck's move to the HOC is itself motiviated by his desire that an object such as (8) represents should be generable by a phrase structure grammar. If one were not to hold this latter goal, then one might be able to resist the conclusion that precedence is not a formal primitive on a par with dominance.

We move, therefore, to another axiomatization, one that allows us to discuss the nonprimitive nature of precedence in a more general setting.

2.3

Higginbotham (1983) has also offered an alternative to the standard axioms and has further discussed the precedence relation.

Unlike McCawley, Higginbotham begins with dominance rather than direct dominance. He correctly notes (1983: 152, n.1) that "systems satisfying [his own axioms] are interchangeable with those satisfying [McCawley's]" *modulo* the change just noted and a concomitant requirement in McCawley's axiomatization that "there is a *unique* root," which ensures that McCawley's domination relation is a partial order (note, however, that Higginbotham's (1983: 152–53) axiom (6) requires of "phrase-markers that display the categorial membership of a string of formatives, those that show that something is an S, an NP, etc.," that they have a unique root). Given this general equivalence between McCawley's and Higginbotham's axioms, I shall not reproduce the latter, but rather focus on those places where their respective discussions differ in ways that bear on our question with respect to the status of precedence.

There are two points to discuss here. One, the more important, is that, if precedence is not a formal primitive, then it is a syntactic relation at best only derivatively. The other is Higginbotham's use of *formatives*—lexical items—as the objects over which the precedence relation is defined. These issues come up in the following statement from Higginbotham (1983: 150–51): "[t]he notion of precedence is to reflect the ordering of formatives in speech . . . [and] [t]hat they will be so ordered is a consequence of the application of the laws of physics to the human mouth . . . reflecting the physics of speech. . . .

I take up the question of *formatives* first. Following McCawley (see 7g above), Higginbotham takes precedence relations between nonterminal nodes to be projections of precedence relations holding between terminals which the respective nonterminals are related to. However, unlike McCawley, Higginbotham explicitly identifies terminals with formatives, calling such elements the *leaves* of a PM. McCawley (7e above) merely defines a terminal as an element in a tree which directly dominates no element in that tree, without further specifying their identity. Higginbotham (1983: 150–51) identifies formatives or leaves as "elements that dominate only themselves."

I think Higginbotham's understanding of precedence in terms of formatives is correct; indeed, it is hard to see what, other than facts of speech, would lead to postulation of a precedence relation. This comes out in each of the nonstandard formalizations with respect to precedence relations among nonterminal nodes. In each of these formalizations, nonterminal precedence relations are determined by means of dominance relations. *Only* terminals are in a precedence relation determinable independently of dominance; but, as we shall see, terminals are in precedence relations for nonsyntactic reasons. Thus, there are no basic syntactic precedence relations. Hence the asymmetry between dominance and precedence.

Despite being correct about formatives as basic to precedence, the way Higginbothom works out his axioms is, I think, somewhat misleading. As argued above in Section 1.2 and as Higginbotham (1985: 555) agrees, the relation of formatives, lexical items, to lexically labelled nodes (i.e., nodes that directly dominate no nodes) is not the part-whole relation which dominance reconstructs—

instantiation, not dominance, is the relation here. Higginbotham (1985: 555) in fact suggests that a formative and a lexically labelled node are nondistinct "points" (i.e., nodes) in a PM; thus, the definitions given in Higginbotham (1983) (e.g., that for leaves just referred to) will technically do the desired work. It is, however, misleading, or at least imperspicuous, to do things this way because formatives are not themselves part of the PM *qua* PM. They are, so to say, parasitic on the lexically labelled nodes they instantiate and from which they are (each) nondistinct. A PM can be complete **as a formal object** without being instantiated by formatives, though it is not then the PM of any particular sentence.

This is similiar to the point raised with respect to Huck (1985) that precedence relations depended on the syntactic analysis of a sentence. Under Higginbotham's analysis, because precedence depends on formatives, precedence relations among nodes depend on the *particular* sentence being analyzed (generated). If there are no formatives, hence no particular sentence, then there can be no precedence relations at all, hence no PM. But this cannot be correct. The well-formedness of a PM as a *formal* object cannot depend on a particular sentence which it may be the PM of. Note the contrast here with respect to dominance.

This leads directly to the first point, the derivative nature of precedence as a syntactic relation. The precedence relation obtains, as Higginbotham suggests, only because of "the physics of speech" and "the human mouth." But how can this be syntax? It can be only if we interpolate the formatives into syntactic structures, as Higginbotham does, because nodes bearing syntactic category labels are not themselves subject to the physics of speech and the human mouth. Precedence, then, is not grounded in the conceptions of category (word class) and structure (nodes) of the syntactic theory assumed by Higginbotham (and by us).

We can contrast precedence with dominance. Given some conception of X-Bar theory (see below), we have a (partial?) theory of possible dominance relations in syntax. This is a theory the content of which is independent of the particular formatives which instantiate a given syntactic structure in that, for example, the presence of heads or the level at which specifiers and complements occur is not in general dependent on choice—or simply presence—of formatives. And, as we have noted, such relations and predicates are not parameterized.

It is well to be as clear as possible on this point. The formal relation of dominance reconstructs an intuitive part-whole relation which itself has independent syntactic reality in the X-Bar theory.[10] It is not clear what intuitive bases precedence might have (distinctness?), and there is, to my knowledge, no independent syntactic theory related to precedence. Thus, where dominance is a nexus of the formal, the intuitive, and the syntactic, precedence is simply the result of "the physics of speech." To reiterate, if we wish to use precedence as a relation in a construction for syntactic structures, we have to (1) use dominance to determine the nonbasic precedence pairs and (2) incorporate elements, viz., formatives, which do not themselves partake of the conceptions assumed in this syntactic theory, viz., nodes and word class labels, in order to determine the basic pairs.[11] In which case, again, it is not clear in what sense precedence remains a primitive formal relation in syntax.

As noted, relying simply on nodes and word class labels, we can provide a substantive, if perhaps incomplete, theory of dominance, viz., X-Bar theory. There is no analogous "theory of precedence" to be discovered in syntax, I believe (*pace* Gazdar & Pullum 1981). To reitierate a point made in Section 0.1 above, this is not to say that there are no linguistic precedence facts, even syntactic precedence facts. Surely there are; the hypothesis, rather, is that precedence is not a ***kind*** and so there is no place, no "module," in syntax in which such facts are localized (or derived, or whatever). It is not a syntactic kind because it is not a formal primitive of syntax, but rather is the result of the "physics of speech." Evidently, then, my view falls in with the analyses of, for example, Stowell (1982) in which an attempt is made to derive precedence facts from interactions of Case and Theta theories, lexical properties, and extended word-formation rules.

To sum up the argument: Higginbotham is correct that precedence is a result of "the physics of speech" applied to formatives and an approach such as McCawley's (1982), which does not recognize this fact, is, for that reason, incomplete. Because, however, neither "the physics of speech" nor formatives derive from the assumed conceptions of the basic concepts of syntax—nodes (structure) and word class labels (category)—precedence cannot be considered a formal primitive of the theory of PMs.

I conclude that we should specify a class of syntactic objects independently of the relation of precedence and the concomitant dependence on formatives and physics. My construction will do just this (see Section 2.5). We move now to another issue in the standard axioms.

2.4

In Section 1.0, I isolated four empirical assumptions encoded in the standard formalization of PMs given in (1); they are repeated in (12).

(12) a. First, there are two primitive relations that are, formally, on a par: dominance and precedence.
b. Second, no node can bear more than one label; this is incorporated into the specification of the relation between the sets N and Q as a function from N to Q.
c. Third, any two nodes are related either by dominance or by precedence, but not by both (Exclusivity).
d. Finally, ancestor and descendant nodes maintain constant precedence relations; that is, if two nodes in a precedence relation each have descendants, then those descendants are also in a precedence relation, and the descendant of the preceding ancestor is the preceding descendant (Nontangling).

We have discussed and rejected using precedence as a basic structuring relation for PMs, and it therefore follows that we have rejected the first, third, and fourth of these assumptions. We turn now to discussing and rejecting the second as well.

The problem with the second assumption is exactly that it is a substantive, empirical point enforced by a formal stipulation. If it is indeed a fact about the grammars of natural languages that they do not allow multiple labelling of nodes with distinct categorial symbols, then we should prefer this to follow from something linguistic. That is, from a formal point of view, there is no more reason to posit a function from N to Q than there is to posit a function from Q to N or, more generally, simply a relation between the two that fails to be a function. As an empirical generalization about grammars, this is exactly the sort of fact that cries out for further explanation, but the approach that incorporates it into the axiomatization of PMs shuts off the explanatory inquiry before it even starts.

I suggest that instead of a function from N to Q, we simply state that there is a relation between the two sets. Notice that, in general, should we wish to have nodes bearing more than one distinct label, this will be ruled out for substantive reasons. For example, should we wish to label a given node with both PP and NP labels, it would follow from X-Bar theoretic considerations that either (1) this phrase has a head that is both P and N or (perhaps) (2) this phrase has two distinct heads, one P and the other N (although this might itself be ruled out by X-Bar Theory). If, on the other hand, substantive syntactic reasons do not exist in a given case to render multilabelling ill-formed, then it seems perverse to rule it out simply for formal reasons. If it makes no (substantive) difference, then it makes no difference.

It is also possible that multilabelling might be desirable. Indeed, in Richardson & Chametzky (1985: 339–40), it is suggested that pronouns instantiate a single node which bears a set of three labels {N, N′, NP}. Whatever the merits of this particular proposal, there seems to be no reason to rule it, or ones like it, out on purely formal grounds. See Section 1.0 of Chapter 2 for more discussion of this proposal.

2.5

Our construction, then, is a simple one that includes only elements and relations found in the other formalizations discussed. We assume two sets: a set of nodes N and a set of categorial labels Q. We assume a (many-to-many) relation between N and Q. Finally, we assume a binary relation on N, "directly dominates" (D), and the reflexive, transitive closure of D, D*. And we take over the first two of McCawley's axioms, repeated here in (10) (though these may be redundant, as noted in note 8).[12] (Note that the parentheticals here refer to PMs, not trees, because these are not trees as defined by linguists.)

(13) a. There is an $x_0 \in N$ such that for every $x \in N$, x_0 D^* x (that is, the PM has a root.)
b. For every $x \in N$, x_0 D^* x (that is, the PM is connected).

And this is all.

Obviously, this is a much more permissive construction for PMs than any others considered. Everything any of the other formalizations allow this will allow also although not vice-versa.

This preferred interpretation of the formalization simply is that syntactic structures are branching structures of a certain (rooted, connected, labelled) sort.[13] In fact, it is not clear that it is necessary or desirable to stipulate that a PM must be rooted, particularly singly rooted. If it is true that syntactic objects have this (these) property(ies), then once more, this may hold not for formal reasons but for substantive ones (see Chametzky 1987b for discussion). As I have discussed this issue elsewhere and nothing I say rides on the root node's existence, I shall simply accept the stipulations.

The question of discontinuous constituents has provoked the alternative formalizations considered above. On the view here adopted, the existence of discontinuous constituents is an entirely empirical issue—although we are not surprised to find them—and whatever allowance or restriction there is on the phenomenon will be a matter for substantive syntactic analysis and theory, as the formalization is maximally permissive in this regard.[14]

2.6

I have argued that formally a PM is constrained only by the relation of (direct/immediate) dominance, by having a single root, and by there being a relation between the sets of nodes and of labels. All other apparent formal conditions are in fact the results of substantive considerations within syntax. It might be wondered why dominance is acceptable. There are two reasons.

One is the existence of X-Bar Theory as a substantive elaboration of the formal relation. This seems, however, to get things backwards, to argue against maintaining even dominance, because, by the sort of reasoning pursued above, the substantive consideration has the apparent formal relation as a by-product. In Section 3, I show that the form of X-Bar Theory I adopt, that of Speas (1990), does not have this result, as it consists only of a single principle, Project Alpha, which itself assumes the dominance relation.

The second reason to maintain dominance is that branching part-whole structures are conspicuously not specific to linguistic theory. Simon (1962) demonstrates that such hierarchical structuring is the "architecture of complexity" with respect to natural systems (those which are the product of evolution) as opposed to artificial systems (those with human engineers). Sampson (1980: 240–41) applies these ideas to linguistics to explain constituent structure, among other things. I partially agree with Sampson. My view is that, indeed, Simon's argument is crucial to understanding why syntactic objects are the sort of things they are, but, no, we cannot get any more out of it than I have here indicated, viz., hierarchical structure.

There might appear to be an unwarrented asymmetry in the use of "the architecture of complexity" to support dominance and the use of "the physics of speech" above to reject precedence. However, some important dissimilarities in the two arguments justify the asymmetry. First, Simon's is a general and abstract idea about natural complex systems of all sorts. "The physics of speech," in contrast, is parochial in more than one way: (1) it is limited to human language and (2) it is not even general there. As Higginbotham himself (1983: 151) notes—though he does not conclude that this observation undermines precedence as formal primitive in syntax—"[i]n a language spoken with two hands we might, pointing here with the left there with the right, simultaneously produce two formatives . . . ." Second, as is elaborated in Section 3, a central part of substantive syntactic theory assumes the dominance relation but, as noted above, this is not true of precedence—this is what we might expect were the former, but not the latter, a formal primitive in the theory of PMs grounded in something both general and extrasyntactic.[15]

3.0

Some reference has already been made to X-Bar Theory and restrictions it may be seen to place on possible dominance pairs. X-Bar Theory has been well-discussed in Stuurman (1985) and Speas (1990), to which readers are advised to turn. I shall simply outline in 3.1 the version of the Theory here adopted, that in Speas (1990); in Section 3.2 I bring this theory together with the formal considerations of Section 2; and finally I offer in Section 3.3 some comments on Kornai & Pullum (1990).

3.1

Speas (1990: 43ff.) proposes "one rule of the base" **Project Alpha** (her (41)).

> (14) Project Alpha: a word of syntactic category *X* is dominated by an uninterrupted sequence of *X* nodes.

Speas defines several other concepts: **Projection Chain, Maximal Projection,** and **Minimal Projection** (her (42) and (43)).

(15) Projection Chain of $X =_{def}$ An uninterrupted sequence of projections of X.

(16) Maximal Projection: $X = X^{max}$ iff $\forall$G which dominate X, G $\neq X$

(17) Minimal Projection: $X = X^0$ iff X immediately dominates a word.

Before discussing (14)-(17), I must amend (14) & (17) in keeping with the policy of distinguishing between the relation between lexical items and the nodes they instantiate and that between nodes and the nodes they dominate. With respect to (17′), the only nodes in a syntactic structure which will immediately dominate nothing are those which are in the instantiation relation with a lexical item.

(14′) Project Alpha: an instantiated node labelled X is dominated by an uninterrupted sequence of X labelled nodes.

(17′) Minimal Projection: $X = X^0$ iff X immediately dominates nothing.

Speas (1990:43) writes that "Project Alpha collapses the labeling function of X-bar theory with the implicit free generation of hierarchical structures." And (1990: 46) that "all structure is projected from the lexical items . . ." I take these quotes from Speas to mean the following. X-Bar theory has been, at least in part, a theory of what labels could be on nodes in a mother-daughter configuration. On the "node admissibility condition" understanding of phrase structure rules (on node admissibility conditions, see McCawley 1968 and Speas 1990: 19-24), structures are not "generated" by the rules but are rather taken as given and either licensed or not, depending on conformance with the conditions (i.e., depending on whether the labels on a mother and its daughter(s) are admitted by a condition). Hence, (14) collapses these by explicitly stating that there is a sequence of nodes labelled X. And, all structure is projected from lexical items because structure is no longer taken as given—structure exists on account of (14), or not at all.

It is not clear that this claim is maintained under (14′). And, I would just as soon uncollapse labelling and generation of structure—

one of my points is that free generation of PMs of the sort allowed by (13) in Section 2.5 above converges with a labelling theory such as that incorporated in (14′). To collapse the two is to lose the possibility of having independent theories converge. In any event, it makes sense to interpret (14′) as a well-formedness condition on hierarchical structures: freely generate any sort of hierarchical structure at all, with any labelling; instantiate those nodes which immediately dominate nothing; check the resulting structure for conformity with (14′). This surely separates labelling from structure generation.

Speas (1990: 43) notes that "all nodes in the sequence will share all syntactic category features" due to the use of the variable in (14′); thus, there is no categorial difference among nodes in the Projection Chain. There is no primitive notion of "bar level" in this framework, and so (16) and (17′) define the maximal and minimal projections in terms of position in the hierarchical structure. Speas follows work by L. Travis in arguing that intermediate "bar levels" have no theoretical status in syntax. Speas claims (1990: 42) that "principles of grammar do not specifically refer to" intermediate levels—and presumably they may not. There is, to be sure, intermediate structure, but this is of an " 'elsewhere' case" nature (1990: 42). The amount of (intermediate) structure is determined by the lexical properties of the head (i.e., by the lexical item in the instantiation relation with the minimal projection) and "the requirement that *all* lexical requirements of the head be instantiated in syntax. . . . The head continues to project until all of the positions in its theta grid have been discharged" (Speas 1990: 45).

It is impossible in this theory to license adjuncts in any significant sense.[16] There can be no adjuncts to maximal or minimal projections, given that these are defined as above. In the former case, the adjoined-to node would fail to meet the definition for maximal projection; in the latter, the adjoining-to node would fail to meet the definition for minimal projection. With respect to intermediate structure, it is "adjunction" all the way down. Following Lebeaux (1988, 1990), Speas argues that this is a desirable result. Chapter 4 elaborates on and defends these assertions, so I leave the matter now.

3.2

I offer now a summation of the theory. The Minimal Phrase Structure Theory (MPST, hereafter) has a single principle, Project Alpha. Maximal and minimal projections are defined structurally. Intermediate levels have no theoretical status. The MPST itself imposes no restrictions on number or position of nonheads; these are determined by other principles, lexical or structural. Adjuncts are not licensed by the MPST.

The formal and substantive parts of our theory come together in the following way. A PM consists of a set of nodes and the (direct) dominance relation. The nodes are associated with labels, names for syntactic categories. In accordance with the MPST, there are no "(bar) levels" in the set of category labels; all the category labels are of the form V, N, P, and so forth. Labelled nodes which directly dominate nothing enter into the instantiation relation with lexical items.

An instantiated PM must obey Project Alpha—and, notice, Project Alpha assumes dominance. Thus, the single formal assumption of the single principle of the substantive theory is also the single primitive of the formal theory.

This is the promised convergence, and it is, I think, quite striking. Since the converging inquiries are supposed to be each independently motivated, it is important to examine objections to either project. We turn, therefore, to objections to the "X-Bar reduction" program of which Speas (1990) represents the zenith.

3.3

Speas (1990: 35-38, 56-60) discusses Pullum's (1985) argument that the program to "eliminate phrase structure rules," adumbrated in Stowell (1981) and pursued by Speas, is largely a shell game. Essentially, Pullum argues that X-Bar restrictions on phrase structure rules have no actual effect on the class of languages which can be generated by a phrase structure grammar and that the same can be said for Stowell's program as well. Speas replies, basically, that Pullum has misunderstood the point of the program laid out by Stowell.[17] Speas claims (1990: 35) that what she says carries over to Kornai & Pullum (1990), as it should if her criticism is apt, because the authors intend this latter to "supercede" Pullum (1985) (Kornai & Pullum 1990: 24 note). I shall not attempt to adjudicate this dispute directly.

Instead, I should like to make two points. The first is that Speas and Kornai & Pullum really are not so far apart. To see this, I must clarify what I take each investigator to be up to and to have found.

Perhaps only with Speas (1990) is the true import of the Stowellian approach clear. The program does not restrict phrase structure rules in particular X-Bar ways (e.g., in terms of restricting all categories to a uniform bar-level projection). It eliminates the X-Bar Theory. Speas (1990: 55) writes "However, rather than increasing the restrictions encoded in the X-bar schema, I have proposed a theory of projection from the lexicon in which the only restriction imposed by X-bar theory is the restriction that sentences have hierarchical structure, and that all structure is projected from a head. All other restrictions on domination relations are to be captured in other modules of the grammar."

If PMs are understood formally to be (just) hierarchical structures, then all the theory adds is Project Alpha, which itself assumes hierarchical structures. Nothing much remains from the content of X-Bar Theory, e.g., cross-categorial structural generalizations and uniform levels are gone. Under the MPST, "all structures are endocentric" (Speas 1990: 46), and this is the only X-Bar theoretic condition that stems directly from the MPST.

Bearing our clarified view of the Stowell-Speas project in mind, we turn to Kornai & Pullum (1990). Kornai & Pullum argue that traditional X-Bar Theory does not constrain the class of describable/generable languages in any significant way (see, e.g. Kornai & Pullum 1990: 42; 47). They also notice (1990: 37) with respect to Stowell (1981) that "the content of [his] theory is to be found not in the universal base component but in other components of the grammar."

Further, they make the following four points about "X-Bar Grammars": (1) that the most important notion in X-Bar Theory is that of "head," (2) that it is possible to dispense with bar levels, (3) that adjunction structures are not licensed by the theory, and (4) that maximal and minimal projections are definable in such a theory (see Kornai & Pullum 1990 42-44; 46-47). Strikingly, in each of these four findings, Kornai & Pullum agree with Speas.[18]

What is puzzling is the apparent antipathy of Kornai & Pullum (1990: 35-39; 47-49) to work in the Stowellian mode. To be fair, it should be noted that they do not—presumably could not—mention the concurrent work of Speas (1990). Still, it would seem that, given their conclusion that traditional X-Bar Theory is not a restrictive theory and the convergence with Speas on what is real and important in X-Bar Theory, they would welcome the attempt to eliminate X-Bar as a contentful "module" of syntactic theory. Paring down the theory of the base to an MPST level and deriving in other components whatever empirical generalizations X-Bar Theory attempted to encode seems, to me at least, to flow rather naturally from Kornai & Pullum's work.

My second point is a comment internal to Kornai & Pullum (1990). They argue (1990: 39-42) that "As long as we permit 'empty categories' the [X-Bar] constraints discussed . . . do not affect the generative power of CFGs [context free grammars] at all. If 'empty categories' are disallowed, the constraints do decrease the descriptive power of CFGs, but the resulting family of languages is not formally coherent . . ." (Kornai & Pullum 1990: 39). Earlier, they write (1990: 27) "that arbitrary CFGs can be emulated by X-bar grammars largely by virtue of this sort of expansion of the category set and the use of *categories realized as the empty string*" (emphasis added). They construe "empty category" as the right-hand side of an "*e*-rule" (a phrase structure rule in which the right-hand side is the empty string *e*) (Kornai & Pullum 1990: 40). Such rules introduce "zero preterminals" (Kornai & Pullum 1990: 41; sensibly, they take lexical categories "as the terminal vocabulary of the grammar" 1990: 26). And they note (Kornai & Pullum 1990: 27) that within GB work "empty categories have multiple uses . . . and they are not eliminable."

Now, it seems that what they call "empty categories" have nothing much to do with the objects that go by that name in GB. Kornai & Pullum (1990: 26) are talking about " 'languages' that are in fact strings of lexical categories rather than strings of words" (a move I endorse). But this means that their "empty categories" are empty lexical categories—as the quotes in the preceding paragraph indicate—which is to say, I suppose, that they are lexical categories of no category. I am not sure I know just how to understand this idea. But, whatever it is, notice that the claim is made that "empty categories" are syntactically empty—they are "zero preterminals." This is clearly not the same as an "empty category" in GB. GB "empty categories" are phonetically empty, but are absolutely present syntactically, perhaps also (morpho-)phonologically. This, indeed, is the point of "trace theory."

So, the Kornai & Pullum claims about grammars with "empty categories" in their sense are, strictly, irrelevant to grammars with GB style "empty categories." Now, it may be that one could show that Kornai & Pullum "empty category grammars" are (formally) equivalent to GB "empty category grammars"; but this they have not done, nor have they indicated that such a move is required.[19] Given this apparent misunderstanding and the convergences noted here, I conclude that Kornai & Pullum (1990) provide no reasons for giving up the Stowellian project carried out by Speas (1990).

4.0

This chapter has argued that formally a PM is a set of node-label pairs ordered by a single relation, (direct) dominance, because the other relation commonly taken to order a PM, precedence, is not naturally understood with the assumed conceptions in the theories of category and of structure. There is, then, a fundamental asymmetry between dominance and precedence, and this asymmetry explains the asymmetry between dominance- and precedence-mediated relations and predicates with respect to parameterization. Precedence-mediated relations and predicates are parochial—thus parameterizable—because there is no basic formal relation of precedence for PMs, hence no *precedence kind* in syntactic theory. Rather, precedence relations depend on formatives, parochial elements *par excellence.* Dominance-mediated relations and predicates, conversely, are universal and nonparameterizable because dominance is the single formal primitive for PMs, forming the basis for a *dominance kind* in syntactic theory—the X-Bar "module."

Our formal view dovetails with the substantive view of phrase structure advocated in Speas (1990), which I call the *Minimal Phrase Structure Theory,* in which nothing is left of X-Bar Theory other than the notion that "heads project"—which assumes the dominance relation. This project of "X-Bar reduction" has been pursued essentially in terms of substantive analysis, yet it converges strikingly with our formal inquiry. The MPST, I suggest, also converges with the investigations of Kornai & Pullum (1990) on several central conclusions, these authors' apparent misgivings about earlier versions of the MPST program notwithstanding, and one of their central objections to the "reduction" program seems to be based on misunderstanding. There is, then, no obvious reason not to pursue our inquiry, and at least *prima facie* theoretical evidence in favor of it.

We turn, therefore, to applications and refinements of the theory. When I refer to the MPST from now on, this should be taken to mean the combination of both the formal and substantive ideas outlined in this chapter and not merely to the views of Speas (1990).

2

The Explanation of C-command

0.0

Not all linguistically significant relations among nodes are among nodes already in a dominance relation. Given that our PMs are defined exclusively in terms of (direct) domination, this fact might seem an embarrassment. But some linguistically significant relations among nodes not related by dominance are no embarrassment at all. Take, for example, the relation of "sister." This is both linguistically important and formally simple to define and understand on PMs in our MPST. "Sisterhood" holds of nodes directly dominated by the same node, which node we call the "mother" of the sisters. It is pleasing that such a formally straightforward and natural extension of our basic relation is also linguistically important, and indeed, we can take it as some support for the MPST that (once again) there is this formal and substantive convergence.

Still, not all linguistically significant relations are among nodes already related by either dominance or sisterhood. Famously, there are the relations of anaphora, which seem to preclude dominance but not to be limited to sisters. For such "nonlocal" relations, linguists have found themselves constructing and adverting to a series of "command relations" (Barker & Pullum 1990; see Section 3), most centrally "C-command." Further, command relations are often invoked to condition other linguistic relations as well, for example, for government.

0.1

In this chapter, I explain why command relations play the role they do in syntactic theory, why and how C-command is central and special within the family of command relations, and why the MPST offers as pleasing and natural a theory in which to understand the centrality of "C-command" as it does for "sister."

I argue further that a particular conception of C-command—that developed, defended, and formalized in Richardson & Chametzky (1985) (R/C, hereafter)—is crucial to understanding why C-command is central. The argument proceeds in two steps. First, I explicate the R/C conception of C-command and show how it fits together with the MPST. Second, I show that standard views obfuscate the explanatory project. This second step takes the form of close analysis of Kayne (1981), the only other work I know of which attempts an explanatory inquiry with respect to C-command; Barker & Pullum (1990), the most extensive investigation of (C-)command within standard assumptions; and some discussions of C-command within GB and Generalized Phase Structure Grammar (GPSG). Both steps are evidently needed if the conclusion of the argument—that it is the nonstandard aspects of the MPST and the R/C approach which allow us to explain C-command—is to be established. I might note that the argument throughout is *theoretical,* in that no language data are adduced or analyzed.

0.2

Once properly posed, it is clear what will not do as an answer to our questions: observations to the effect that this or that command relation (e.g., C-command) is required to mediate this or that linguistic phenomenon (e.g., binding relations). It is the existence of such observations, the fact that the patterns we seek to understand require adverting to a command relation **and not something else,** that calls out for explanation. And by its very nature, **such an explanation will not be linguistic;** that is, if we want to understand **why** command relations are relevant to linguistic phenomena, invoking their relevance to linguistic phenomena will get us nowhere.

To anticipate: C-command is the basic command relation. It is nonlinguistic in the following sense. It is the unique relation which nonarbitrarily exhaustively factors a PM while respecting hierarchical structure. The nonlinguistic nature of the relation follows from the fact that C-command is definable for any branching structure regardless of the sorts of labels its nodes bear. C-command is a generalization of the sister relation. Precisely what these statements mean is explained in Section 1.

0.3

The chapter is organized as follows. Section 1 reviews and expands on the characterization of C-command found in R/C. Section 2 discusses Kayne's (1981) attempt to replace C-command with his notion of *unambiguous path.* Section 3 discusses the foundational formal work on the family of command relations by Barker & Pullum (1990) and includes a new formalization of the R/C view of C-command. Section 4 considers the fate of C-command in Government & Binding—May (1985) and Chomsky (1986a)—and in (early) Generalized Phrase Structure Grammar—Gazdar (1982) and Fodor (1983). Section 5 briefly describes another command relation—M-command—in the framework developed and shows how it relates to C-command. Section 6 is a general stock and leave taking.

1.0

C-command is a relation between nodes in a PM. R/C argue for reorienting our understanding of C-command. The suggestion is that, instead of asking, "Does node A C-command node B?" we should rather ask, "Which set contains all and only the nodes which C-command node B?." There are two distinct moves here. First, we "take the point of view" of the C-commandee rather than the C-commander. Second, we move from a relation between two nodes to a relation between a node and a set of nodes. Shifting our perspective in these ways allows for the relatively straightforward statement in (1).

> (1) For any node A, the C-commanders of A are all the sisters of every node which dominates A.

This assumes, as is usual, that nodes dominate themselves. The statement in (1) reconstructs the intended extension of a "standard" statement of C-command as in (2) (see Reinhart 1981), *modulo* the changes in perspective noted above (see R/C for demonstration).

> (2) Node A C-commands node B if the first branching node dominating A also dominates B, and neither A nor B dominates the other.

Various technical and empirical advantages of (1) over (2) are pressed in R/C, but these are orthogonal to the present investigation, and so shall be ignored.

One further point from R/C requires discussion. R/C (337-40) argue that there is (and ought to be) no nonbranching domination in a truly well-behaved phrase structure theory. Their suggestion that pronouns instantiate a single, multiply labelled node, noted in Section 2.4 of Chapter 1, is part of this argument. We could add this general provision outlawing nonbranching domination (as a stipulation) to the MPST. As R/C recognize, the issue, though technical, is not entirely unimportant, as the stipulation would allow us to identify the unique minimal factorization of a phrase marker (see below). However, this is both inelegant and not clearly necessary. R/C inventory the types of nonbranching domination found in the linguistic literature and find some four types. One type uses functional labels such as, for example, "subject" or "topic," as the label for a mother to a node labelled with, for example, NP. R/C dismiss this as the confusion that it is. Another sort allows for exocentric labelling; for example, giving a node labelled NP as mother to a node labelled S (or S′). This is impossible within the MPST. Then there is the relation between a Minimal Projection and a lexical item. Understanding this as domination has been rejected in the MPST, having been replaced by the instantiation relation (see Section 1.2 of Chapter 1). All that is left, then, is the case of nonbranching domination within a Projection Chain. But this is just the case where the MPST would allow multiple labelling of a single node instead. We can, then, maintain two very general formal conditions on PMs: (1) we allow nonbranching domination and (2) we allow multiple labelling of nodes. Indeed, the possibility of the latter reduces the need for the former to zero.[1]

1.1

Let us examine the tree diagram in (3).

(3)

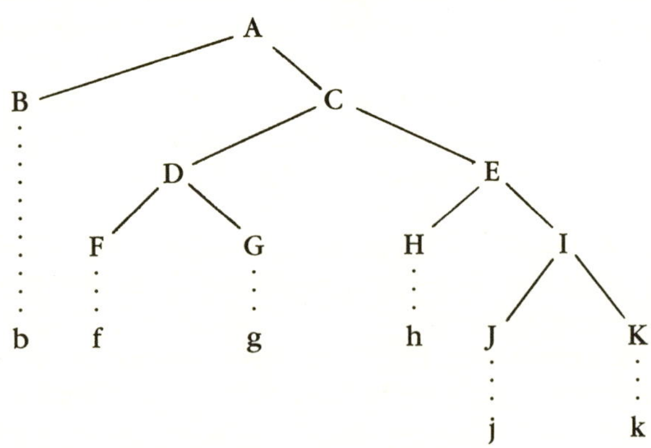

If we ask of a node, say that labelled G, what is the set of C-commanding nodes of G, we see that it is {F, E, B}, according to (1). In addition to being the correct set, we can observe some other interesting properties of this set. Only nodes which are not in a dominance relation to one another can be in the C-command relation; this follows immediately from (1). From this we further suggest part of the reason that C-command is such a central relation in syntax. If precedence is not a primitive relation in the way dominance is, then we might expect that some other formal relation, itself parasitic on dominance, would form the basis for further relations between nodes not in a dominance relation. C-command, I contend, is that relation. Examination of (1) and (3) helps reveal why.

We can see that the notion of C-command embodied in (1) is both entirely formal and parasitic on dominance. It is formal, as inspection of (3) reveals, because the set of C-commanders is determinable without recourse to any specifically linguistic predicates or relations. All we need have reference to, ultimately, is our single primitive relation, *direct dominance.* From this, again, we can define both its reflexive, transitive closure—dominance—and the mother and sister relations (see Barker & Pullum 1990: (18) and Section 3.4 have for formal statements). And then we have everything necessary for (1). Because (3) is an arbitrary tree diagram, it is clear that there is nothing intrinsically linguistic about C-command; since it is constructed out of dominance, itself a "linguistics free" predicate, C-command is also independent of substantive linguistic content. On this view, C-command is a generalization of the sister relation: to C-command a node is to be the sister of a node that dominates that node.

Further, and even more significantly, inspection of (3) reveals the following. The set of C-commanders of G (or any node) is the set of nodes which offers what we can call the **minimal factorization**[2] of the PM in question with respect to the node G (in R/C, this set is somewhat misleadingly called the "*minimal string*" for G). That is, there is no other set of nodes that, when unioned with the set {G}, is both smaller than the set in question (has fewer members/a smaller cardinality) and also offers a complete, nonredundant constituent analysis of the structure.[3] Thus, the set {A, G} is smaller than {B, F, G, E} and provides a complete constituent analysis, but it is redundant—it is not a factorizaton—in that the constituent A contains the constituent G; similarly {B, G, C} is complete but redundant (C contains G). In general, any set that contains a distinct node that dominates the node whose C-commanders we seek is redundant (and disallowed by

(1)). The set {B, F, G, H, I} is complete and nonredundant—it is a factorization—but it is larger than the set {B, F, G, E} and, further, to obtain this set would require a formal relation rather more complex than the simple sister generalization of (1). The set {B, G, E} is incomplete (F is neither contained in it nor dominated by anything in it), hence not a factorization.

We see, then, what our way of viewing C-command allows us. Undertanding C-command as a generalization of the sister relation provides a formal relation that holds between nodes not in a dominance relation. And, that relation provides the minimal complete analysis of the tree. This minimal completeness seems to be just what one would want from such a relation, in that any other relation among nodes not in the dominance relation would be arbitrary in a way C-command is not. That is, we would need to explain just **why** we did not have a **complete** analysis of the structure (i.e., a factorization)—why the **particular** left out nodes are left out and not any others—or **why** we did not have the **minimal** analysis—why the **particular** extra nodes (from the minimal point of view) are included and not any others.

Let us look at an example involving nonminimal factorizations (we can take incomplete analyses to be nonstarters). Referring to (3), repeated here, we would have to explain why either of {B, F, H, I} or {B, F, H, J, K} should be chosen, for these are the only sets besides {B, F, E} which offer a factorization of (3) with respect to {G}. There is no formal reason to choose the former from among the three available factorization sets—it is simply an arbitrary factorization—but we might choose the latter because it is the **maximal** such set.

(3)

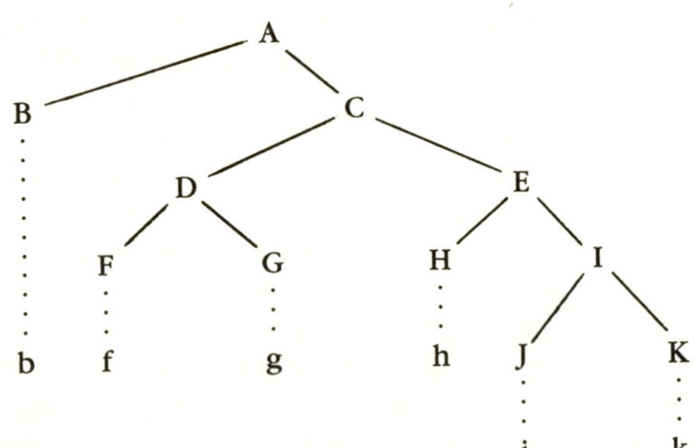

Evidently, the maximal set is unique, just as the minimal set is and as no other set is. There is, however, a significant difference between the minimal and maximal sets. The maximal set is just the set of (pre)terminals not dominated by the target node. It therefore denies the relevance of all dominance relations not involving the target node for all further relations involving the target. Thus, of the two nonarbitrary sets, only the minimal set requires the full branching hierarchical structure—the full phrase marker. This difference is clearly highlighted in the formal construction of the minimal set, which we get to by means of a generalization of the sister relation, itself straightforwardly constructed from our single primitive, direct dominance. There is no such straightforward formal construction for the maximal set that flows so naturally from our single primitive relation; even though it is easy to establish, the maximal set bears no obvious relation to direct dominance, unlike the minimal set.

Notice that the invocation of hierarchical structure in the decision for the minimal set versus the maximal set is not an importation of substantive linguistic notions into the formal construction. Branching diagrams based on the direct domination relation are representations of arbitrary hierarchically structured objects.[4] It is most natural that further relations among nodes in such objects will advert to the fact of such structure. Natural, but not, nonetheless, inevitable; it might well turn out, in a given empirical inquiry, that a largely nonhierarchical relation—such as that represented by the maximal set—is the one which the facts dictate choice of. But we should be surprised if this were so, and if the facts consistently led us to such choices, then our initial commitment to hierarchical objects based in direct dominance would need rethinking. If the natural formal extensions of our basic formal concepts are empirically otiose, this is evidence that our bases are ill-conceived—just as the empirical applicability of such extensions supports those bases.

1.2

This concludes the characterization of the R/C view. C-command is a generalization of the sister relation, so it therefore holds between nodes not in a dominance relation. It is entirely formal and parasitic on (direct) dominance. Such a relation is expectable within MPST-based syntax because not all possible relations hold among nodes in a dominance relation, and so some further way of picking out possible relata is required. Although the set picked out by (1) is not the only possible such set of non-dominance-related nodes, we have argued that it—uniquely—nonarbitrarily factors a PM while respecting the existence of hierarchical structure. It is thus an extremely natural set—in fact, the most natural one, I claim. We turn now to some other views.[5]

2.0

Kayne (1981: 129) asks the right question: "Why should there exist a c-command requirement?" He here is asking specifically about the requirement that an antecedent C-command an anaphor, but he later generalizes to all uses of C-command. I shall argue that though he asks the right question, and approaches answering it from the right direction, nevertheless, Kayne's notion of *unambiguous path* is inferior to the account of C-command developed in Section 1.

2.1

Kayne's answer is given in two slightly different forms. He first (1981: 130) suggests that C-command "is 'close to' the standard dominance relation" and that this distinguishes well-formed from ill-formed binding relations.[6] Obviously, there is a sense in which I agree that the explanation of C-command lies in its "closeness" to the standard notion of dominance, as I have already shown. But Kayne then develops his central notion of an *unambiguous path,* which he believes "brings out this 'closeness' to the dominance relation" in a way that diverges from our own understanding of C-command.

We reproduce Kayne's (1981: 131-32) definition of *unambiguous path* (the parentheticals are also Kayne's):

> Let a path P (in a phrase structure tree T) be a sequence of nodes ($A_0 \ldots A_i, A_{i+1} \ldots A_n$) such that
>
> (4) a. $\forall i, j \quad 0 \leq i, j \leq n \quad A_i = A_j \rightarrow i = j$
> (P is a sequence of distinct nodes; we want to exclude from consideration paths that double back on themselves.)
> b. $\forall i \quad 0 \leq i < n \quad A_i$ immediately dominates A_{i+1} or A_{i+1} immediately dominates A_i
> (A path is a sequence of adjacent nodes.)

An unambiguous path in T is a path $P = (A_0 \ldots A_i, A_{i+1} \ldots A_n)$ such that:

(5) $\forall i \quad 0 \leq i < n$

a. if A_i immediately dominates A_{i+1}, then A_i immediately dominates no node in T other than A_{i+1}, with the permissible exception of A_{i-1}.

b. if A_i is immediately dominated by A_{i+1}, then A_i is immediately dominated by no node in T other than A_{i+1}, with the permissible exception of A_{i-1}

(Informally put again, an unambiguous path is a path such that, in tracing it out, one is never forced to make a choice between two (or more) unused branches, both pointing in the same direction).

As Kayne's parenthetical remarks indicate, a path is a sequence of distinct, adjacent nodes in which no node occurs more than once (no "doubling back"). A path is unambiguous just in case no node on it represents a "choice point," where we can understand this latter term (not one that Kayne uses) in the following way. A node in a path is a choice point just in case there is more than one way in which that path could be continued from that node; in other words, more than one distinct, adjacent node exists which is not already in the path (i.e., would not require "doubling back" to add it to the path). Implicit in this way of talking is the assumption that unambiguous paths are constructed asymmetrically; that is, an unambiguous path from an anaphor to its antecedent does not imply that there is also an unambiguous path from the antecedent to the anaphor (Kayne 1981: 130).

As already noted, Kayne suggests that his notion of unambiguous path should replace C-command anywhere the latter appears. He shows (132-33) that the two notions are not equivalent when the substitution is made in the definition of *government.* In particular, (mutual) C-command holds among the daughters in a structure in which a mother has more than two daughters, whereas in such a structure there is no unambiguous path from any one daughter to any other (because the other daughters constitute distinct nodes adjacent to the mother which are not already in the path). Therefore, Kayne is led to reanalyze, for example, English double object constructions not as a V with two NP sisters, but as a V with a single sister (he labels it S), which itself has the two NPs as its daughters. I am not primarily interested in such issues, however, and so do not pursue them.

2.2

Kayne (1981: 131) explicates the relation between dominance and unambiguous paths in the following way. Both the relations "dominates" and "is an antecedent of (under the binding principles)" are mediated by unambiguous paths. That is, if a node is to dominate another node or if a node is to be the antecedent for another node, then there must be an unambiguous path from, respectively, the dominated node or the anaphor to the dominating node or the antecedent. Notice, too, that Kayne's construction can be understood to take the "point of view" of the "commandee," although not, of course, in those terms.

It is worth examining the relation of dominance to unambiguous path. It appears that Kayne is suggesting, obliquely, that dominance is not the basic relation in syntax but, rather, that unambiguous path is. This appears to be so because, apparently, he is taking dominance as a special case of an unambiguous path. If this is not the suggestion, then we are left to wonder **why** this particular generalization of dominance is significant. If dominance is still the basic primitive (and in Kayne's definition of unambigous path, which assumes trees as given, it seems to to be), then our "why question" arises. Why should this particular generalization of dominance play any role—what is special or natural about it formally? If, on the other hand, dominance is to be replaced by unambiguous path as the basic primitive, then, evidently, the definitions will have to be reworked, and at least some mention of this fundamental change in the theory should be made. Kayne does not indicate any recognition of the need to address either of these issues: either some formal justification, beyond the empirical observations and arguments he makes, for why the particular generalization of dominance should be important or some discussion of the replacement of dominance by unambiguous paths.

Notice, further, what would happen if we reconstrued unambiguous paths as a relation between a node and a set of nodes—let us call this set P. All nodes which dominate a node would be in the set connected to that node by unambiguous paths (i.e., in P). Thus, P would not pick out the set of potential antecedents for an anaphor, for example. Indeed, the set P seems to have no motivation whatsoever. There is no evident formal reason to collect all the nodes connected to a given node by unambiguous paths nor is there any linguistic reason to do so. The linguistic uses to which Kayne puts unambiguous paths all make reference not to P but to that subset of P which does not contain nodes which dominate the node which "generates" the set. This set, of course, is just the set of nodes which C-command the "generator," with the added condition that all branching is binary. The set P, then, is constructed only so that reference may be made to the subset that, essentially, is C-command; the more general relation of unambiguous path appears to be simply artifactual.

It is worthwhile to more directly compare C-command, as here understood, with unambiguous paths. Formally, neither relation contains the other. C-command contains pairs of nodes which are daughters of a mother which is more than binary branching, while unambiguous paths do not connect such sisters (Kayne 1981: 133). C-command does not contain nodes in the dominance relation, while unambigous paths do connect nodes so related. C-command, to reiterate, is a generalization of the sister relation, this latter defined in terms of the basic primitive direct dominance. The definitions are entirely straightforward; with unambiguous paths, there are possible equivocations with respect to the identity of the basic primitive relation. With C-command, the irrelevance of nodes in the dominance relation is part of the characterization of the set in question, so that artifactual detours are avoided, unlike with unambiguous paths. As shown in Section 1, C-command is unique among relations which hold between nodes not related by dominance because it represents the minimal factorization of the PM containing the C-commandee and its C-commanders. Any other relation either requires arbitrary nodes (because it is neither the minimal nor the maximal factorization of the PM) or, if it is the maximal factorization (hence nonarbitrary in the nodes it includes), it denies the relevance of the full hierarchical structure. By contrast, there is no motivation for the set P, the set of nodes "generated" by tracing unambigous paths. Such motivation as Kayne adduces is, on the one hand, essentially empirical, which effectively forecloses the explanatory project, and, on the other, refers only to a subset of (C-commanders in) P.

Notice further that if Kayne's empirical arguments are good, we can, after all, incorporate them into a C-command-based approach simply by stipulating that all branching is binary. There is a loss here because contrary to many who purportedly follow him in this, on Kayne's approach binary branching is not stipulated but rather entailed given the unambiguous path requirement. Alternatively, we might take it as an empirical generalization that, for at least some linguistic relations, just those C-commanders that are also connected by an unambiguous path are licit relata. That is, we maintain the set of C-commanders as our basic set of potential relata, and then we impose, in particular cases, for empirical reasons, the further unambiguous path condition. This seems to be on the right track, as the motivation for C-command is not essentially empirical and linguistic, while that for unambiguous paths is.

In sum, then: Kayne asks the right question ("why C-command?") and has the correct intuition ("it is related to dominance"), but in developing the intuition to answer the question, he attempts to replace C-command with unambiguous paths and this attempt fails, once C-command is correctly understood.

3.0

Barker & Pullum (1990) ask not "why C-command?" but rather "what is a command relation?". They provide a formal definition that is general enough to allow as specific instances the various "command relations" that have appeared in the linguistic literature (e.g., command, C-command, M-command). They are providing a means for understanding what all these relations share, what mathematical properties any such relation might have, and what makes each relation different from the others. I shall argue that their investigation has two major flaws, where the first leads directly to the second: (1) the formalization takes the point of view of the commander, not the commandee and (2) they do not appreciate the central, founding place of C-command in the family of command relations.

3.1

The crucial definitions are (4) and (5) (Barker & Pullum's (1) & (2)).

(4) $UB(a, P) = \{b: b >^{D} a \ \& \ P(b)\}$

(5) $CP = \{\langle a, b \rangle: \forall x \ [(x \in UB(a, P)) \rightarrow x \geq^{D} b]\}$

Definition (4) defines the set of *Upper Bounds* (UB) for a node (a) with respect to a predicate (P); it says that a node is in that set just in case it both has property P (e.g., if P is **being a maximal projection** and a node is a VP, then this condition is satisfied) and properly dominates **node a** (*proper domination* is dominance without reflexivity; thus, a node cannot be its own UB). Definition (5) defines *command relation.* It says that **node a** *P-commands* (the command relation *generated* by the property P) **node b** just in case every upper bound for **node a** with respect to property P dominates (N.B., *dominates,* not *properly* dominates) **node b.** Thus, if P is **being a maximal projection,** then (5) says that **node a** *M-commands* **node b** just in case every node which both is a maximal projection and properly dominates **node a** also dominates **node b.** Which is the same as saying that **node a** *M-commands* **node b** just in case every distinct (from **node a**) maximal projection dominating **node a** also dominates **node b.**

C-command is defined by way of defining a predicate, **is a branching node,** and substituting this predicate for the variable P in the definition (5). Barker & Pullum give (6) as a definition for this predicate (their (20)).

(6) $P5 = \{a: \exists x,y[x \neq y \;\&\; aMx \;\&\; aMy]\}$

The symbol M represents the relation "is the mother of," for which Barker & Pullum also provide an explicit definition (their (19); see (8) below). So, a node is in the set defined by (6) just in case it is the mother of two distinct nodes. Substituting into (5), we see that **node a** *C-commands* **node b** just in case every branching node distinct from **node a** that dominates **node a** also dominates **node b.** As Barker & Pullum point out, it is not necessary to say anything about the **first** branching node nor require that **node a** be dominated when defining C-command; these follow from the general definitions. The definition (4), of UB, ensures that the commander is dominated by the predicate satisfying node(s), and the universal quantifier in (5) obviates the need for any reference to **firstness** (obviously, a set containing all P-satisfying nodes distinct from **node a** which dominate **node a** must contain the first such node). While there is a great deal more to their paper, not all of it is relevant to present concerns.

3.2

Perhaps because it does not address the explanatory issues, Barker & Pullum's (1990) paper has the capacity to obscure them. The principle point obscured is the singularity of C-command. There is no recognition in the paper that C-command—or any command relation (but see the discussion of "IDC-command" below)—has a status different from that of any other command relation. Concomitantly, there is no hint as to **why** command relations should play any—let alone such a central—role in syntax. Again, this is not their aim, so it may be uncharitable to criticize them on this score. But, I claim, there is the possibility that this central point will be not merely unexpressed but, because unappreciated, unnecessarily difficult to express when pointed out. The discussion by Barker & Pullum does not distinguish among command relations along an "essentially linguistic" versus "essentially not linguistic" parameter. Therefore, a relation such as C-command, which is essentially not linguistic, is conflated with relations such as "M-command" and "S-command" (= "command"), which are essentially linguistic in that they depend on specifically linguistic predicates for their definition. Barker & Pullum fail to see this central distinction because their formalization takes the point of view of the C-commander rather than the C-commandee. Their viewpoint allows the fundamental insight that C-command is the unique minimal factorization of a PM with respect to a given node to be buried, perhaps inexhumably so.

We move now to a comparison of Barker & Pullum and R/C.

3.3

Barker & Pullum's assumptions differ from those in R/C in a number of ways. One is that for Barker & Pullum (1990: 4) all command relations are reflexive. This is obviously not true of C-command as defined here. If it were true, that might seem to be no bad thing: in that case, the set of C-commanders for a given node would exactly minimally factor the PM. Under current assumptions, it is the union of the set of C-commanders and the singleton set containing the node in question that factors the PM, as noted above. This suggests that a reformulation incorporating Barker & Pullum's reflexivity property might be an improvement. However, I think that this is not so.

The "minimal factorization" of a PM is always with respect to some node. That is, it is only relative to a given node that a set of other nodes is the minimal factorization of the PM in question (an "absolute" minimal factorization would evidently be just the root node). The R/C account of C-command reconstructs the node dependence of the notion "minimal factorization," while a Barker &

Pullum-style approach would lose it. The node being C-commanded would have no distinct status in determining the set under a Barker & Pullum-style reformulation. In Section 3.4 I nevertheless provide both sorts of formalizations.

Barker & Pullum (1990: 10–11) also assume that dominance and command relations may overlap. They provide no reasons for so doing—they do cite "formal convenience"—and do not endorse the only arguments in the literature that they know of supporting this view.[7] In defense of their position, they write that they "are aware of no authors who give definite motivation for the exclusion." The view here espoused provides definite motivation, as discussed in Section 1: the MPST needs a formal relation other than dominance for relating nodes, and our "dominance-free but dominance-based" construction for C-command allows us to understand C-command—the (unique) minimal factorization of a PM with respect to a given node—as that relation.

It is worth noting that Barker & Pullum's position also leads them to an odd argument with respect to Langacker's (1969) "command" ("S-command" as they call it). Langacker's original definition included a clause to the effect that nodes in the command relation were not also in the dominance relation. Their reconstruction of this relation, which neither includes such a "nondominance" condition in the definition of the generating property for this command relation (P1—see their (10)) nor has it as a consequence of the general definition of command relation ((5) repeated here) into which P1 is substituted, leaves out this part of Langacker's relation. Their justification for this move is that, when Langacker came to apply (S-)command in mediating pronoun-antecedent relations, he additionally required that a pronoun not simultaneously precede and command its antecedent. Given this, the "nondominance" requirement in the definition of (S-)command is redundant.

(5) $CP = \{\langle a, b\rangle : \forall x\ [(x \in UB(a, P)) \rightarrow x \geq^{D} b]\}$

But this is surely a peculiar argument. It rests on conflating an application of the relation—to pronoun-antecedent relations—with the relation itself. In this case, since this is, apparently, the only application of (S-)command, the point does not appear very sharply. But suppose there were many applications, and in each case it were to turn out that dominance and command should not overlap. As Barker & Pullum (1990: 11) note, in their framework such non-overlap "should be made to follow from other considerations"; this could easily miss a significant generalization.

Consider the situation somewhat more abstractly. There is a relation, call it C, which has two conditions which must be met for its satisfaction, call them C_1 and C_2. There is a second relation, call it R, which also has two conditions which must be met for its satisfaction: one is C, the second we can call B. Now, it happens that meeting B entails meeting C_1. Therefore, with respect to R, C_1 is redundant given B. Should we therefore eliminate C_1 from C? This is exactly what Barker & Pullum have done with respect to (S-)command. Clearly, we should do as they have done only if **both** (1a) either R turns out to be the only (possible) application of C or (1b) all other applications of C independently entail C_1 **and** (2) there is no independent theoretical reason to maintain C_1.[8]

Barker & Pullum seem unaware of the need to argue for the relevant version of either (1a) or (1b). And in Section 1 we have already begun the argument that our version of (2) does not hold—the argument is that dominance cannot overlap with any command relation. The argument continues immediately below in the discussion of (7) "IDC-command" and again in Section 3.4.

Further, the redundancy which Barker & Pullum locate crucially depends on the Exclusivity Condition on PMs (repeated here from Chapter 1 (1)), according to which nodes are in a dominance relation if and only if they are not in a precedence relation. But, the MPST being advocated here gave up the Exclusivity Condition when it gave up precedence as a formal primitive. Thus, the redundancy is gone, too.[9]

Exclusivity Condition:

$$(\forall x, y \in N)\ ((\langle x, y\rangle \in P \vee \langle y,x\rangle \in P) \leftrightarrow (\langle x, y\rangle \notin D \ \&\ \langle y, x\rangle \notin D))$$

Barker & Pullum also do not share the R/C views concerning either nonbranching domination or, it seems, the relation between lexical items and (pre)terminals. As noted, R/C argue that there is no nonbranching domination at all and that the relation between lexical items and (pre)terminals is not (direct/immediate) domination but rather instantiation. This difference comes out in Barker & Pullum's discussion of IDC-command ("immediate dominance command," from Pullum 1986):

(7) a IDC-commands b if and only if a's mother dominates b.
(Barker & Pullum's (21))

(1) For any node A, the C-commanders of A are all the sisters of every node which dominates A.

If one adopts the R/C views, then this relation collapses into C-command, as comparison of (7) with (1), repeated here, reveals. This is so because on R/C assumptions all mothers will be branching, (pre)terminals are not mothers, and command and dominance are disjoint. This is a significant result because Barker & Pullum (1990: 16) show that IDC-command "is the most restrictive (smallest) of all command relations. Another way to put this is that a pair ⟨a, b⟩ is in the IDC-command relation if and only if ⟨a, b⟩ is in every command relation." The significance of the identity between (7) and (1) is that it shows again the basic nature of C-command. It is C-command that is the core—smallest—relation in the family of relations which Barker & Pullum investigate. We have begun to see why this should be so from the point of view taken here; it is heartening that the different perspective taken by Barker & Pullum can be seen to converge on this result. We return to the discussion of the status of C-command among the family of command relations in the next section, which reformalizes the R/C approach to C-command.

3.4

I present here a formalization of present ideas in the spirit and formalism of Barker & Pullum for comparison with that of Barker & Pullum. I repeat definitions (4) and (5), for *Upper Bound* and *command relation,* respectively, and in (8) give Barker & Pullum's definition (18) for *mother.*

(4) $UB(a, P) = \{b: b >^{D} a \; \& \; P(b)\}$

(5) $C_P = \{\langle a, b\rangle: \forall x \; [(x \in UB(a, P)) \rightarrow x \geq^{D} b]\}$

(8) $M = \{\langle a, b\rangle: a >^{D} b \; \& \; \sim\exists x[a >^{D} x >^{D} b]\}$

In (9), we define the set of commmanders of **node a** with respect to a **property P.**[10]

(9) Set of P(roperty)-commanders of node a:
$CP(a) = \{b: \sim a \geq^D b \ \& \sim b \geq^D a \ \& \ \forall x[P(x) \ \& \ x >^D b \rightarrow x \geq^D a]\}$

This says, first, that the commanders of node a with respect to **property P** are a set. It then says in the first two conjuncts that the members of this set are not in a dominance relation with **node a.** Finally, the third conjunct says that the members of this set are properly dominated by all the nodes having **property P** which dominate **node a.** C-command is the relation that results from substituting the property "mother of b," derivable from (8), for P in (9). In this case, the second conjunct of the antecedent of the conditional is always satisfied; that is, if a node satisfies "mother of b" then it necessarily satisfies "properly dominates b." Thus, the conditional reduces to simply $\forall x[xMb \rightarrow x \geq^D a]$, that is, all the nodes whose mothers dominate **node a.** Given the rest of (9) and R/C assumptions, this is equivalent to (1), as we desire.

Consider again the relation between this conception of C-command and IDC-command: as pointed out above, C-command is equivalent to the set of IDC-commanders for a given node, under R/C assumptions. As also noted above, Barker & Pullum (1990: 16) show that IDC-command "is the most restrictive (smallest) of all command relations. . . . a pair ⟨a, b⟩ is in the IDC-command relation if and only if ⟨a, b⟩ is in every command relation." From our point of view, we can understand the two parts of this statement in the following ways. First, C-command is the smallest / most restrictive command relation because the relation P is "mother of b," and any other relation that satisfies the other antecedent conjunct "properly dominates b" will necessarily include the nodes which satisfy "mother of b" (given the other conditions in (9)), but not vice-versa. The second, more formal part of the statement becomes, under R/C assumptions, that the set of C-commanders of a node is the intersection of all command relation sets for that node—in other words, only nodes which are in every command relation set for a node are in the C-command set for that node.

C-command is foundational for the family of command relations in that every other command relation is a superset of C-command.

If we wish to allow command relations to be reflexive, as Barker & Pullum unwarrantedly do (but I do not), then we must change the relation in the first two conjuncts in (9) (repeated here) from *dominance* to *proper dominance;* this allows for the case of self-domination (i.e., it allows a = b) but no other cases of dominance. Symbolically, it looks as in (10)

(9) Set of P(roperty)-commanders of node a:
$CP(a) = \{b: \sim a \geq^D b \;\&\; \sim b \geq^D a \;\&\; \forall x[P(x) \;\&\; x >^D b \rightarrow x \geq^D a]\}$

(10) Set of P(roperty)-commanders of node a, reflexive:
$CP(a) = \{b: \sim a >^D b \;\&\; \sim b >^D a \;\&\; \forall x[P(x) \;\&\; x >^D b \rightarrow x \geq^D a]\}$

3.5

Barker & Pullum seek to reconstruct the definitions of various command relations found in the syntax literature within a suitably explicit and general formalism to allow for investigation of the mathematical properties of the relations so reconstructed. This is an important project. Unfortunately, given that all command relations in the literature (other than in R/C) have been formulated from the point of view of the commander and in terms of pairs of nodes, this reconstruction simply inherits—and perhaps even exacerbates—some undesirable properties. In particular, the central place and unique character of C-command is obscured, and given this paper's singular status as a general formal framework for studying command relations (as well as "mate relations" and "government", Barker & Pullum 1990: 16–18), this could well have deleterious implications for research which aims at explanation along the lines of the present inquiry.

4.0

We turn now to C-command in GB and (early) GPSG practice.

4.1

Despite certain problems in the statement of its definitions (see Pullum 1989 and Chapter 4 here), Chomsky (1986a) can be taken to make two proposals concerning C-command. One is directly about C-command, the other is about dominance, hence indirectly about C-command. The first suggestion (Chomsky 1986a: 8) is similar in intent, it seems, to the more general project of Barker & Pullum. Chomsky (1986: 8 (13)) defines C-command as in (11).

(11) α C-commands β iff α does not dominate β and every γ that dominates α dominates β.

Chomsky suggests that this represents a "general way" to understand C-command, and that values for γ might be restricted to maximal projections or to branching categories, depending on the empirical context, apparently. That this is conceptually related to Barker & Pullum's work seems clear.

The other suggestion Chomsky makes (1986a: 7) is actually to follow May (1985: 56–58) in revising the notion of dominance. The specific proposal is that in adjunction structures a node must be dominated by all "occurences" of the adjoined-to category in order to count as dominated by (the node labelled by) that category. That is, if a node (labelled) X is adjoined to a node (labelled) Y, X is not "new dominated" by Y, because it is "old dominated" only by the adjunction structure mother (labelled) Y, not by both that node and the adjoined-to (Y-labelled) node. The adjoined-to node and the mother of the adjunction "do not constitute distinct categorial projections" but rather are a single "multi-membered projection," and it is dominance by a projection that matters (May 1985: 56–57). I discuss and clarify these notions in Chapter 4; for present purposes, it is enough to see that they lead to changes in what C-commands what, as can be readily grasped.

These works are less concerned with C-command in itself and more interested in which command relation is most useful for particular syntactic purposes—with the added oddity that whichever command relation this turns out to be is thereby given the (honorific?) name "C-command."

4.2

The moves made in Chomsky (1986a) effectively preclude an explanatory approach to C-command. If we understand "C-command" as in (11) above, which is a less formal analogue of Barker & Pullum's work, as noted, then we run into the sorts of problems set out in Section 3.2. True C-command is conflated with various other command relations, and the founding nature of C-command for this family is obscured. Once more, essentially linguistic relations (e.g.,

M-command) are run together with the essentially nonlinguistic C-command. Using "C-command" for whatever command relation seems to be empirically warranted by the investigator's research at least tacitly suggests that there is no deeper, pre-empirical, theoretical account of C-command to be looked for or found. And this is wrong.

These observations carry over to the revision in the dominance relation. Actually, this is not strictly so, as the dominance revision runs together the distinction between nodes and labelled nodes, whether the labels are linguistic or something else. Still, the general point holds, in that a purely graph-theoretic relation between nodes has been changed to one that holds in a substantive application of graph-theoretic concepts. There is nothing wrong with such a substantive relation, if it is empirically motivated, except that there seems to be no reason to use the term "dominance" for this new linguistic relation, as this can do little except create confusion, it seems to me (see Chapter 4 for discussion and reformalization). To reiterate, given the empirical nature of the relation, explanatory insights of the sort sought in the present work cannot be forthcoming. And, again, it is possible that such terminological moves may (unintentionally) stop such investigations before they begin.

4.3

Within "canonical" GPSG, C-command apparently plays no role; thus, the term does not appear in the index to Gazdar, Klein, Pullum, & Sag (1985), and this is, to my knowledge, an accurate indexing of the book with respect to this term. In earlier expositions, however, claims were sometimes made regarding C-command. The general claim was basically the following. C-command conditions need not be explicitly stated in the grammar. Rather, they follow from the form and content of the rules used to analyze the dependencies apparently mediated by C-command. For example, Gazdar (1982: 174) writes: "Note also that the familiar c-command condition on the relation between the controlling expression and the controlled "hole" simply follows from the use of context-free phrase structure rules to generate this kind of construction: in a rule of the form $[_{\alpha}$ a b/a] or $[_{\alpha}$ b/a a], a cannot help but c-command the hole in b/a. But the c-command condition on binding has to be separately stipulated in theories which employ transformations like Controlled Pro Deletion or wh-movement to handle unbounded dependencies."

Similarly, Fodor (1983: 175): "This [c-command] condition will always be met in the case of the ungoverned dependencies, since the correlation between the presence of a filler in a sentence and the presence of a gap can only be ensured in this nontransformational system by having one and the same phrase structure rule introduce both the filler and the highest slashed node over its gap. In other words, a linking rule for an ungoverned dependency must be such that it provides, as sister to the slashed node it introduces, a node of the same syntactic category as follows the slash, to serve as the filler."

The central idea in early GPSG, then, was to treat C-command conditions as an "emergent property," as it were, of the system of rules and representations. The predicate itself seems to have had no actual status within the framework.

4.4

The "emergent property" approach to C-command in (early) GPSG ultimately stems from the fact that "any dependency between non-sisters, such as between an antecedent and trace, could only be licensed by a tree-walking path." (Fodor & Jones 1987: 209) But this fact does not in itself assure that C-command is the emergent property. Any two nodes can be connected by a "tree-walking path" in a rooted, connected graph. Thus, for example, it is consistent with the "tree-walking path" requirement that the nodes labelled F and J in (3) (repeated here) be connected. Of course, there is no C-command between the nodes (F, J) connected by the tree-walking path.

(3)

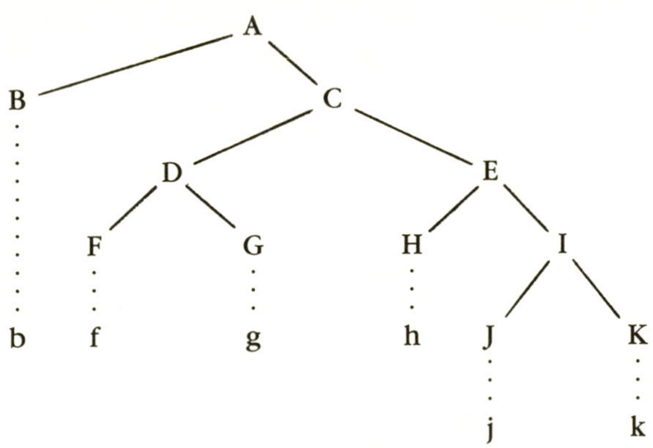

It was, in fact, conditions on the form of "linking rules"—the rules that introduced into the tree the "slashed-category" which carried information about the presence of a "gap"—that assured that the C-command relation held (Fodor 1983: 175). It is not at all clear that one could not have constructed a "GPSG" in which linking rules did not have this property, but rather allowed, for example, that the node labelled F be a filler for a gap located at the node labelled J in (3). The emergent status of C-command, then, seems radically contingent in GPSG, stemming as it does, apparently, from empirically driven conditions on the form of linking rules at least as much as from the tree-walking path requirement. The true nature of the special status of C-command does not come through on this analysis. There seems to be no theoretical reason for C-command and not, say, M-command to be the emergent property. This issue—the status of C-command—is worth discussing further.

There are evidently two possibilities with respect to the status of C-command restrictions as an emergent property of a GPSG. Either, as just suggested, the status is contingent and there could be a GPSG without such an emergent property or C-command restrictions are a necessary (side-effect) property of a GPSG. We have already discussed the first alternative; let us, therefore, examine the second case.

Now, with respect to our putative relation above between the nodes (F, J), a "GPSG with C-command necessary" could not license a tree-walking path connecting them. There might seem to be no great loss in this particular case, but consider the situation with respect to other command relations. As has been discussed, other command relations are supersets of C-command, and other command relations (e.g., M-command, see Section 5) are adverted to in the syntactic literature. If it were a necessary property of any GPSG that nonsister dependencies be mediated by the emergent property C-command, then this would seem to rule out even other command relations. However, perhaps this need not be so: C-command's necessity need not imply the impossibility of other mediating relations. Nonetheless, there is a problem here.

Holding that C-command restrictions necessarily emerge from the form and content of the rules and representations of any possible GPSG has great explanatory promise, but the promise is predicated on C-command being the **only** relation which mediates nonsister relations. If other (command) relations are needed, either they must be stipulated or they have to emerge too. If they are stipulated (both what they are and what linguistic relations they mediate), then some explanatory power is lost. For one thing, such stipulations must be explicitly stated somewhere, unlike an emergent property, thus creating an asymmetry between C-command and other (command) relations. But, perhaps not all explanatory force is lost: the core command relation—C-command—is a necessary property of such a grammar, whereas other command relations—supersets of C-command—are stipulated, empirical findings. This is not so terrible; much worse would be if some other command relation were the necessary one. Still, given that, by hypothesis, (some) nonsister relations are necessarily mediated by C-command in such a grammar, we might wonder about why there should be any role for other command relations. If the grammar must use C-command, why should it also use other unnecessary command relations?[11]

Consider the difference here between the hypothetical GPSG and our MPST-based theory. In our approach, C-command is not a necessary property of grammars; it is a straightforwardly definable relation in a PM, but grammars might not require it—for example, the maximal factorization might be what grammars require. It is a natural formal relation in our theory, but its linguistic applicability is contingent. On this view, it is perhaps less surprising that other command relations are also contingently useful in linguistics. C-command has a different formal status from other command relations in our theory, but in the grammar they are all on a par: it must be stated which command relation mediates which linguistic relation. In the GPSG, the different status of C-command is internal to the grammar: C-command, but not other command relations, is an emergent that is not stated. It seems to me that the hypothetical GPSG gets things exactly wrong here. C-command and other command relations do not differ in how they "go about" their substantive linguistic work; they differ because C-command is not "essentially linguistic" and other command relations are.

Let us turn to the alternative "GPSG with C-command necessary" in which other command relations need not be stipulated, but are themselves emergents from the rules and representations. In this case, apparently, each nonlocal dependency would have its restricting command relation as a side effect of the rules and representations needed for its analysis. C-command, then, would have no special status among the family of command relations, other than perhaps being most commonly the emergent property. I take it that though it would be a remarkable feat to construct a grammar in which each nonlocal dependency did, in fact, provide its mediating command relation as a side effect, nonetheless we might feel that something signficant had been missed. Namely, the fact of there being a family of command relations, with C-command at its core.

I conclude that there would be something unsatisfactory about each of the three GPSG alternatives: (1) C-command as a contingent emergent property (2a) C-command as a necessary emergent property, with other command relations stipulated; and (2b) C-command as a necessary emergent property, and all other command relations also emergents. The importance of this conclusion and the discussion that led to it—and of the disappearance of (any discussion of) C-command from more recent GPSG—should be clear. Once more, the approach does not lead us to understand the fundamental fact about C-command—its formal nature that places it at the core of all command relations—but rather obscures it.

5.0

We have completed the analysis and explanation of C-command itself. It is a generalization of the sister relation and as such has a distinguished, founding place among the command relations. And, as Barker & Pullum have taught us, there is a family of command relations. Among those which linguists have adverted to are (S-)command, Kommand, and M-command. Let us examine this last one from our point of view to see exactly how it relates to (our theory of) C-command.

5.1

For the purposes of discussion, we follow Barker & Pullum (1990: 13) in assuming "a class of nodes defined as maximal projections," identifiable as "a set MAX of labels." The property P in (9) (repeated here) is then M, as in (12) (see Barker & Pullum 1990: 13 (15))

(9) Set of P(roperty)-commanders of node a:
$CP(a) = \{b: \sim a \geq^D b \ \& \sim b \geq^D a \ \& \ \forall x[P(x) \ \& \ x >^D b \rightarrow x \geq^D a]\}$

(12) $M = \{z: z \in MAX\}$

Looking now at an example, we can see that in (13), the M-commanders of V_2—that is, substituting V_2 for node a and M for P in (9)—form the set $\{NP_1, NP_2\}$ (the subscripts on V and NP appear simply to distinguish one from the other). These are the only nodes which are not in a dominance relation with V_2 and for which it is true that every maximal projection that properly dominates them also dominates V_2. Neither N nor PP is in this set because each is properly dominated by NP_1, which does not dominate V_2. The C-command set for V_2 is also $\{NP_1, NP_2\}$. Because every set is a superset of itself, the M-command set is a superset of the C-command set, as the theory requires.

(13)

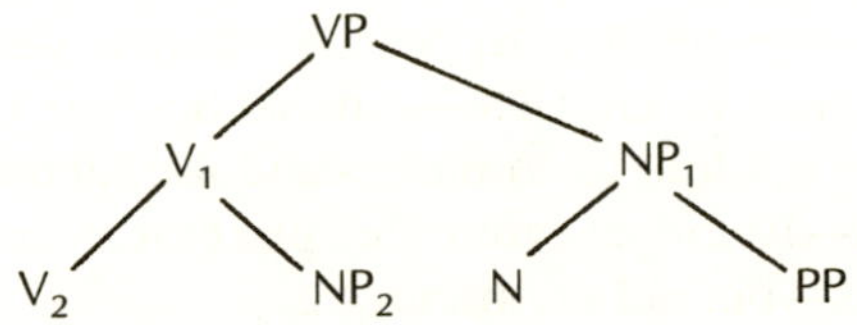

Picking another node, we can see that the M-command set for N is $\{PP, V_1, V_2, NP_2\}$. None of these is in a dominance relation with N and for each of them it is true that all the maximal projections that properly dominate it also dominate N—for PP these are NP_1 and VP, while for the other three it is just VP. The C-command set for N is $\{PP, V_1\}$. Thus, the M-command set is a superset of the C-command set and V_2 M-commands, but does not C-command, N, as is often thought to be empirically desirable, say, for government relations.

5.2

We thus see that the view here developed allows for new insight into M-command and the domain of command relations in general. M-command—and any other command relation—is a superset of C-command, an insight unavailable on other views. No view that does not "take the point of view of the commandee," as does R/C, would be likely to yield this result, although, of course, it could be incorporated into an alternative.

6.0

The fundamental fact about C-command is that it is nonempirical and nonlinguistic. I have argued that the most explicit and detailed attempts to understand (C-)command within standard assumptions actually obscure this fundamental fact. C-command is a formal, graph-theoretic relation which founds a family of further command relations, themselves involving substantively linguistic predicates. It is the most restrictive of command relations in that other command relations are supersets of C-command.

C-command is a generalization of the sister relation and so is a relation parasitic on (direct) dominance and complementary to dominance. It provides the unique nonarbitrary factorization of a PM that respects the full facts of hierarchical structure.

Command relations are ubiquitous in current syntactic practice, and this is no accident. The strength of the present proposal is that, by taking the point of view of the commandee and embedding C-command within the MPST-based approach to syntax which has only the single formal primitive (direct) dominance, it alone makes clear why this is so.

3

Coordination

0.0

In this chapter and the next I develop what I call the "extended base." The idea here is that there are PMs which are not projected from the lexicon but which nevertheless fall under the MPST. That is, even though these PMs are not simply the result of projection from the lexicon, they are still subject to the theory of the base (the MPST). The theory of the base is the theory of well-formedness for PMs, and the content of that theory, recall, is essentially Project Alpha and the definitions of Minimal and Maximal Projections.

The "secret" of the extended base is combining of well-formed PMs. Thus, in each of this chapter and Chapter 4 an operation is defined for combining PMs projected from the lexicon to form a new PM. For the new object to be a well-formed PM, it must meet the conditions of the MPST. This, then, is the meaning of the "extended base": given the set of well-formed PMs projected from the lexicon in accordance with the MPST, we can augment that set with combining operations on its members that return objects which also meet the conditions of the MPST. Essentially, then, we have something like an algebra consisting of the set of PMs and two combining operations which enlarge the original set. We might alternatively think of this in terms of a recursive definition for PMs, in which the outputs of the recursive clauses must also meet the conditions on the basic clause.

0.1

In this chapter I apply the theory as so far adumbrated to the analysis of the syntax of coordinate conjunction constructions (CCC, hereafter). The analysis is a recasting of that developed in Chametzky (1987a), which itself refines and formalizes the ideas put forward in Goodall (1987). This analysis of CCC is called the "three-dimensional" (3-D) or "union-of-phrase-markers" approach.

Section 1 of this chapter presents the central desideratum for a theory of the syntax of CCC—the "law of coordination of likes"—and introduces a formal construction on "basic" PMs that achieves this desideratum. The construction and further manipulations of it are novel, so several examples are worked through in some detail. Section 2 addresses some conceptual and technical issues that arise with respect to the construction merely exemplified in Section 1. Section 3 steps back a bit to offer some theoretical perspective on the analysis, with a particular eye toward motivating the apparently arbitrary formal construction. A novel aspect of this analysis is that the conjunction words (*and, or, but*) are not present in the syntax, and indeed, these different types of CCC are all analyzed as having the same syntax. Section 4 presents an immediate and central empirical result (discussed first in Chametzky (1987a)) due to this aspect of the analysis, in hopes of increasing its plausibility. However, it is clear that the CCC types must be distinguished, and doing so with this analysis requires adopting an unorthodox grammar organization independently argued for by Hornstein (1985-86; 1987). This, too, is discussed in Section 4, as is conjunction placement. Section 5 summarizes the argument and findings.

0.2

An informal characterization of the "leading idea" of this approach is the following. The intuition behind the transformation of *conjunction reduction* was correct, despite myriad difficulties in actually stating that transformaton. That intuition is that coordinate structures are "derived" structures, with the inputs to the "derivation" being the syntactic structures of complete sentences, and that the derivaton somehow "factors out" and "eliminates" material common to the inputs. Resolving the difficulities requires not giving up the intuition but rather giving up formalizing it as a transformation.

Instead of using transformational operations for moving, regrouping, or deleting constituents, the union of phrase markers approach analyzes the syntactic structure of CCC as arising from the operation of *set union*. This analysis retains a "derivational" characterization of CCC. It also obviously requires that syntactic structures be sets, which they are not in the MPST—a PM is a 4-tuple consisting of two sets (nodes, labels) a relation between these sets, and the reflexive, transitive, antisymmetric relation D* (dominance) on the set of nodes. This is discussed in Section 1.1.

0.3

It is perhaps slightly misleading, though nonetheless helpful, to analogize the 3-D approach to conjunction reduction as I just did. It might be more accurate to suggest that the approach is a refining of the idea of *generalized transformations,* from the pre-Chomsky (1965) version of transformational grammar. Indeed, both the account of CCC in this chapter and the analysis of adjuncts proferred in the next can be understood in this way, I believe (I owe the generalized transformation idea to Lebeaux 1988; 1990 and to Speas 1990; 1991).

To reiterate the crucial idea: Separate full PMs are combined into a new single PM. Under this analysis, both the inputs and the output of the operation must conform to the well-formedness conditions on PMs, viz., the MPST. In this sense—and this is one of the central claims being advanced in this book—coordination and adjunct adding are ways of augmenting the set of base structures, rather than mappings to S-structures. We move now to the analysis of CCC.

1.0

The crucial property of CCC is that, in general, only like syntactic categories conjoin (there are questions and problems here that I put aside; see Sag, Gazdar, Weisler, & Wasow 1985; Chametzky 1987a; Dowty 1988; Steedman 1989 for discussion in various frameworks). Put differently, likeness of syntactic category is necessary and sufficient for coordinate conjunction (not all theories agree that syntactic categories are crucial, though all agree on some sort of "alikeness restriction"). Call this generalization the law of coordination of likes (LCL, hereafter) (see Williams 1981, for a statement).

Our primary desideratum, then, is to derive this generalization, rather than to stipulate it, within the theory of PMs we are developing.

1.1

According to Goodall's (1987) original version of the 3-D theory, a *compound PM* is defined as in (1) (see Higginbotham n.d. and Chametzky 1987a: 31-45 for discussion). Such a compound PM is the PM for a CCC in the earlier theory. However, we cannot use this definition.

(1) C, the compound PM of PMs A and B, $=_{def}$ A ∪ B

According to (1), a compound PM is the union of two PMs. As reiterated in Section 0.2, in the MPST PMs are not sets but rather 4-tuples, so we cannot simply perform set union on such objects. We can use (1) in the following way.

From any PM we can uniquely construct an object we can call the D*-set. The D*-set for a PM is the set of pairs of label-node pairs from the PM in which the nodes are in the D* (dominance) relation, where the first member of the pair dominates the second. Technically, the members of the pairs in the D*-set are themselves pairs of a label and a node, and only the nodes are in the dominance relation. For perspicuity, we shall write the members of such pairs not as label-node pairs but simply with the labels. Thus, the D*-set will look like a set of pairs of labels. As noted, the D*-set is unique for each PM, and, conversely, there is a unique PM for any D*-set. For CCC, we can start with two PMs, construct their respective D*-sets to "go proxy" for them, and then perform set union on the D*-sets. Finally, we can recover the complete PM that corresponds to the union, should we wish to.

Perhaps the best way to explain how (1) works in our theory is by means of examples. In our examples, we shall substitute D*-sets for PMs, and refer to these objects simply as PMs. Let us suppose, then, that we wish to form a compound PM from the PMs for the sentences in (2). The PMs (= D*-sets) are given in (3)—(3a) the PM for (2a), (3b) the PM for (2b)—with lexical instantiation notated by means of X/wxyz. Different label-category tokens are not notated to indicate distinctness (label-category tokens are important to, and discussed in, Chapter Four).

(2) a. That kid drank some sodas.
b. That kid ate some donuts.

(3) a. {(S, S),
(S, NP),
(S, VP),
(S, Det/that),
(S, N/kid),
(S, V/drank),
(S, NP),
(S, Det/some),

(S, N/sodas),
(NP, NP),
(NP, Det/that),
(NP, N/kid),
(VP, VP),
(VP, V/drank),
(VP, NP),
(VP, Det/some),
(VP, N/sodas),
(NP, NP),
(NP, Det/some),
(NP, N/sodas),
(Det/that, Det/that),
(N/kid, N/kid),
(V/drank, V/drank),
(Det/some, Det/some),
(N/sodas, N/sodas)}

b. {(S, S),
(S, NP),
(S, VP),
(S, Det/that),
(S, N/kid),
(S, V/ate),
(S, NP),
(S, Det/some),
(S, N/donuts),
(NP, NP),
(NP, Det/that),
(NP, N/kid),
(VP, VP),
(VP, V/ate),
(VP, NP),
(VP, Det/some),
(VP, N/donuts),
(NP, NP),
(NP, Det/some),
(NP, N/donuts),
(Det/that, Det/that),
(N/kid, N/kid),
(V/ate, V/ate),

(Det/some, Det/some),
(N/donuts, N/donuts)}

The union of these two is quite straightforward and is given in (4). Notice that there is only one occurrence of any ordered pair, because in sets multiple occurrences of an element are meaningless. Thus, the fact that a pair such as (S, S) occurs in both PMs (indeed, this particular pair occurs in every PM) does not mean that it occurs more than once in the compound PM. Thus, by using set union, we immediately get the "factoring out" noted earlier with respect to conjunction reduction. (The PM in (4) is identical to that in (3a) except that the last seven pairs are those from (3b), which do not occur in (3a).)

(4) Union of (3a) & (3b)

{(S, S),
(S, NP),
(S, VP),
(S, Det/that),
(S, N/kid),
(S, V/drank),
(S, NP),
(S, Det/some),
(S, N/sodas),
(NP, NP),
(NP, Det/that),
(NP, N/kid),
(VP, VP),
(VP, V/drank),
(VP, NP),
(VP, Det/some),
(VP, N/sodas),
(NP, NP),
(NP, Det/some),
(NP, N/sodas),
(Det/that, Det/that),
(N/kid, N/kid),
(V/drank, V/drank),
(Det/some, Det/some),
(N/sodas, N/sodas),

(S, V/ate),
(S, N/donuts),
(VP, V/ate),
(VP, N/donuts),
(NP, N/donuts),
(V/ate, V/ate),
(N/donuts, N/donuts)}

It is probably useful to discuss an object such as (4). Only a single VP labelled node is represented in (4), even though there are two input VPs, one from each of (3a) and (3b). This property leads to the "3-D" name; the subparts of the original VPs are still dominated by VP but bear no dominance relation to one another. They are "parallel structures" in Goodall's (1987) terms—any precedence relation between them is not a matter of syntax but rather results directly from the temporal ordering of speech.

1.2

We turn now to locating "conjoinable categories" in a compound PM. First, we form the *symmetric difference* of A and B. That is, we form the set of all pairs that are in one or the other but not in both of the PMs in the compound; call this set D. For the examples (3a) & (3b) this is given in (5a).

Now we form two sets from D: the set F, given in (5b), of all categories that appear as first elements in the pairs in D, and the set I, given in (5c), of all instantiated categories that appear as second elements in the pairs in D.

Any member of F that appears in D with every member of I is a "conjoinable category" with respect to the input PMs.[1]

(5) a. Symmetric Difference of (3a) & (3b)

D = {(S, V/drank),
(S, N/sodas),
(S, V/ate),
(S, N/donuts),
(VP, V/drank),
(VP, N/sodas),
(VP, V/ate),
(VP, N/donuts),

(NP, N/sodas),
(NP, N/donuts),
(V/drank, V/drank),
(V/ate, V/ate),
(N/sodas, N/sodas),
(N/donuts, N/donuts)}

b. First elements of members of D

F = {S, VP, NP, V, N}

c. Instantiated second elements of members of D

I = {V/drank, N/sodas, V/ate, N/donuts}

In the example, the "conjoinable categories" are S and VP (but not either NP or N). Indeed, S is always a possible value—it is always possible to conjoin full sentences[2]—so for purposes of discussion we can, in each particular case, leave it out. Thus, the set D specific to the example is (6), not (5). And the only conjoinable category specific to these inputs is VP.

(6) Symmetric difference of (3a) & (3b), minus S

D = {(VP, V/drank),
(VP, N/sodas),
(VP, V/ate),
(VP, N/donuts),
(NP, N/sodas),
(NP, N/donuts),
(V/drank, V/drank),
(V/ate, V/ate),
(N/sodas, N/sodas),
(N/donuts, N/donuts)}

1.3

We now examine some other examples that illustrate some properties not exemplified in the above example. We then turn to some discusssion of the construction itself.

In (7), we have examples in which coordination of lexical categories is a possibility. Example (7c) is the PM for (7a); (7d) that for (7b).

(7) a. That kid is a shooter.
    b. That kid is a passer.

    c. {(S, S),
    (S, NP),
    (S, VP),
    (S, NP),
    (S, Det/that),
    (S, N/kid),
    (S, V/is),
    (S, Det/a),
    (S, N/shooter),
    (NP, NP),
    (NP, Det/that),
    (NP, N/kid),
    (VP, VP),
    (VP, V/is),
    (VP, NP),
    (VP, Det/a),
    (VP, N/shooter),
    (NP, NP),
    (NP, Det/a),
    (NP, N/shooter),
    (Det/that, Det/that),
    (N/kid, N/kid),
    (V/is, V/is),
    (Det/a, Det/a),
    (N/shooter, N/shooter)}

    d. {(S,S),
    (S, NP),
    (S, VP),
    (S, NP),
    (S, Det/that),
    (S, N/kid),
    (S, V/is),
    (S, Det/a),
    (S, N/passer),
    (NP, NP),
    (NP, Det/that),
    (NP, N/kid),

(VP, VP),
(VP, V/is),
(VP, NP),
(VP, Det/a),
(VP, N/passer),
(NP, NP),
(NP, Det/a),
(NP, N/passer),
(Det/that, Det/that),
(N/kid, N/kid),
(V/is, V/is),
(Det/a, Det/a),
(N/passer, N/passer)}

The set D with respect to (7) is given in (8a), F is given in (8b), and I in (8c).

(8) a. Symmetric difference of (7c) & (7d), minus S

D {(VP, N/shooter),
(VP, N/passer),
(NP, N/shooter),
(NP, N/passer),
(N/shooter, N/shooter),
(N/passer, N/passer)}

b. First elements of D (8a),

F = {VP, NP, N}

c. Instantiated second elements of D (8a),

I = {N/shooter, N/passer}

The possible "conjoinable categories" are VP, NP, and N—all the members of F (= 8b). Notice that N is a possible "conjoinable category," though it might appear not to be on first inspection of (8a). But, the question is one with respect to categories, and there is no difference in category between the differently instantiated N labelled nodes in (7) & (8a)—thus N is a member of F (= 8b).

In (9), we have examples in which not all the second members of pairs in D are members of I; that is, not all are (instantiated) lexical categories: (9c) is the PM for (9a), (9d) that for (9b), (9e) is the set D, (9f) is the set F, and (9g) is the set I. The only "conjoinable category" is VP.

(9) a. Some cats sit on some mats.
b. Some cats eat many sardines.
c. {(S, S),
(S, NP),
(S, VP),
(S, PP),
(S, NP),
(S, Det/some),
(S, N/cats),
(S, V/sit),
(S, P/on),
(S, Det/some),
(S, N/mats),
(NP, NP),
(NP, Det/some),
(NP, N/cats),
(VP, VP),
(VP, V/sit),
(VP, PP),
(VP, NP),
(VP, P/on),
(VP, Det/some),
(VP, N/mats),
(PP, PP),
(PP, NP),
(PP, P/on),
(PP, Det/some),
(PP, N/mats),
(NP, NP),
(NP, Det/some),
(NP, N/mats),
(Det/some, Det/some),
(N/cats, N/cats),
(V/sit, V/sit),
(P/on, P/on),
(Det/some, Det/some),
(N/mats, N/mats)}

d. { (S, S),
(S, NP),
(S, VP),
(S, NP),
(S, Det/some),
(S, N/cats),
(S, V/eat),
(S, Det/many),
(S, N/sardines),
(NP, NP),
(NP, Det/some),
(NP, N/cats),
(VP, VP),
(VP, V/eat),
(VP, NP),
(VP, Det/many),
(VP, N/sardines),
(NP, NP),
(NP, Det/many),
(NP, N/sardines),
(Det/some, Det/some),
(N/cats, N/cats),
(V/eat, V/eat),
(Det/many, Det/many),
(N/sardines, N/sardines)}

e. Symmetric difference of (9c) & (9d), minus S

D = {(VP, V/sit),
(VP, PP),
(VP, P/on),
(VP, Det/some),
(VP, N/mats),
(PP, PP),
(PP, NP),
(PP, P/on),
(PP, Det/some),
(PP, N/mats),
(NP, Det/some),
(NP, N/mats),
(V/sit, V/sit),

(P/on, P/on),
(Det/some, Det/some),
(N/mats, N/mats),
(VP, V/eat),
(VP, Det/many),
(VP, N/sardines),
(NP, Det/many),
(NP, N/sardines),
(V/eat, V/eat),
(Det/many, Det/many),
(N/sardines, N/sardines)}

f. First elements of D (9e)

F = {VP, PP, NP, V, P, Det, N}

g. Instantiated second elements of D (9e)

I = {V/sit, P/on, Det/some, N/mats, N/sardines Det/many, V/eat}

2.0

We turn now to several issues about the construction. It appears somewhat formally arbitrary. Why does it have the form it does: the symmetric difference, the instantiated lexical categories that appear as second members of pairs? What, precisely, is the meaning of the "conjoinable category?" Where are the conjunction words (*and, or, but*)?

2.1

In order to address these issues, we have to think some about CCC. CCC are not purely formal. That is, they are of an ineliminably linguistic, as opposed to graph-theoretic, nature. This is hardly surprising, I suggest—CCC are, after all, a contingent syntactic phenomenon, in the sense that there is no purely formal requirement that such structures exist in grammar. A crucially linguistic fact about CCC is that (non)identity of the terminal string is a determinate of conjoinability options, as I now explain.

We are asking how to combine two distinct PMs into a single PM. Set union is the obvious formal move. But, only insofar as sentences differ does this question of combining arise. If they do not differ, then, of course, they are not different sentences, and the question of combining their distinct PMs cannot arise because the PMs are identical. The procedure for forming set D, using "symmetric difference" as just outlined, picks out those places where the PMs differ, which is what is called for. While at first it seems odd and arbitrary, the symmetric difference is thus exactly right.

Well, not exactly right; it is the differences in the terminal string that matter for CCC, and as we have seen, the symmetric difference—set D—includes pairs without instantiated lexical categories as members. That is why we need to form the further set I, of instantiated lexical categories dominated by some other node. The requirement on choosing members from the set F means that the "conjoinable categories" are just those categories that label the nodes which dominate the entire differing stretches of the respective terminal strings. In other words, the "conjoinable categories" are the constituents which these differing instantiated lexical categories are part of.

2.2

The meaning of "conjoinable categories" can now be understood. They locate the possible place(s) for conjunction placement. Conjunction words, as noted, do not appear in the input PMs or the compound. The claim being made here (and defended at length in Chametzky 1987a) is that the syntax of CCC with *and* and *or* (and *but*) is identical. Differences between them are located exclusively in PF and LF. Notice that if we wanted to include conjunction words (or some sort of marker for CCC "type") in the inputs, then we could not say that the PM for such an input was the PM for the otherwise identical sentence that was not input to compounding. On theoretical grounds, this seems absurd.

Should we wish to introduce conjunction markers in the formation of compounding, we should then be forced to do something other than set union—something perhaps not obviously set theoretic at all—in the construction. The construction as given introduces nothing that was not present in the inputs. Theoretically, the burden of argument falls on those who would have conjunction markers present in the syntax. Chametzky (1987a) is largely devoted to arguing that this burden cannot be met—empirical arguments are given there for preferring the syntax to be "conjunction-free"—and that objections to the "conjunction free syntax" program can be met, see Section 4 for discussion.

2.3

A technical question arises with respect to what Speas (1990: 44 - 45) calls the "lexical index" of a word. This index "seems to be necessary to distinguish multiple instances of the same word in a given structure." Thus, in order that there be two, not just one, maximal V projections in (10) (example (45) from Speas 1990: 45), the instances of the verb *make* and their respective Projection Chains are distinguished from one another by means of the "lexical index" annotation.

(10) You must make the TAs make their students work hard.

For the compound PM theory, the following issue arises. Given that there is a single label on a "locus node" (that is, a node labelled by a conjoinable category in a PM) that dominates the differing stretches of the respective terminal strings and that these differing stretches will have distinct lexical items as their heads (or, distinct instances of the same lexical item), each such item having its own lexical index, what is the index on the "locus node?" That is, in a compound PM we have two parallel Projection Chains that share a single dominating locus node that must be a part of both Chains, but the Chains are headed by items with different lexical indices. My suggestion here is straightforward, although entirely technical. We can consider the original lexical index itself as a set containing an integer and then the locus node's index will be the union of the two Chain lexical index sets. Recall, in this connection, that the identity of categories relevant to compounding is one that ignores differences in lexical instantiation; in other words, it is type, not token, identity that is relevant. This technical move makes both the compounding operation and the "compound index" the result of set union, an aesthetically pleasing formal confluence.

We turn now from these largely technical issues to somewhat larger theoretical points in an attempt to better motivate the analysis.

3.0

What has been suggested is an augmentation of the set of base PMs, the creation of an "extended base" whose members are still subject to the conditions of the MPST (e.g., Project Alpha). Because PMs are themselves only partially ordered sets (by means of the dominance relation), the union of two PMs to include parallel structures does not require relaxing or otherwise changing well-formedness conditions. This is in contrast to the original versions of the 3-D theory in Goodall (1987) and Chametzky (1987a), in which dominance and precedence totally order a PM. Thus, in the earlier theory, the syntactic structure of CCC is not a well-formed PM. Indeed, part of the content of the earlier theory is the altering of the notion "well-formed PM" to include CCC structures in which some elements do not partake of either dominance or precedence relations with one another.

3.1

Since the locus node is a single labelled node, it follows that coordination is always of constituents and, further, of like categories. Thus, the LCL is derived. If either of these were not the case—coordination either of nonconstituents or of nonlike categories—then the MPST would be violated in the resulting putative PM. Specifically, there would be ill-formed Projection Chains.

While it might seem that the results with respect to constituents and like categories—our derivation of the LCL—are the contingent and gerrymandered results of an arbitrary formal construction, it is not totally so: if combining PMs is to result in a PM, the output must meet the MPST. What is true is that there might be other ways to combine PMs (indeed, there is at least one other such way, adding of adjuncts, discussed in the next chapter) or no combined PMs at all.

The formal construction is perhaps not so arbitrary, either. As noted previously, union is the obvious way to combine two sets; union just is the combining of sets. Further, the union of two sets can itself be partitioned into (1) the intersection of and (2) the symmetric difference between the two sets. The intersection, in the case of CCC, represents overlap that is "factored out"; the symmetric difference, potential conjoinable categories. From a set theoretic point of view, the points where unioned sets respectively overlap and differ is a very natural partition. Indeed, in the absence of information about the nature of the members of the sets in question, it is difficult to imagine another partition that has a comparable naturalness. Which is a roundabout way of suggesting that no partition of the result of the union operation has greater formal generality.

We move now from the construction itself to an empirical result of the analysis and to the organization of a grammar incorporating such an analysis.

4.0

In Section 4.1, a central empirical consequence of the analysis in the realm of anaphora is discussed. Section 4.2 outlines the grammar organization advocated by Hornstein (1985–86; 1987), arguing that our analysis of CCC both requires something like this organization and converges with this one in particular. Section 4.3 pursues the somewhat technical issue of conjunction placement.

4.1.0

Certain patterns of anaphoric dependencies in CCC seem to counterexemplify the structural Binding Conditions on such dependencies. As I shall demonstrate, the 3-D analysis exactly predicts these patterns.

4.1.1

Consider (11) and (12) (we shall examine further anaphora patterns in CCC in Section 4.1.4).

(11) a. *She$_i$ and I consider Sue$_i$ a lucky person.
b. *Cyndi and she$_i$ consider Sue$_i$ a lucky person.
c. *She$_i$ considers Sue$_i$ a lucky person.
d. Near her$_i$, Sue$_i$ saw a snake.

(12) a. *Sue$_i$ considers Cyndi and her$_i$ lucky.
b. Sue$_i$ considers Cyndi and herself$_i$ lucky.
c. *Sue$_i$ considers her$_i$ lucky.
d. Sue$_i$ considers herself$_i$ lucky.

In (11), (a) and (b) pattern with (c) rather than with (d) with respect to "backward anaphora" possibilities. In (12) we find that the coreference possibilities in the CCC examples (a) and (b) pattern just as those in (d) and (c). In both cases, the CCC examples show anaphora patterns exactly like those found in sentences where the position occupied by the conjoined structures is occumpied by a nonconjoined NP. Put differently, the conjoineed structure apparently "isn't there" as far as anaphora is concerned.

Given rather common assumptions, the facts in (11), at least, present a rather large problem. The first of these assumptions is that CCC are branching structures. That is, the assumption is that there is a node with the same label as the conjuncts superordinate (usually mother) to the conjuncts, as in (13).

(13) $[[\text{Cyndi}]_{NP}$ and $[\text{Sue}]_{NP}]_{NP}$ like each other.

The other assumption is that there is a particular set of structural conditions on anaphora possiblities, viz., the Binding Theory. In the Binding Theory, *Bound* means "C-commanded by" and "coindexed with" while *Free* means "not bound."

(14) Binding Theory

Condition A: an anaphor is Bound in its governing category.

Condition B: a pronominal is Free in its governing category.

Condition C: an r-expression is Free.

4.1.2

Given these assumptions, we have a problem. If the structures of the conjoined phrases are as in (13), then (11a) and (11b) ought not to work as they do (the examples in (12) pose no problem). Rather, (11a) and (11b) should be like (11d). In the latter **her** fails to C-command **Sue** because of the PP-labelled node which dominates **her** and **near,** and therefore Condition C is not applicable and coreference is possible (although not required). In (11a) and (11b), given a structure such as (13), neither of the conjuncts C-commands the NP **Sue,** so, again, Condition C should be inapplicable and coreference possible; but, of course, it is not.

Undoubtedly, it is possible to fix up the Binding Conditions, or define a different command relation, or alter the notion of dominance (see Chapter 4) to account for these facts. However, the point is surely to not make any *ad hoc* repairs, but rather to have the facts fall out from what we already need. I shall therefore simply ignore such possibilities.

4.1.3

For the problem at hand the important fact is that a compound PM nowhere contains the conjunction word **and** or a new superordinate node dominating the conjuncts—the conjuncts, recall, are "parallel structures," with NP being their locus node (Section 2.3). In set union, the operation which forms a compound PM, nothing new is created, and therefore no such new superordinate node is possible in principle.

One might well ask, and reasonably so, where then **is** *and* if not in the PMs for CCC? Goodall's (1987: 32–34) answer, developed independently of any concern for anaphora questions, is that the conjunct words are placed when a CCC is linearized in interpretation to PF.[3] He gives few details, and there are possible equivocations (see Chametzky 1987a: Chapter 1 for discussion and resolution of these issues), but crucially for present concerns, the conjunction word placement occurs in PF interpretation (see Section 4.2 for some further discussion). In other words **and** not in the syntax, there is no superordinate branching node which keeps the subject conjuncts from C-commanding the rest of the sentence, and so the facts in (11) are no problem or surprise. The problem is (dis)solved without special stipulation. There are other problems, however, to which we now turn our attention.

4.1.4

Let us consider a few more facts.

(15) a. *Cyndi$_i$ and Sue$_j$ considered herself$_{i \text{ or } j}$ lucky.
b. *Cyndi$_i$ and Sue$_j$ considered her$_{i \text{ or } j}$ lucky.
c. *Cyndi$_i$ and Sue$_j$ considered them$_i$ lucky.
d. Cyndi$_i$ and Sue$_j$ considered themselves$_{i \text{ and } j}$ lucky.

On the usual assumptions about constituency (i.e., (13)) and the Binding Theory, (15b) should be grammatical because neither NP **Cyndi** nor NP **Sue** C-commands **her** and therefore Condition B should not be operable, allowing coreference. Correctly, the 3-D analysis rules this out. All is not quite so simple with this data set, however.

If (15b) is out, then presumably (15a) should be in. Under the 3-D analysis, the C-command relations of subjects to the rest of the sentence are the same when the subject is conjoined as when it is not. That is to say, the C-command relations between the conjunct subjects and the rest of the sentence in a compound PM are the same as the relations between the subjects and the rest of the sentences in the input PMs. Therefore, (15a) should be well-formed, because the sentences in (16) are good.

(16) a. Cyndi_i considered herself_i lucky.
b. Sue_j considered herself_j lucky.

There are, however, still further facts to consider. I include the (?) in (17) out of deference to other speakers, as my judgment here is that (17) is fine. Notice that the indexing on the reflexive **herself,** "i or j" here has to mean that **herself** does not corefer with the collectivity, Cyndi and Sue. This is in contrast with the i and j indexing on *themselves* in (15d) (I discuss such indexing and its interpretation more fully below).

(17) (?)Cyndi_i and Sue_j each considered $\text{herself}_{i \text{ or } j}$ lucky.

Although **each** evidently forces a distributed reading on the example, it does not change the relevant C-command relations between the subject and the rest of the sentence. If the indexing is syntactically ill-formed in (15a), then it is still ill-formed in (17), and no amount of lexical semantic forcing should be able to change that. It is quite impossible that there should be a Binding Theoretic difference between (15a) and (17).

The difference, I suggest, is semantic *cum* pragmatic. Lexical plurals, it should be noted, show a referential indeterminacy. Thus, in (18), **them** and **they** each allows both an interpretation that the group as a group (was) said good-bye to (by) me and an interpretation that I (was) said good-bye to (by) each of the individuals in the group(s) (perhaps separately) (for some discussion, see Higginbotham 1985: 571; Williams 1986: 280–81; Chametzky 1987a: 140ff.).

(18) a. I said good-bye to them.
b. They said good-by to me.

I suggest that this same referential indeterminacy is at work in (at least some) CCC with **and.** There is, however, this difference: in the CCC there is a heavy pragmatic favoring of the collective interpretation. The favoring is so heavy, in fact, that it may take the overt presence of the distributive forcing **each** to enable us to overcome it out of context. That it can be so overcome—cancelled—is some evidence that the collective interpretation is, indeed, pragmatically favored and not semantically required.

Thus, (15a) ceases to be syntactically ill-formed, and becomes, instead, simply uninterpretable for pragmatic reasons. Syntactically, it is assimilated to (17). But we have not addressed (15d), repeated here.

(15) d. Cyndi$_i$ and Sue$_j$ considered themselves$_{i\ \text{and}\ j}$ lucky.

The problem now is how this example can be well-formed if (17) and (15a) are also. Since the nodes in the C-command relation are the same in the compound PM as in the input PMs, this would seem impossible. However, recall that there is but a single NP node in the subject position of the compound PM (viz., the locus node discussed in Section 2.3). Recall as well that there is no nonbranching domination in the MPST, but rather there can be multiple-labelling of a single node (see Chapter 2, Section 1.0). Thus, the node labelled NP is also labelled N and is instantiated by both Cyndi and Sue. Now, this node C-commands the reflexive, and as just suggested above, the collective reading is heavily favored for such CCC. Therefore, we should not be at all surprised that this example is well-formed, too.

It may be helpful to go through the example (17) in detail. I am assuming (1) nonce labels QP & Q for **each** and (though nothing depends on it) (2) a "flat" VP with four daughters: QP, V, NP, AP (on the position of **each** in VP, see Sportiche 1988 and consider the interpretation of, e.g., *The boys each want to leave and the girls do, too,* and, on the lack of a so-called "small clause," Carrier & Randall 1992: 226–27). The input sentences and their PMs are given in (17a) & (17b), and their compound PM is given in (17c). The only difference between (17a) & (17c) is the last three lines of (17c). Examination reveals that there is, indeed, only one **herself** in the compound PM, as pointed out in the text (though it is in more than one dominance pair, of course).

(17) a. Cyndi each consider herself lucky.

{(S, NP), (S, VP), (S, QP), (S, NP), (S, AP), (S, N/Cyndi),

(S, Q/each), (S, V/consider), (S, N/herself),(S, A/lucky),
(NP, NP),(NP, N/Cyndi),
(VP, VP), (VP, QP), (VP, NP), (VP, AP), (VP, Q/each),
(VP, V/consider), (VP, N/herself), (VP, A/lucky),
(QP, QP), (QP, Q/each),
(NP, NP), (NP, N/herself),
(AP, AP), (AP, A/lucky),
(N/Cyndi, N/Cyndi), (N/Cyndi, NP),
(Q/each, Q/each), (Q/each, QP),
(V/consider, V/consider),
(N/herself, N/herself), (N/herself, NP),
(A/lucky, A/lucky), (A/lucky, AP)}

b. Sue each consider herself lucky.

{(S, NP), (S, VP), (S, QP), (S, NP), (S, AP), (S, N/Sue),
(S, Q/each), (S, V/consider), (S, N/herself),(S, A/lucky),
(NP, NP),(NP, N/Sue),
(VP, VP), (VP, QP), (VP, NP), (VP, AP), (VP, Q/each),
(VP, V/consider), (VP, N/herself), (VP, A/lucky),
(QP, QP), (QP, Q/each),
(NP, NP), (NP, N/herself),
(AP, AP), (AP, A/lucky),
(N/Sue, N/Sue), (N/Sue, NP),
(Q/each, Q/each), (Q/each, QP),
(V/consider, V/consider),
(N/herself, N/herself), (N/herself, NP),
(A/lucky, A/lucky), (A/lucky, AP)}

c. {(S, NP), (S, VP), (S, QP), (S, NP), (S, AP), (S, N/Cyndi),
(S, Q/each), (S, V/consider), (S, N/herself),(S, A/lucky),
(NP, NP),(NP, N/Cyndi),
(VP, VP), (VP, QP), (VP, NP), (VP, AP), (VP, Q/each),

(VP, V/consider), (VP, N/herself), (VP, A/lucky),
(QP, QP), (QP, Q/each),
(NP, NP), (NP, N/herself),
(AP, AP), (AP, A/lucky),
(N/Cyndi, N/Cyndi), (N/Cyndi, NP),
(Q/each, Q/each), (Q/each, QP),
(V/consider, V/consider),
(N/herself, N/herself), (N/herself, NP),
(A/lucky, A/lucky), (A/lucky, AP),
(S, N/Sue),
(NP, N/Sue),
(N/Sue, N/Sue), (N/Sue, NP)}

The symmetric difference between (17a) & (17b)—set D—is given in (17d). The set F is (17e), and the set I is (17f).

(17) d. Symmetric difference of (ia) & (ib), minus S

D = {(NP, N/Cyndi), (N/Cyndi, N/Cyndi), (N/Cyndi, NP), (NP, N/Sue), (N/Sue, N/Sue), (N/Sue, NP)}

e. First elements of D (iia)

F = {NP, N}

f. Instantiated second elements of D (iia)
I = {N/Cyndi, N/Sue}

According to this, both NP and N are "conjoinable categories," which is to say that they each label a locus node. But, they label the same node, so this is an acceptable result. According to the proposal to be made in the text, this locus node will bear as its referential index {i, j}, the union of the indices of the input NPs, and the single **herself** NP in the compound PM will bear the new notation {i}/{j} as its index. According to the new Binding definition given in (21) below, the two indices of the reflexive **herself** will each be bound by a member of the locus node's index, as we desire.[4]

As hinted at in the preceding exposition, an important, though largely technical, question remains to be answered. Exactly how does the Binding work in examples (17) and (15d)? That is, if Binding entails being coindexed, what are the indices on the respective nodes in question, how do they get that way, and how are they to be interpreted?

I suggest the following. As with the "lexical index" discussed in Section 2.3, so with the "referential index" here (whether the two might be collapsed is an issue I do not explore here). That is, we will consider the referential index to be a set containing a letter or an integer. The referential index on the locus node in a compound PM is then the union of the referential indices of the conjuncts. We can also allow that plural items may (though, unlike a locus node, they need not) have a referential index with cardinality greater than one.[5] Thus, in particular, a plural item such as **themselves** could have such an index. Hence, (15d) would actually look as in (19). I have indicated the indices of the component sentence subjects **Cyndi** and **Sue** without indicating that the locus node they both instantiate is indexed {i,j} because the two-dimensionality of the page does not allow us to easily represent the true structure of the sentence. Enclosing *Cyndi and Sue* in brackets and indexing the bracket would misleadingly suggest that there is an **and**-including syntactic constituent here, which is what the 3-D analysis crucially denies.

(19) Cyndi$_{\{i\}}$ and Sue$_{\{j\}}$ considered themselves$_{\{i,j\}}$ lucky.

To account for (17), repeated here, more needs to be said, however. We need a bit of new indexing notation, an explanation for this notation, and a new notion of Bound.

(17) Cyndi$_i$ and Sue$_j$ each considered herself$_{i \text{ or } j}$ lucky.

Instead of (17), then, we shall have (17′), with the new bit of notation. It should be understood as indicating "simultaneously *either,* but not both together."

(17′) Cyndi$_{\{i\}}$ and Sue$_{\{j\}}$ each considered herself$_{\{i\}/\{j\}}$ lucky.

How does this bit of notation arise? Recall that the inputs to the compound PM for (17′) are the PMs for (20a & b).[6]

(20) a. Cyndi$_{\{i\}}$ each considered herself$_{\{i\}}$ lucky.

b. $Sue_{\{j\}}$ each considered $herself_{\{j\}}$ lucky.

Now, in the compound PM, there is only one **herself;** that is due to the collapsing aspect of union of phrase markers. However, nothing prevents the two input instances of **herself** from having different referential indices. In such a case, where there is no conjoining (of **herself**), hence no locus node, the notation {i, j} is unavailable. But in exactly such an instance, I suggest, we get the new notation {i}/{j} on the NP(and N)-labelled node that **herself** instantiates.

We cannot yet understand the relations in (17′) as Binding, however, because Binding requires coindexing and the new notation is different from that on the locus node subject. I therefore propose a revised definition of Binding, (21), which covers all the cases.[7] Recall that referential indices are assumed to be sets.

(21) x Binds y iff x = y and
$x \in A$, $y \in B$ where
XP_A C-commands XP_B

Under (21), Binding is a relation between indices. We therefore also need a new way to interpret Binding so that it can lead to coreference between NPs. In the spirit of Reinhart (1983: Chapter 7; see Williams 1986: 276f. for an approving summary), who argues that the grammar provides only for a single "bound anaphora" condition which applies to all pronouns (both "pronominals" and "anaphors") I propose (22).

(22) If x Binds y, then interpret $NP_{\{y\}}$ as a variable bound to $NP_{\{x\}}$

I bring up one last bit of data, (23).

(23) *Sue considered $himself_{\{i\}}$ and $himself_{\{i\}}$ lucky.

On standard analyses of CCC, the reflexives would form a branching constituent and C-command each other in their governing category. Therefore, should they be indexed as indicated, they would Bind each other and the example would be grammatical. Of course, the example is ungrammatical. And, on the 3-D analysis, there is no constituent containing the conjuncts and no C-command relation between them (they are "parallel structures"), so there can be no Binding relation between them. Hence, the indexing as given is ungrammatical, as desired.[8]

We have seen that the 3-D analysis, on account of not having **and** in the syntax or any new superordinate node dominating the conjuncts, can immediately handle some otherwise puzzling anaphora patterns in CCC. With some extensions that are, it is hoped, not too unnatural, the system can analyze further anaphora facts. The claim is not being advanced that no other analysis could handle such facts; it is obviously the case that accomodations could be made to include them. Rather, the point is being made that this analysis *requires* that the facts be essentially as they are; our theory would have to make accomodations were the facts other than what they are.

We move now to the question of conjunction choice and placement, because it is evident that a theory arguing that syntax does not distinguish **and** structures from **or** structures must nonetheless make this distinction somewhere.

CCC with different conjunctions differ both in meaning and pronunciation (in that **and** and **or** are different words) but the respective meanings and pronunciations are themselves correlated, so any analysis of CCC must encode a systematic relation between the semantics and phonology / phonetics of CCC. Standard analyses meet this desideratum by inserting conjunction words into syntactic structure and interpreting this structure both sematically and phonologically / phonetically. That is, the systematic relation between the meaning and pronunciation of CCC derives from the fact that each of these is fed by the syntactic representation containing the conjunction word.

Because our analysis abjures the insertion of conjunction words into the syntax, this standard approach is not open to us. What we shall need instead is a grammar organization in which there is a direct feeding relation between the representations of meaning and pronunciation. Obviously, there are two possible such organizations: "meaning" feeds "pronunciation" or "pronunciation" feeds "meaning." In principle, neither is preferred a priori. Luckily, there is independent reason to choose one of these options, to which we now turn. However, it should be borne in mind that our theory does not rise or fall with the particular grammar organizaton we now take up. We use it for concreteness, because it is independently motivated, and because there are, as we shall see, convergences between it and our inquiry. Nonetheless, the two are independent.

4.2.0

Hornstein (1985-86; 1987) has argued for the grammar organization in (24) against the standard "T-model" of (25). We discuss (24) directly.

(24)

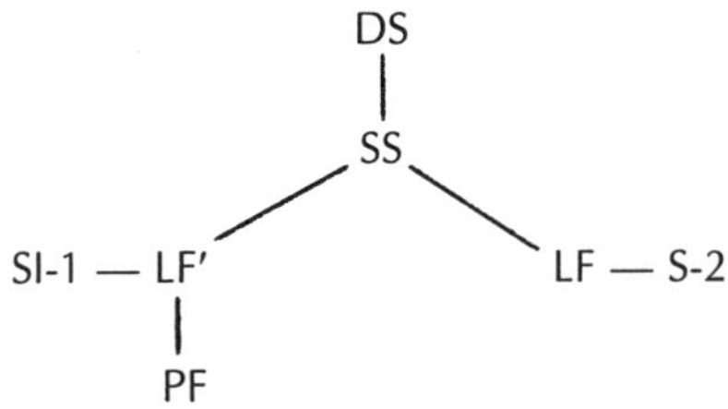

(25)

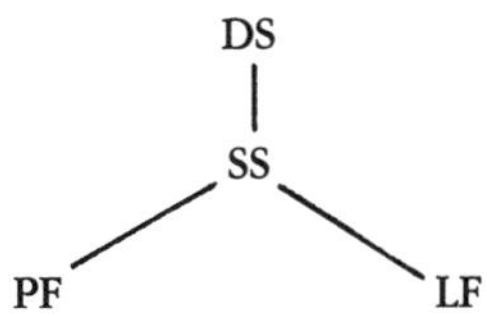

4.2.1

Hornstein (1985-86: 301) argues that "in natural language there are two fundamentally different kinds of interpretive processes." These are represented by LF′ and LF in (24).[9] There are two differences between the two sorts of processes. First, LF "underlies those aspects of interpretation concerned with *internominal dependencies*" whereas LF′ "is the locus of *non*-nominal relationships" (Hornstein 1985-86: 302). Second, LF′ feeds PF, phonetic form, but LF does not have any direct relation to PF.

The internominal dependencies are those which are generally taken to fall under Binding Theory and quantification. The nonnominal relationships are those in which at least one of the relata is not nominal. Hornstein (1985-86: 302) lists "opacity, scope of negation, modal scope, adverbial modification, and predication" for these.

That two sorts of phenomena can be characterized in this way does not, however, argue that they should be represented as in (24). Hornstein (1987) demonstrates the independence of the two sorts of phenomena. He shows that there are various noninteractions which are explicable if the grammar is organized as in (24), but which are mysterious on the more standard (25). However, this demonstration of independence does not by itself argue for the feeding relation between LF′ and PF in (24). Hornstein (1985-86) argues for this relation by means of interactions between plausibly PF processes with some non-nominal relations, such as, cliticization with scope of negation (1985-86: 303-6), and intonation contour, adjectival scope, and predication with focus / presupposition (1985-86: 313-15).

It should be noted that none of Hornstein's arguments in any way involves CCC, so that, insofar as it is motivated, the motivation for (24) is entirely independent of current concerns. And, conversely, insofar as our analysis of CCC supports Hornstein's model, this is further independent evidence.

In fact, CCC do give independent support for Hornstein's proposal. Larson (1985a) (as discussed in Chametzky 1987a: Chapter 3) provides evidence that **or** CCC interact with scope of intensional verbs (i.e., opacity), with scope of negation, and, like adverbs, with scope of auxiliary verbs (modals included). I turn to some data that exemplify these interactions.

4.2.2

The initial datum is (26) (see Larson 1985a: 218 (1)). This example, according to Larson, is three-ways ambiguous, as discussed next.[10]

(26) Mary is looking for a maid or a cook.

This sentence contains a familiar ambiguity between the *de dicto* and *de re* readings, available also in the component sentences given in (27).

(27) a. Mary is looking for a maid.
b. Mary is looking for a cook.

So, for (26), we can adopt Larson's (1985a: 218) informal logical presentations for the respective readings.

(28) a. Mary is looking for ((a maid) or (a cook)).
b. For some x, a maid or a cook, Mary is looking for x.

Now, (26) has as well a third reading not available for examples such as in (27), a second *de dicto* reading, which is the reading of interest, the so-called "wide-scope **or** reading," represented in (29).

(29) Mary is looking for (a maid) or Mary is looking for (a cook).

This is a "disjunction reduction" reading which can be brought out be continuing (26) with "*but I don't know which.*" There is actually a further reading for (26), apparently unnoticed previously. It is quite predictable, a "wide-scope" *de re* reading, represented in (30).

(30) For some x, a maid, Mary is looking for x or for some y, a cook, Mary is looking for y.

Larson (1985a: 221-23) argues that **either** is the marker of the scope of a disjunction; he analyzes **either** as part of the coordinating conjunction. It is, as it were, an English word that serves as a "left-parenthesis." We shall be concerned only with the data demonstrating the interactions alluded to previously.[11]

4.2.3

The ambiguities noted in (26) but not in (27) indicate the interaction between opacity and CCC.

The examples in (31) (Larson 1985a: 223-24 (9)-(10)) illustrate interaction between scope of negation and CCC, as discussed directly below. (Judgments are from Larson 1985a.)

(31) a. Mary isn't looking for a maid or a cook.
b. Mary isn't looking for either a maid or a cook.
c. (?)Mary isn't either looking for a maid or a cook.
d. ??Mary either isn't looking for a maid or a cook.
e. ??Either Mary isn't looking for a maid or a cook.

Larson suggests that in (31a) **or** cannot have scope wider than **isn't** and that (31b)-(31e) demonstrate that negation bounds on the left the possible positions of **either.** The most interesting example is (31c), which according to Larson (1985a: 224) "is interpreted as the negation of the sentence *Either Mary is looking for a maid or a cook*"; that is, **or** has scope wider than **look for,** but narrower than negation.

The examples in (32) show the relative freedom of occurrence of **either.** McCawley (1983) has shown that adverbs occur in all positions relative to auxiliaries in which we see **either** appearing in

(32). Assuming that **either** is an indicator of disjunction scope, these examples illustrate both the interaction of CCC with auxiliary scope (including modals, (32i)) and a parallel with adverb scope.

(32) a. Sherlock may have been pretending to have been (looking for) a burglar or a thief.
b. Sherlock may have been pretending to have been either (looking for) a burglar or a thief.
c. Sherlock may have been pretending to have either been (looking for) a burglar or a thief.
d. Sherlock may have been pretending to either have been (looking for) a burglar or a thief.
e. Sherlock may have been pretending either to have been (looking for) a burglar or a thief.
f. Sherlock may have been either pretending to have been (looking for) a burglar or a thief.
g. Sherlock may have either been pretending to have been (looking for) a burglar or a thief.
h. Sherlock may either have been pretending to have been (looking for) a burglar or a thief.
i. Sherlock either may have been pretending to have been (looking for) a burglar or a thief.

This concludes the data survey showing the interactions of CCC with LF′ relationships. It is, I think, quite striking that such convergences should exist between these independently arrived at theories. They are independent not only in the areas analyzed, but also in another way, one that bears specially on the MPST project.

The analysis of CCC developed is largely formal (although not exclusively so—the actual lexical items matter), relying on set theoretic manipulations, whereas the motivations for Hornstein's reorganization of the grammar are entirely substantive. This is the sort of formal-substantive convergence that we have noted to be desirable in general. We have increasing amounts of evidence that the MPST is particularly good at delivering such convergences.

We move now to the question of conjunction placement and interpretation, a somewhat more purely technical issue.

4.3

Conjunction placement is done in the mapping from S-structure to LF′. The proposal is simply that a representation of conjunction type—say a "logical connective" & or v—is placed in a compound PM. The resulting object is no longer a well-formed PM, because the connective is not part of any dominance pair(s). But this does not matter, because there is no requirement that an LF′ be such a well-formed PM.

It might be objected that this is an unprecedented sort of procedure, introducing a meaning-bearing element in the course of derivation, under no apparent general constraints. But, if someone objects that meaning-bearing elements may not be introduced except at D-structure or S-structure, then there is no way at all to argue for the present analysis against such a person. It is, after all, a central claim of the analysis that at least some meaning-bearing and phonologically realized elements are not part of the (pre-LF′) syntax, viz, the conjunction words. And the putative objector takes it as (part of) a constraint on possible grammars, apparently, that no such discrepencies may exist.

It is not immediately obvious that such an alternative view is in any clear way more constrained than the present view. Its advocate would be willing to license elements in, say, base structures, entirely on semantic and phonological grounds—at least from the point of view of the present analysis. That is, if the present analysis is correct that conjunction words have no syntactic effects, then the alternative would be in the position suggested in the previous sentence. And if the issue now comes down to whether the current analysis is correct in regard to the lack of syntactic efficacy of the conjunction words, then there is no longer an issue with respect to a priori constraints on grammars, as the hypothetical objector originally maintained. This is as it should be, I believe.

Further, as to the apparent unconstrained nature of the "connective placement" procedure, I say the following. The analysis is committed to the construction of a new and distinguished syntactic object, the compound PM. Our new procedure refers only to this new and distinguished object. This perhaps offers hope for constraining such procedures.

Interpretation of an LF′ structure with a logical connective is straightforward. Semantically (SI-1), it can receive the cross-categorial Boolean interpretation that has become common (e.g., Gazdar 1980; Partee & Rooth 1983; Keenan & Faltz 1984). This interpretation would be applied to (the interpretation of) a conjoinable category. Phonological interpretation would be as whatever the conjunction words (or morphemes) might be in the language in question. Placement of the conjunction item is also a language particular phenomenon, and this analysis suggests why this is so, because the connective is not involved in any syntactic constituency relations.

These proposals provide an explanation of two problems that have been noted in the interpretation of CCC. The first is that, despite multiple occurrences of a conjunction word in a pronounced string, there is only one conjunction meaning in a CCC (Gazdar, Klein, Pullum, & Sag 1985: 228). Since we here separate out conjunction word placement from logical interpretation—the former being language particular in a way the latter is not—this is no longer surprising or problematic.

Second, as Carlson (1983: 73, 81-84) discusses with respect to Latin *-que,* a conjunction word (morpheme) can appear "too low" in the structure, that is, attached to the "wrong thing," relative to where its interpretation requires it to be. In (33) (from Carlson 1983: 73), *-que* is attached to the demonstrative *eas,* even though the conjoining would be of PPs, not of the demonstrative with anything else. Again, our separation of conjunction item placement in the string from logical interpretation and application to a conjoinable category renders this fact much less mysterious than in other analyses.

(33)

ob	easque	res
because(of)	these-and	things

'and because of these things'

Details of actual conjunction morpheme placement are left to the grammars of particular languages. That is, no general claim is advanced that is meant to cover, say, English *and* and Latin *-que.* The attempt here has been to develop an analysis of the nonparochial aspects of CCC. We have now reached the end of the exposition of that analysis and move to a brief review of its high points.

5.0

The formal aspects of the analysis seem to me most compelling. Union combines two sets. Sentence structures can be understood as sets (PMs). CCC are the combining of sentences, the result subject to the MPST. The formally most general partition of a union is (almost) exactly what we need empirically to derive the most general condition (viz., the LCL) on CCC. Because set union adds nothing new, there are no conjunction words in the syntax and there is no constituent containing the conjuncts. These idiosyncratic properties of the analysis predict otherwise problematic patterns of anaphoric dependencies in CCC. These properties also mandate a nonstandard grammar organization. Such a grammar organization has been suggested on entirely independent empirical grounds and in an entirely substantive mode, and—remarkably—it converges with our largely formal proposal for CCC analysis.

Once again, close thinking about and manipulation of the resources of the MPST is more revealing than simply adding new types of machinery to our analytic tool box.

4

Adjuncts & Adjunction

0.0

Coordination is not the only way in which PMs can be combined. In this chapter we examine another way: adjunction. In fact, we have two topics often treated together which are in fact distinct: **Chomsky-adjunction** (C-adjunction, hereafter), a syntactic movement operation found, for example, in the mapping from S-structure to LF; and **adjuncts,** nonargument modifiers related to the head of a Projection Chain. We shall examine one account of adjuncts which involves an operation called "Adjoin Alpha"; I shall use "Adjunct Adding" for its analogue in our MPST-based theory. With respect to C-adjunction, I shall argue that there can be no such rule, though the structures it putatively gives rise to may, in fact, be correct.

It is really not surprising that these two topics have been run together. They share, so it seems, a structural configuration unique to them, exemplified in (1). The crucial fact of such a structure is that the mother and one of the daughters have the same label.

A terminological note: in both constructions I shall call an "adjoined-to element"—a daughter such as XP in (1)—the "host."

(1)

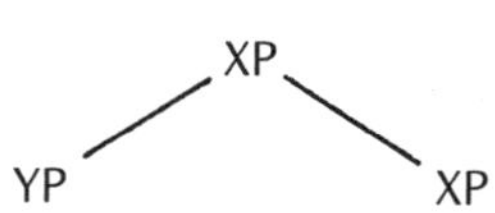

To anticipate: adjoining (in both senses) is a situation in which a mother and daughter do not have different labels. Much remains to explicate in this brief statement, particularly the phrase "do not have different labels." I shall propose that in the case of adjuncts, mother and daughter have the same label **token,** whereas in C-adjunction, the mother may have no label at all. The explication takes the form of clarifying, revising, and sometimes rejecting ideas found in, on the one hand, May (1985; 1989) and Chomsky (1986a) and, on the other, Lebeaux (1988; 1990) and Speas (1990). The former two authors deal with C-adjunction, while the latter two deal with adjuncts.

We have seen that the operation used in coordination "adds nothing" when PMs are combined, and utilizes the most general partitioning of the union of two sets. Adjoining, in both senses, also "adds nothing," though how they do not add—to be made precise below—is interestingly different from, even complementary to, that explicated in the analysis of coordination.

0.1

The chapter is organized as follows. I begin with C-adjunction. First, I discuss C-adjunction as a transformation, showing that no such rule is possible (Section 1). In Section 2 I discuss node labelling, asking what principles at which strata mandate labels on nodes. The general conclusion is that principles mandating labels are D-structure principles, except for the Projection Principle. Section 3 moves to May (1985; 1989) and Chomsky (1986a). I both discuss, clarify, and reformalize the May / Chomsky ideas and argue that much of their work is theoretically questionable. In addition, I argue that a different understanding of the Projection Principle would allow the new mother node in an adjunction structure to remain unlabelled, thus eliminating not only the C-adjunction rule but also C-adjunction structures.

Section 4 presents the proposals for adjuncts of Lebeaux (1988; 1990) and Speas (1990). In Section 5, I discuss, clarify, and develop an MPST-based version of the ideas from Section 4, arguing that Adjunct Adding is the second process by means of which the extended base is derived. In doing so, I reject as telling a class of data taken to be central by both Lebeaux and Speas. I argue that (1) our MPST theory is silent about such data, (2) Lebeaux has an account of these facts but no theory, and (3) Speas has presented other facts that both counterexemplify Lebeaux's account and render her own theory incoherent.[1] My claim is that a silent theory is better than either no theory or one that says the wrong things. A central finding is that adjuncts, the result of Adjunct Adding, do have the characteristic adjunction structure (1), but on account of independent principles of the theory of the base, the MPST. Section 6 reviews the main findings.

The goals throughout are theoretical and explanatory. We attempt the construction of theories of adjuncts and of C-adjunction within the overall context of the MPST. The explanatory goal is structural and categorial: we wish to understand **why** adjuncts and C-adjunctions have the particular phrase structures that they do and no other structure. We will consider the project successful to the extent that we offer an explicit, MPST-based theory that meets the explanatory goal. We turn now to C-adjunction.

1.0

It is widely held that there is a syntactic rule which mediates the relation between structures such as those in (2a) and (2b). This is the rule I shall call *C-adjunction*. The crucial properties of C-adjunction are (1) it is a movement rule, (2) it creates a new node, (3) the new node is the after movement mother of the moved element and a second node, and (4) the new mother node bears the label of its nonmoved daughter (the host). C-adjunction is supposed to be part of both the D-structure to S-structure mapping and the S-structure to LF mapping.

(2) a.

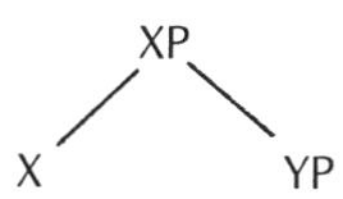

b.

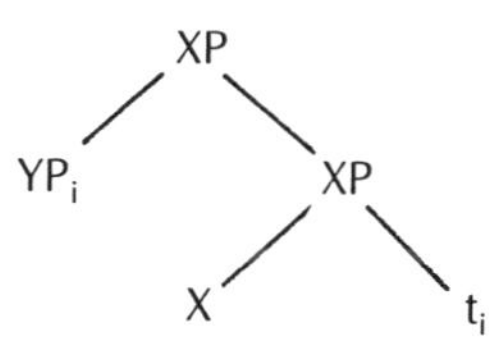

I demonstrate in what follows that though these structures may be correct, there is no such rule.

1.1

The argument is theoretical, by which I mean that no new (or, for that matter, familiar) data are crucial to it. I argue that on theoretical grounds, a rule with the properties described in 1.0 cannot exist. The argument moves from very general considerations in the theory of transformations to more particular ones in the MPST. On the other hand, I offer a conceptual argument for (unlabelled) node creation and adjunction, which argument involves a new understanding of "structure preservation."

The primary conclusion is that if there is an adjunction rule, it cannot be C-adjunction, because the adjunction rule does not label the new mother node.

1.2

C-adjunction is a holdover from the Standard Theory (and before). It combines both a movement and copying function (and also node creation, of course). In fact, within the Standard Theory C-adjunction was one of the so-called "elementary transformations" (see, e.g., Bach 1974: 84-87), so that its component parts were themselves unanalyzed. C-adjunction, then, was one of the building blocks for a theory that allowed vastly greater power and scope to transformations than is currently considered desirable. Heny (1979: 335), writing specifically about the theory elaborated in Chomsky's *Logical structure of linguistic theory* (1955/1985), offers what should seem a compelling—and negative—evaluation of such a theory to those who share contemporary assumptions:

> There is something highly unsatisfactory in the account, perhaps typified by the dissatisfaction and suspicion one feels in regard to the claim embodied in the use of elementaries in a number of grammatical transformations, as if genuine significance could be attached to that. But this is an inevitable consequence of the more basic claim that the operations of deformation, permutation, and adjunction (and compounds of these) form a significant inventory of operations which serve to define the [structural] relations [among sentence "types"] in question in an interesting way. Much of the recent work in linguistic theory, in so far as it has been seriously concerned at all with the formal properties of transformational operations, rather than arguing against specific transformational analyses, has been an attempt to further constrain the power of these rules. Chomsky's restriction of the core grammar to just one movement rule with unspecified target reflects a growing conviction that whatever structural relations do hold between sentences, these will not be captured by defining operations corresponding to the elementaries.

Under the current view of transformations, we should be suspicious of C-adjunction. It clearly cannot be simply a case of "Move Alpha"; it is not even a case of "Affect Alpha." It cannot be "Affect Alpha" (or "Move Alpha") because it affects more than one element. There is movement of one element, and then creation and labelling of an entirely new node. It therefore follows that there can be no transformation of C-adjunction, unless it is an unreducible, sui generis primitive.

Suppose, though, that we want to allow there to be an adjunction rule. We might motivate it conceptually in the following way. If movement is not to be structure preserving, perhaps it must be structure creating; hence, movement and node creation are not "really" distinct. Rather, they are the two parts of what it means to be a "nonstructure preserving" rule (see Section 3.5.1 for further discussion).

However, even if we were to allow a single rule to both move one element and create a new node, it is not at all clear that we should also permit the rule to stipulate a label on that new node. Minimally, we should like that much to follow from some general principles. Node creation by itself does not entail labelling (see Section 2 below for discussion).

1.3

We are led, then, to investigate the conditions on the labelling of nodes. In the next section I argue that, while there are general principles at work in this area, only one applies to the strata in a derivation that are held to be post C-adjunction. Thus, there is one nonstipulative way to label the new node, though there exists no general requirement that it be labelled at all.

2.0

In this section we investigate node labelling within the MPST. Two cases are to be examined: heads and nonheads, respectively. We begin with heads.

2.1

Recall from Section 3.1 of Chapter 1 that there is but a single "*X*-barish" principle in the MPST: Project Alpha. I repeat both Speas's version ((14) from Chapter 1) in (3a) and our revision ((14′) from Chapter 1) in (3b).

(3) a. Project Alpha: a word of syntactic category X is dominated by an uninterrupted sequence of X nodes.

b. Project Alpha: an instantiated node labelled X is dominated by an uninterrupted sequence of X labelled nodes.

Project Alpha licenses the Projection Chain, and each link node in the Chain is, at its level of structure, the head daughter. These head links are identifiable on account of the (type identical) labels they bear, this label identity being what Project Alpha mandates.

Thus, projection, regulated by Project Alpha, is one means of node labelling in the MPST. It pertains to heads only. We turn now to nonheads.

2.2

Nonhead daughters are not determined by Project Alpha. They "are present only in virtue of the licensing relation that they bear to a node in the projection [chain]." (Speas 1990: 45) Further, "[t]he reason that the head and its complement are dominated by a projection of the head has to do with the requirement that *all* lexical requirements of the head be instatiated in syntax." (Speas 1990: 45). Here, "head" means the labelled node-lexical item pair that takes part in the instantiation relation, where the lexical item provides the "lexical requirements" referred to by Speas. A head in this sense projects a Chain that provides sufficient structure to allow that "all of the positions in its theta grid have been discharged." (Speas 1990: 45) In sum, "D-structure contains all and only phrases which are licensed by theta theory" where this includes both specifiers and complements, but, as noted in Section 3.1 of Chapter 1, not adjuncts (Speas 1990: 54, 60f.).

Nonhead, nonadjuncts are thus selected for by the head. Given that heads select syntactic categories and that labelled nodes are the structural realization of syntactic categories, it follows that the labels of nonheads are licensed due to selection by the head.[2]

We can see that in this theory there are two means for licensing labelled nodes: projection and selection. In each case, the particular labels are determined by the properties of particular lexical items. We can also note that every node in D-structure will be labelled, because nodes will exist only on account of projection or selection. These two mechanisms, it should be stressed, are part of the theory of the base, the theory of well-formed D-structures.

2.3

We are now in position to ask what principles determine node labels at strata other than D-structure. For nodes that have been licensed at D-structure, we can presume that nothing more need be said; they bear the labels which have allowed them to be licensed in the base. In the case of adjunction, however, we are dealing precisely with a node that is not licensed at D-structure, but rather comes into being only at another stratum, either S-structure or LF. What principles, then, determine the label on a node not present at D-structure?

There is one such principle: the Projection Principle.[3] On any current version, the Projection Principle requires that the structurally represented lexical requirements of a lexical item be identically represented at every stratum (see Section 3.4.1 for a different understanding of the Projection Principle). As we have just seen, the labels on nodes in D-structure representations exist on account of lexical properties of heads. Thus, if at D-structure a structure such as (2a), adapted here in (3a), were licensed as a subphrase marker, it would be so licensed because some other head selects XP—for concreteness, say, as a subcategorized complement to some node labeled Z.

(3) a. b.

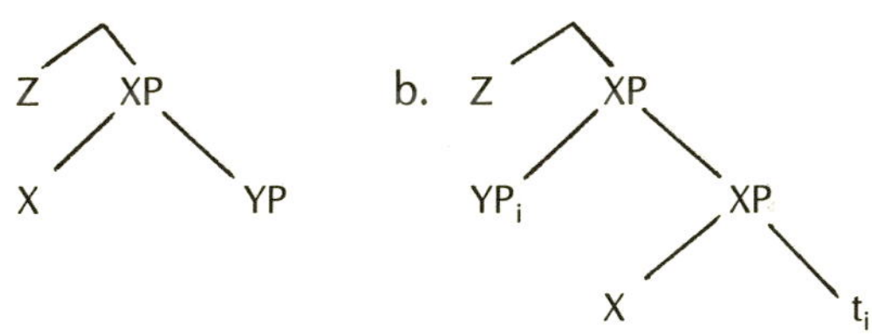

But then, if there were an adjunction which created a new node mother to the moved YP and the original node labelled XP, then this new mother node must also be labelled XP or the Projection Principle would be violated because otherwise Z would no longer be sister to a node labelled XP, as its lexical entry requires (3b).[4] It will presently be of some significance that the Projection Principle is not a principle that holds only of non-D-structure strata.

We see, therefore, that there is no need for a rule which includes the "copying function" of C-adjunction, because the label on the mother node will follow from a general principle. I now argue that there is not only no need for C-adjunction, but also compelling theoretical grounds to disallow this rule. This might seem pointless, but it is not. Theoretically, it is desirable to show that what is not necessary is also not possible, because then we can claim to have explained its supernumerary status.

2.4

Recall from Sections 2.1 and 2.2 that labels are required due to the particular properties of lexical items. If there is a rule of adjunction, then as a transformational rule it is exactly not the case that its properties result from the particular requirements of lexical items. Thus, any label that results from a transformational rule could not be due to particular lexical requirements; but, it has just been pointed out that all labels result from particular lexical requirements. Therefore, there can be no transformationally mandated labels.

It might be objected that the argument in the preceding paragraph only establishes that transformationally mandated labelling would have to be entirely general—not subject to specific lexical requirements. And, it could be argued, C-adjunction is exactly that: the general rule is "copy the label on the host node, whatever it is."

The objection is theoretically misguided, however. It assumes that, in the absence of any principle requiring it, a non-D-structure licensed node must nevertheless be labelled. The theory implicit in such a view therefore involves two distinct modes of labelling. The first is that which is part of the specification of well-formed D-structures as structural realizations of lexical properties in syntax. The second is an unmotivated extension of the purview of transformations into label copying. This view thus suggests that labelling is not a *kind* within the theory of grammar; it is instead a disjunctive object. Further, there is no reason, on this view, that adjunction should be C-adjunction; the unmotivated label on the mother merely has to be something that can be specified independently of individual lexical properties. Thus, it could be the label on the adjoining element or it could be any third label distinct from the adjoiner and adjoinee; both of these are general in the required way. Indeed, on this view, we would need to **explain** why adjunction does not take these other forms or why it does in some languages and not in others; but such "problems" are spurious, and it is a mark of the wrongheadedness of the C-adjunction rule view that it must lead to such pointless activity.[5]

On the view advanced here, node labelling is a theoretical kind. To reiterate, all labels are licensed by individual lexical requirements, as a part of the specification of well-formed D-structures. It therefore follows that there can be no transformationally mandated labels, as transformations do not enforce individual lexical requirements. It therefore also follows that there are no principles requiring labels which hold only at strata which differ from D-structure due to the application of transformations. If the derivation of S-structures and LFs is by means of transformations, and transformations cannot mandate labels, then it would be impossible to satisfy any principle which required at either S-structure or LF a label not present at D-structure. The Projection Principle, recall, is a condition on all strata, including D-structure, which is exactly why it can require labelling the new node.

If there is a transformational rule of adjunction, it is not C-adjunction—instead, it simply creates an unlabelled new mother node.

2.5

We have seen that both the theory of transformations and the theory of the base separately and together lead to the conclusion that a C-adjunction rule does not exist. Nonetheless, C-adjunction structures apparently do exist. In current work the two are run together. I therefore turn to May (1985; 1989) and Chomsky (1986), who analyze C-adjunction structures assuming a C-adjunction rule.

3.0

May (1985: 56-57) initiates, Chomsky (1986: 7) follows, and May (1989: 91-92) formalizes an approach to C-adjunction structures that involves redefinition of two basic syntactic predicates: *category* and *dominates.* May and Chomsky apparently provide independent and mutually supporting justifications for C-adjunction structures in that they analyze distinct areas: May explores the mapping between S-structure and LF; Chomsky works on the D-structure to S-structure relation. May develops his notions on the basis of the analysis of scopal relations; Chomsky concentrates on the notion "government." I have nothing to add to the data analyses.

I begin by presenting and discussing May's (1989) definitions and Chomsky's (1986) less formal analogue (Section 3.1.0). I then offer a reformalization that meets possible objections to the May / Chomsky position (Section 3.1.1). Next, I move on to discussion and analysis internal to the respective proposals of May and Chomsky

(Sections 3.2 & 3.3). Finally, I propose an alternative version of the Projection Principle that has the effect of not requiring any label at all on the new mother in an adjunction structure (Section 3.4) and offer a conceptual justification for adjunction and new node creation that involves a rethinking of "structure preservation" (Section 3.5). Section 3.6 summarizes the argument and findings.

3.1.0

May (1989: 91-92 (15)) provides the following definition.

(4) Theory of Adjunction
 (i) A Category C = $\{n_1, \ldots, n_n\}$
 (ii) C dominates $\alpha =_{df} \forall n \in C$ (n dominates α)

The intent of the definition is that "categories are sets of nodes, and to be dominated by a category is to be dominated by every member node." (May 1989: 92) When combined with his stipulation that there is a rule of C-adjunction, (4) allows May (1989: 92 (16)) to derive (5), "the primary theorem" of his theory of adjunction.

(5) Adjuncts are not dominated by the categories to which they are adjoined.

Chomsky (1986: 7 (12)) endorses May's proposals, and offers his own statement.[6]

(6) α is dominated by β only if it is dominated by every segment of β.

I turn now to objections and a response.

3.1.1

Pullum (1989) has suggested that (6) is incoherent, as it explicates the crucial term on its left side—"dominated"—by means of the identical term on its right side. The same might also be said for May's definition (4ii). May further does not distinguish between nodes and labelled nodes; apparently he takes the latter as his primitives. It is also never stated what values the variable α is to take. Presumably, May is assuming a primitive relation of "dominance" that holds between pairs of labelled nodes. He then wants to say that this same relation also can hold between a set of labelled nodes and a single labelled node.[7] I shall provide a reformalization that respects the node versus label distinction and that avoids objections of the sort raised by Pullum (1989).[8]

We assume the transitive, reflexive, asymmetric relation of "dominance" between pairs of unlabelled nodes. A labelled node is itself a pair, ⟨n,l⟩, of a node and its associated label. We can now define two new relations **l-(abelled) domination** and **c-(ategory) domination** and the notion Category as in (4′). (4′a) is not a biconditional because l-dominance is not required for dominance. The intent of (4′b) is that a Category is a set of labelled nodes all of which have the same label. And (4′c) says that, whenever all members of a Category l-dominate a labelled node, then that Category c-dominates the labelled node; I do not define a "dominance relation" between Categories, though we could.[9]

(4′) n = node, l = label, N = labelled node, that is, ⟨n,l⟩

a. ⟨n,l⟩ l-dominates ⟨n′,l′⟩ only if n dominates n′
b. A Category C $=_{def}$ {⟨n_i,l⟩}
c. A Category C c-dominates N iff (∀: N′ ∈ C) (N′ l-dominates N)

Using (4′), we would restate (5), May's "primary theorem" of the theory of adjunction, as (5′).

(5′) Adjuncts are not c-dominated by the Categories to which their hosts belong.

I move now to internal analysis and discussion, first of May's "theory of adjunction" and its "primary theorem," then to a further apparent empirical need for something like the "primary theorem," Chomsky's (1986: 9 (17)) notion of "exclusion."

3.2

We begin by considering May's "primary theorem" (5), repeated here.

(5) Adjuncts are not dominated by the categories to which they are adjoined.

How does May derive this theorem? He does so by constructing his new notions of "category" and "dominance"; in all cases other than C-adjunction structures, these reduce to the familiar versions of these notions.[10] The purpose of his revisions, in fact, is to allow the structure created by the C-adjunction rule to be ignored. This should give us reason to pause and ponder: what might it be about the rule of C-adjunction that forces us to revise basic notions in order to ignore the result of C-adjunction? The answer is quite clear and is indicated in May's definitions themselves: it is the label on the mother node, the node created and labelled by the C-adjunction rule, that forces the revisions. More perspicuously, it is the label on the new mother node that must be ignored. And why, we now ask, is the mother labelled as it is? Because the adjunction is C-adjunction. And why is it C-adjunction? Because . . . it is so stipulated. At this point, even if we did not have the earlier theoretical demonstration of the nonexistence of a C-adjunction rule, we would be unhappy on grounds completely internal to May's account. The "theory of adjunction" consists of two parts: (1) a stipulation of a C-adjunction rule and (2) ad hoc revisions of basic predicates that undo a main result of part (1).

On the other hand, we have seen that C-adjunction structures can be theoretically motivated even without the C-adjuncton rule. And it is these structures, not the rule which purportedly creates them, which force May's revisions. In other words, the problem with the first of the two parts of May's "theory of adjunction"—the stipulation of the rule of C-adjunction—has disappeared under our analysis.

However, there is still a problem with the second part—the derivation of the theorem, either in the form of May's (5) or (5′). The new or revised predicates are still ad hoc.[11] The only role they play in the theory of grammar is to allow us to derive (5) or (5′). Why not simply **stipulate** (5) instead, thus avoiding either possibly incoherent revisions or totally new definitions? No generality is lost; indeed, May's "theory of adjunction" hardly seems like more than an indirect, roundabout way of stipulating (5).

As noted already, however, Chomsky (1986a: 9 (17)) adds a new concept, "exclusion," which apparently adds empirical content to the "theory of adjunction." We must now examine "exclusion."

3.3

Chomsky (1986a: 9 (17)) defines "exclusion" as in (7).[12]

(7) α excludes β if no segment of α dominates β.

Chomsky (1986a: 9 (18)) then goes on to offer a definition of "government" in terms of "exclusion"—(8)—which he contrasts with an earlier version (1986a: 8 (14)) in terms of "dominance" (or "inclusion" as he sometimes says)—(9).

(8) α governs β iff α m-commands β and there is no γ, γ a barrier for β such that γ excludes α.

(9) α governs β iff α m-commands β and every barrier for β dominates α.

As he points out, under (8), but not (9), in a C-adjunction structure, if the host node is a barrier with respect to something it dominates, then the adjoined element can govern across that barrier, because this barrier does not exclude the adjoiner.

At various points in the text (e.g., 1986a: 29-30, 45-46, 81-83), Chomsky argues that (8) is empirically superior to (9). This, then, seems to indicate that the "theory of adjunction" should not be replaced by a stipulation of May's (5).

Appearances can mislead. As Chomsky (1986a: 9) himself notes, "[a]part from adjunction structures, the definitions of 'government' in terms of exclusion and domination coincide." In other words, there is no adjunction-independent motivation for "exclusion." Given this, what the clause in (8) concerning "exclusion" amounts to is another roundabout stipulation: hosts are not barriers with respect to their adjoiners. The use of the new definitions of "dominance" and "exclusion" may make this less than clear, but it is nonetheless true. The definitions give the appearance of something general, but once more there is nothing general here. There is only one new structure covered by the new definitions, C-adjunction structure.

So, it seems we could replace the "theory of adjunction" with two stipulations: (5) and "hosts are not barriers with respect to their adjoiners."[13] Still, there is often discomfort with stipulations, at least *eo nomine*. Alternatively, accepting the revisions in Section 3.1.1, we can do away with (7) and (8) and instead have (9′).[14] In the C-adjunction structures at issue, if the host is a member of a barrier for β, then the like-labelled new mother will be too, and the mother will l-dominate α, achieving the desired result.

(9′) α governs β iff α m-commands β and some member of every barrier for β l-dominates α.

Nonetheless, there remains something odd. Let us compare (9′) with the "primary theorem," repeated here in its (5′) version.

(5′) Adjuncts are not c-dominated by the Categories to which their hosts belong.

The oddity here is that the entire point of May's "theory of adjunction" is that adjoiners are, in some sense, outside that to which they are adjoined; conversely, the point of Chomsky's analysis is that, in some sense, they are not. A potential advantage, then, of the formulations in Section 3.1.1 and the revisions in (5′) and (9′) is that they make precise what "in some sense" comes down to in each case—c-dominance in the one, l-dominance in the other.

Along with this advantage, however, the formulations of Section 3.1.1 also have an inherited flaw. They are still entirely ad hoc. Just as in May's and Chomsky's proposals, these serve merely to allow us to pick out and talk about C-adjunction structures in a roundabout way. None of the new concepts used in any of the analyses of C-adjunction structures have any use anywhere else in the theory of grammar. This should make us worry.

3.4.0

If the concepts developed in the analyses of C-adjunction have no generality, then perhaps it is wrong to develop such concepts. Perhaps a stipulative approach is better just because it avoids a spurious appearance of generality. In trying to judge this issue, we should ask why, in this particular case, we seek to develop the particular new concepts that we do.

The answer is a familiar one: it is the label on the new mother node that leads us to our new concepts. Because this label is identical to that on the host, it is natural to revise or extend our notions of "category" and "dominance" to try to account for the apparent idiosyncracies of C-adjunction structures. But if the apparent idiosyncracies are true idiosyncracies, then, as suggested, this may be a misleading way to talk about them, lending a false appearance of explanatory depth.

The new mother's label—the problem—is forced by the Projection Principle, as discussed above. Perhaps, then, this is evidence that there is something wrong with the Projection Principle as it is usually understood. A deep principle of grammar ought not to treat ad hoc revisions of basic predicates as natural.

3.4.1

Suppose, then, that the Projection Principle should be understood in something like the following way: different syntactic strata do not represent different lexical properties for the same lexical item. In general, this will not give different results from the usual sort of understanding, which says that the Projection Principle requires that the structurally represented lexical requirements of a lexical item be identically represented at every stratum. There is one case, however, where they can differ: adjunction.

We are taking the adjunction rule to be one that simply creates a new node which is mother to the moved element and the host (see Section 3.5.1). This new node has no label—a transformational rule, recall, cannot create a label (Section 2). In Section 2 it was shown that heads select and project syntactic categories and that labelled nodes are the structural realization of syntactic categories. It therefore follows that no head selects or projects an unlabelled node. Hence, the introduction of an unlabelled node into a phrase marker at one stratum cannot be the introduction of anything that represents lexical information not present at another stratum. Therefore, the revised understanding of the Projection Principle would allow the unlabelled node introduced by the adjunction rule to remain unlabelled. And if it remains unlabelled, we will not be led into the various ad hoc revisions that worry us.

3.4.2

It is probably good to be extremely clear about what is being claimed here. The claim is not that, for example, being the sister of an unlabelled node is the "same thing" as being the sister of a node labelled with a maximal projection—clearly these are "different things." Rather, the claim is that the first situation cannot be one that any lexical item **requires** due to its lexical selection (or projection) properties. Thus, such a structure cannot be the representation of any lexical requirement at all. It therefore cannot, in particular, be the representation of a lexical requirement not represented at some other stratum.

The argument goes as follows. (1) All structure at D-structure is licensed due to lexical requirements. (2) All lexical requirements represented at post-D-structure strata are also represented at D-structure. (3) All lexical requirements are syntactically realized as requirements for syntactic categories. (4) All syntactic categories are realized in structure as labelled nodes. (5) An unlabelled node does not realize a lexical requirement in structure. (6) Therefore, introduction of an unlabelled node at a post-D-structure stratum cannot introduce structure that represents a lexical requirement not represented at D-structure.

The crucial point is (2). This corresponds to the Projection Principle. But, it will be objected, (2) is too weak. It only requires no new lexical satisfaction at post-D-structure strata. It does not require that all D-structure lexical satisfaction be preserved. In fact, this is never actually required. All that is generally required is that D-structure lexical satisfaction be **recoverable** at other strata—that, in a way, is the point of trace theory. It is, for example, a **Chain** that satisfies Theta requirements. Because adjunction will also leave a trace, the lexical requirement licensing the moved element is recoverable. And, the lexical requirement licensing the host is also recoverable: since unlabelled nodes cannot represent lexical requirements, they are invisible when determining whether such requirements are met. Only the host is available for local satisfaction of a lexical requirement; the unlabelled new node is invisible, and the moved element is part of a Chain that satisfies other lexical requirements.

3.4.3

Notice, now, that if we accept the argument just given, then May's (5) follows trivially, reverting to the usual notion of "category" (= labelled node), rather than either of the revisions.

> (5) Adjuncts are not dominated by the categories to which they are adjoined.

Thus, any result which (5) ensures also follows if we allow the new mother to remain unlabelled and without further revision or stipulation. But, what of Chomsky's "exclusion" on this proposal? Clearly it cannot be an immediate consequence, because, as noted previously, it "in some sense," denies (5).

As also pointed out above, Chomsky's definitions also serve to pick out only one new structure, adjunctions. We could, therefore, simply rewrite (8) (repeated here) as (10). It may appear that (10) is stipulative in a way (8) is not, but this is not true. The stipulation is buried in (8), packed beneath the definitions of "exclusion," "dominates," and "segment," but, again, these definitions combine to pick out exactly one case, "unless α is adjoined to γ." And, under our new proposal, we have no independent need for May's (or Section 3.1.1's) revisions of "dominate" and "category" (or "segment").

(8) α governs β iff α m-commands β and there is no γ, γ a barrier for β such that γ excludes α.

(10) α governs β iff α m-commands β and for every γ, γ a barrier for β, γ dominates α, unless α is adjoined to γ.

Or, if one likes (8) as it is, we can rewrite (7) (repeated here) as (11) (I make (11) a biconditional, unlike Chomsky's (7)), and then continue to use (8).

(7) α excludes β if no segment of α dominates β.

(11) α excludes β iff α does not dominate β and α and β are not sisters directly dominated by an unlabelled node.

This does not have exactly the same extension as (7), because under (11) in an adjunction structure neither daughter of the new node excludes the other, but under (7) only the adjoiner excludes the host (but not vice versa, of course, as this result is the whole point of the series of definitions). This does not matter, however, because such lack of exclusion has no (unwanted) consequences.

3.4.4

The only motivation for C-adjunction structures is the Projection Principle. If we change our understanding of the Projection Principle, there need not be any C-adjunction structures. C-adjunction would now be a theoretically otiose stipulation, so anything that invoked it should simply go around in a circle, extending to no other structures or facts. And this is exactly what we have found.

3.5.0

We have seen that each of May and Chomsky's proposals is on its own terms ad hoc and stipulative, widening the class of cases only to include C-adjunction structures. There is thus no independent justification that either proposal can lend to the other or to C-adjunction structures more generally. There is no compelling empirical argument for C-adjunction structures. The lack of empirical need for C-adjunction structures would be explained by the lack of a theoretical possibility for them. The new understanding of the Projection Principle would allow the mother to remain unlabelled, removing the theoretical justification for C-adjunction structures.

Although I have argued that a C-adjunction rule does not exist and C-adjunction structures need not exist, I have continually left open the possibility that there can be a rule of adjunction. In Section 1.2, a brief conceptual motivation for having an adjunction rule was adumbrated. I now return to this topic.

3.5.1

The suggestion I wish to make is that all substitutions are structure preserving, whereas all adjunctions are non-structure preserving. More explicitly, I suggest that it is definitional of "non-structure preserving" that it mean "adjunction." An adjunction is explicitly structure creating, so in an obvious sense it cannot be structure preserving, and I propose we accept this sense.[15] By definition, then, all nonadjunctions—that is, all substitutions—are structure preserving. The structure they preserve is structure licensed at D-structure. This fits well with, for example, Chomsky's (1986a: 5) reformulation of wh-movement as movement to the specifier of CP position, rather than as "adjunction to COMP," as in earlier work.[16]

"Structure preservation" in something like the original sense of Emonds (1976) might better be called "label (or category) preservation" instead. It is not about either movement or structure as such but rather the (im)possibility of mismatches between labels on moved elements and on landing sites in substitutions. It cannot be an issue with respect to "non-structure-preserving" rules (adjunctions) in our sense, because these create unlabelled nodes. Let us suppose, then, that "label preservation" is a fact about all and only substitutions.

It was pointed out in Section 1.2 that C-adjunction cannot be "Move Alpha" for the simple reason that more than one thing is affected. Suppose, though, that the movement part of adjunction is an instance of Move Alpha. That is, there are two sorts of movement: structure-preserving to a pre-existing position (label preserving substitutions) and non-structure preserving to a nonexisting position.[17] Now, in the second sort of movement, if the moved element is to remain a part of the phrase marker, a new node must be created to reintegrate the moved element; that is, adjunction must happen.[18] If this reasoning is sound, then we are committed to node creation and adjunction as part of the theory of grammar. We should like other evidence of its existence. Our analysis of adjuncts in terms of "Adjunct Adding" (Section 5) will provide such independent evidence. Before we take up adjuncts, however, I summarize the argument concerning C-adjunction.

3.6

Although there cannot be a C-adjunction rule, there is need for node creation and adjunction. This process is available both at D-structure for creating "extended base structures" that integrate adjunct phrases into existing phrase markers (Section 5) and in the derivation of the strata S-structure and LF for integrating the result of movements to non-existing positions. As we shall see below in Section 5, in the former case the new node is labelled, because an extended base structure is still subject to the theory of the base and the resulting structures have the typical adjunction structure (1) (repeated here). In the latter cases, presence of a label depends on how the Projection Principle is understood. On familiar understandings, the mother is labelled and C-adjunction structure (2) (repeated here) results, with the concomitant obscurantist "theory of adjunction." On the revised understanding of Section 3.4, the new node need not be labelled, hence the "primary theorem" is a trivial consequence, and the construction specific nature of "exclusion" is transparent.

(1)

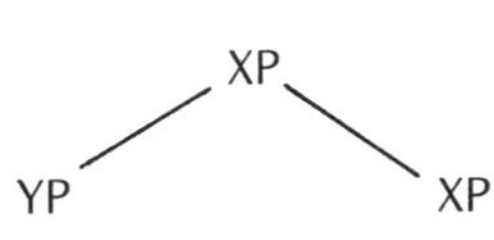

(2) a.

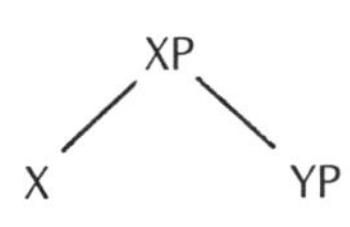

b.

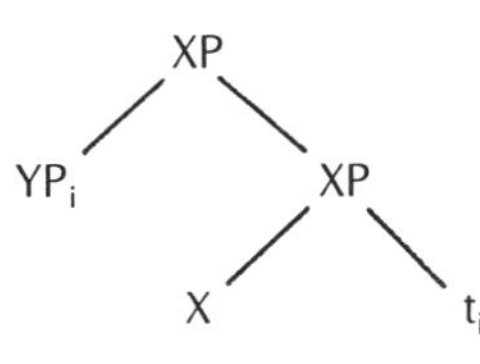

The unjustified assumption that all nodes must be labelled is what causes syntacticians to propose a C-adjunction rule. Both the assumption and the rule are inheritances from earlier stages in generative grammar. Under examination, neither stands up today. We move now from C-adjunction to adjuncts.

4.0

We noted in Chapter 1 that the theory elaborated in Speas (1990) does not allow for adjuncts as part of the set of base structures. This follows from the lack, in the MPST, of categorial distinction among the labels on the nodes in the Projection Chain—lack of "bar levels"—as we now make clear (see Speas 1990: 48-56, for discussion of bar levels).

There are three possible cases to consider: adjunct attachment to the maximal projection, to the minimal projection; and to an intermediate node. We can immediately rule out this last possibility. There are no "intermediate categories" as such, and therefore, any apparent base adjunct would be structurally identical to the nonadjunct structure. Hence there can be no such thing as a distinct base adjunct with respect to intermediate nodes. An adjunct attached to an intermediate node would appear to be simply an incorrectly projected Chain.

There can be no adjuncts with respect to the Minimal Projection. Or, rather, if there were, they, too, would dissolve into non-adjunct structure. This is because the *Minimal Projection* is defined as the node in the Projection Chain which does not directly dominate anything. The mother of the adjunct and the host (the Minimal Projection) does not meet this definition and so is simply another member of the Projection Chain.

Finally, there can be no base adjuncts with respect to the Maximal Projection. The *Maximal Projection* is defined as, essentially, the member of the Projection Chain which is not directly dominated by any other member of the Projection Chain. Hence, it is necessarily unique, and in any putative base adjunct structure, the mother of the adjunct and host would become the Maximal Projection.

4.1

There is a further issue here. It follows from the MPST that base adjuncts are impossible, as just demonstrated. But it also seems to follow that there can be no nonbase adjuncts, for the same reason as with the base structures: no categorial distinctions are made among the labels on the nodes in the Projection Chain. Any adjunct attached below the level of the Maximal Projection would simply be another member of the Projection Chain; any attached above the Maximal Projection becomes the Maximal Projection. A total ban on adjuncts seems to be an undesirable result and not one that Speas (1990) endorses (or discusses).

A resolution to this difficulty, one that appears consistent with the practice in Speas (1990), is the following. Suppose that that the Minimal and Maximal Projections are fixed—notated—at base structure. That is, the definitions given in Chapter 1 for these two are to be understood as relabelling instructions. Now, the Minimal and Maximal Projections of a Projection Chain will bear unique labels in the base, and the possibility is opened up that there can be "postbase" adjuncts. We return to this in Section 5.2.

There is a further theoretical reason to suppose that there are no base adjuncts. As Speas (1990: 49) notes, it has been suggested "that D-structure may be a representation which includes only heads and their arguments." And, as Speas also points out, Lebeaux (1988; 1990) has provided empirical argument for this suggestion and the beginnings of a way to implement it.

4.2

Lebeaux (1988: 133-58; 1990: 21-41) argues at length for the proposition that D-structure consists of "a set of structures, in which the "argument-of" relation holds in pure way within each structure . . . but the relation of adjunct-of holds between structures" (Lebeaux 1988: 139; 1990: 25). He further suggests (1988: 142, 1990: 28) a reason for this: " [i]f . . . the Projecton Principle holds, and (with respect to this issue [formation of the base]) only the Projecton Principle, then it would require additional stipulation to actually have adjuncts present in the base."[19] We note in passing that combining PMs in this way requires that a "well-formed PM" need not be rooted in a node labelled S.[20]

Lebeaux (1988: 148; 1990: 33) proposes the rule Adjoin Alpha to combine PMs. His discussion of the rule itself is limited to the following: "Let us assume that this always involves Chomsky-adjunction, copying the node in the adjoined-to structure. Like Move-α, Adjoin-α applies perfectly freely, ungrammatical results ruled out by general principles, interpretive or otherwise."

Speas (1990: 49) interprets Lebeaux's proposal to mean that "adjuncts are added to the phrase marker after D-structure." In Section 5, I offer a different proposal.

In addition to the conceptual arguments, Lebeaux (1988: 146; 1990: 31) adduces empirical evidence in favor of Adjoin Alpha.

(12) a. *He_i believes the claim that John_i is nice
b. *He_i likes the story that John_i wrote
c. *Whose claim that John_i is nice did he_i believe.
d. Which story that John_i wrote did he_i like.

(13) a. *He_i destroyed those pictures of John_i.
b. *He_i destroyed those pictures near John_i.
c. *Which pictures of John_i did he_i destroy.
d. Which pictures near John_i did he_i destroy.

Examples such as (12d) had been contrasted with such as (13c) by van Riemsdijk & Williams (1981): the unexpected well-formedness of (12d) they called an *antireconstruction effect.* They suggested that the crucial difference between these examples lay in "degree of embedding." Lebeaux's further data argue that this cannot be the right answer. Rather, the contrasts between (12c) and (12d) and (13c) and (13d) lead to what Speas (1990: 50 (54)) calls

(14) *Lebeaux's Generalization:*
Coreference is OK if the R-expression is in a fronted adjunct (the relative clause and the **near**-phrase [in (12) & (13)]), but is not OK if the R-expression is in a fronted argument.

According to Lebeaux (1988: 150-51; 1990: 35-36) Adjoin Alpha offers an account of the data in (12)-(13) in the following way.

Adjoin Alpha is an operation that combines PMs. Move Alpha is an operation within a single PM. Thus, unless further stipulations are made, we should expect the latter to occur with perfect indifference with respect to the former; that is, both on PMs that are prior to adjunct attaching and those that are the result of adjunct attaching. Further, Lebeaux argues, it is necessary to assume that Condition C of the Binding theory applies at every level throughout a derivation, marking ungrammatical any PM in which an R-expression is C-commanded by a coindexed pronoun. We turn now to how this actually works.

4.3

Lebeaux (1988: 154-55; 1990: 37-39) illustrates his proposal with respect to the examples in (15) (his 1988: 154 (50); 1990: 37 (50)).

(15) a. *Whose examination of John_i did he_i fear?
b. Which examinations near John_i did he_i peek at?

In (15a), the D-structure is a single PM to which Adjoin Alpha has not applied—there is no adjunct in (15a). At D-structure, the coindexed pronoun *he* C-commands *John,* a violation of Condition C of the Binding Theory. Fronting of the wh-phrase by Move Alpha does not obviate this violation, given Lebeaux's two assumptions (1) that Condition C applies at all stages in a derivation and (2) "that starred sentences may not be 'saved' by additional operations." (Lebeaux 1988: 152; 1990: 36) Thus (15a) is accounted for.

Two D-structure PMs underlie (15b): one for *He peeked at which examinations* and one for the adjunct *near John.* Move Alpha can apply either before or after Adjoin Alpha. If Adjoin Alpha applies first, then there is a Condition C violation, which, again, cannot be fixed by movement. On the other hand, if movement happens before adjunct attaching, there is never a Condition C violation. Move Alpha gives something like *Which examinations he peeked at;* Adjoin Alpha results in *Which examinations near John he peeked at.* Thus, there is a licit derivation of (15b), and the difference between it and (15a) is neatly accounted for. However, things are less neat than they seem, as we now see.

4.4

Speas (1990: 51-52 (59)-(62)) adds further data which somewhat becloud Lebeaux's clear picture of the nature of adjuncts.

(16) **Temporal location** vs. **locative**
a. In Ben_i's office, he_i is an absolute dictator.
b. *In Ben_i's office, he_i lay on his desk.

(17) **Rationale** vs. **benefactive**

a. For $Mary_i$'s valor, she_i was awarded a purple heart.

b. *For $Mary_i$'s brother, she_i was given some old clothes.

(18) **Temporal** vs. **locative**

a. On $Rosa_i$'s birthday, she_i took it easy.

b. *On $Rosa_i$'s lawn, she_i took it easy.

(19) **Temporal** vs. **instrumental**

a. With $John_i$'s novel finished, he_i began to write a book of poetry.

b. *With $John_i$'s computer, he_i began to write a book of poetry.

As Speas points out, these examples all have fronted adjunct PPs, but they differ with respect to presence or absence of the antireconstruction effects. With locative (16b) & (18b), benefactive (17b), and instrumental (19b) phrases, there are no such effects; with temporal (16a), (18a), and (19a) and rationale (17a) phrases, the effects obtain.

Speas argues that under Lebeaux's approach to adjuncts, it therefore follows that locative, benefactive, and instrumental adjunct phrases cannot be added by means of Adjoin Alpha. This is because, if they could be so attached, then they, too, would show the antireconstruction effects; that is, there would be, for each of the ill-formed (b) examples in (16)-(19), a licit derivation analogous to that just sketched for (15b).

Speas concludes from this that there are actually two sorts of adjuncts: (1) those showing antireconstruction effects, which are added by Adjoin Alpha; (2) those which do not show the effects, which are present in the PM from the start. Speas (1990: 52) suggests that the latter sort are theta marked and governed by the verb, even though they are not part of the verb's theta grid; she calls them *theta-marked adjuncts.* She adds as well (1990: 54) that these adjuncts are "likely . . . [to be] equivalent to the class which has traditionally been called VP internal adjuncts."

4.5

There is much that is attractive about this approach to adjuncts, but there is also much to be discussed, clarified, and ultimately, rejected—or so I shall argue. In the next section, I turn to these tasks.

5.0

Recall that Chomsky (1986a) stipulates that adjunction (which may or may not include adjuncts, however) is always to a maximal projection and that Lebeaux (1988: 148, 1990: 33) writes, "Let us assume that this always involves Chomsky-adjunction, copying the node in the adjoined-to structure. Like Move-α, Adjoin-α applies perfectly freely, ungrammatical results ruled out by general principles, interpretive or otherwise."

Recalling our discussion in Section 3, we now might wonder about these statements. Why always to a maximal projection, supposing this holds of adjuncts? Why Chomsky-adjunction? Which "general principles?" So, for example, why should the mother node be labelled with the same label as that of the host and not either the adjunct's or some third label, or none at all? Why not daughter-adjunction, for that matter? Which, if any, of the considerations in Section 3 holds of adjuncts? One might be tempted by an empirical answer to such questions: a VP with a PP adjunct, for example, patterns distributionally with VPs without such an adjunct. Such temptations must be resisted, however, because they merely restate the problem to be solved: why VP and not, say, PP? To approach such issues explanatorily, we require a **theory** of adjuncts, to the development of which we now turn.

5.1

Our theory of adjuncts should meet two desiderata. The first is to explain the sorts of stipulated properties noted in the previous section. The other is to allow for the special structural properties of adjuncts. I propose that these can be met in the following way.

The output of *Adjunct Adding,* as I shall call our version of Adjoin Alpha, must meet the conditions on D-structures; that is, PMs with adjuncts are a subspecies of base structures, just as CCC structures are. But, PMs with adjuncts, although a subspecies of base structures, cannot be **merely** base structures; we have seen that the

MPST cannot allow adjuncts in the base. Therefore, they must be distinguishable from ordinary base structures while satisfying, say, Project Alpha and the definitions for Maximal and Minimal Projections. Is it, in fact, possible to simultaneously satisfy these desiderata? We examine this question in the next section.

5.2

In Section 4.1 it was suggested that the definitions for Maximal and Minimal Projections be understood as relabelling instructions. We therefore have a Projection Chain of the following form: XP . . . (X) . . . X^0; that is, two distinguished labels (Maximal and Minimal) and an "elsewhere" case. In a PM with an adjunct, we have two such Projection Chains, an XP chain and a YP chain. Suppose the YP structure is the adjunct; the XP structure, the host.

If we attach to XP, the new mother node cannot bear a third, distinct label, Z, because in that case we have a non-Projection Chain: Z is not itself a head nor is it a projection of either X or Y. I postpone discussion of the mother bearing either an X or Y label.

If we adjoin to an intermediate level, there are two familiar problems. One is apparent reference to intermediate structure, the possibility of which is denied by Speas (1990). More important, in my view, is the other: as noted in Section 4.0, nothing is distinctively "adjunctive" about the resulting structure if the mother node is labelled X. It is structurally identical to a base structure without any adjunct. Because more structure is present than the head requires and nothing distinguishes this structure from an ill-formed Projection Chain, it, too, should simply appear (from the point of view of the MPST) to be an ill-formed Projection Chain.[21] This suggests that adjuncts are figments of the analyst's imagination, with no grammatical reality, a conclusion I reject. Finally, if the mother node is labelled Y (or Z), then we have an ill-formed Projection Chain.

Attachment to the Minimal Projection also results in ill-formed Projection Chains if the mother is labelled either Y or Z. If it is labelled X, then the mother and the host have different labels. If it is X^0, then the labels are the same, but the new mother node does not meet the definition for a node to be so labelled: it directly dominates other nodes.

Consider now daughter-adjunction. If PMs are exclusively binary branching (Speas 1990: 39), then this is ruled out for all cases except the Minimal Projection. However, daughter-adjunction would remove the Minimal Projection from the frontier of the PM graph, thus removing it as the site for interface with the lexicon and PF. If binary branching is not assumed, nothing in the MPST immediately rules out daughter-adjunction, I believe. Kayne's (1981) unambiguous path condition, which does not stipulate binary branching, does require it in cases where some further relation—such as government—is to hold between nodes. As noted in the discussion of unambiguous paths in Chapter 2, it may be that for such substantively linguistic reasons—such as government—the unambiguous path condition should be included in syntactic theory. If so, then in general daughter-adjunction would be ruled out because it would create undesirable ambiguous paths

We return to the case of Maximal Projection. Suppose the mother node is labelled X. This node now meets the definition for the Maximal Projection; it is relabelled XP. We now have a classic adjunct structure. But, we have a node labelled XP which does not meet the definition for Maximal Projection, viz., the original XP. Ought it no longer be so labelled, but rather be labelled merely X? Because it has been suggested that the definitions are relabelling instructions, we apparently cannot appeal to the familiar idea that labels cannot be changed. Perhaps, though, the relabelling construal is incorrect, for just this reason. Instead, we can suggest that the nodes meeting the definitions must always bear these respective labels. Recall, as well, that, unlike Speas (1990), we do not "collapse labelling and generation" of structure. We take labelled PMs as given, then instantiate them; if the resulting instantiated PM meets the lexical requirements of the head(s) and the definitions of the Projection Chain and Minimal & Maximal Projections, it is licensed.

Thus, the nodes meeting the definitions bear the labels XP and X^0 always and forever. Adjunct Adding creates a new node that must be integrated into the PM. If it is an X (or Y) it is definitionally the Maximal Projection in the new combined PM, hence it too bears XP (YP). Any other position or label choice results in an ill-formed Projecton Chain. However, the host XP (YP) retains its label; all labelled nodes do always. Because a constructional process is involved, we can get a structure which both meets the conditions on base structures after the process and is not a possible original base structure.

The theory as outlined allows only Adjunct Adding to maximal projections and the resulting structures are identical to those putatively created by C-adjunction (though without a trace). It does not decide which is the adjunct and which is the host, nor does it determine which of XP and YP labels the mother node. I take these last to be nonstructural issues in the sense that they depend on how the notion of "modification" is cashed out; Speas (1990: 60ff.) elaborates on ideas from Higginbotham (1985; 1989) in presenting an approach in which satisfaction of lexical argument structure requirements mediates the "modification" relation.

The approach outlined is the fullest account of adjunct structure I know of and the only one that suggests principled reasons for many observations about the structural nature of the phenomenon. However, it runs up against the empirical arguments adduced by Lebeaux (1988; 1990) and Speas (1990) discussed in Sections 4.2–4.5, a confrontation we now turn to.

5.3

The central empirical claim of Lebeaux's (1988; 1990) approach to adjuncts is that "antireconstruction" data—repeated here—are immediately handled.

(12) a. *He_i believes the claim that $John_i$ is nice
b. *He_i likes the story that $John_i$ wrote
c. *Whose claim that $John_i$ is nice did he_i believe.
d. Which story that $John_i$ wrote did he_i like.

(13) a. *He_i destroyed those pictures of $John_i$.
b. *He_i destroyed those pictures near $John_i$.
c. *Which pictures of $John_i$ did he_i destroy.
d. Which pictures near $John_i$ did he_i destroy.

We repeat as well what Speas (1990: 50 (54)) calls

(14) *Lebeaux's Generalization:*
Coreference is OK if the R-expression is in a fronted adjunct (the relative clause and the *near*-phrase [in (12) and (13)]), but is not OK if the R-expression is in a fronted argument.

The manner in which Lebeaux's approach to adjuncts works was outlined in Section 4.3. It crucially relies on two assumptions: (1) Adjoin Alpha and Move Alpha stand in no determinate order with respect to each other and (2) "Condition C is not earmarked for any particular level—it applies throughout the derivation" (Lebeaux 1988: 151; 1990: 35).

The theory of adjuncts advocated here cannot account for the data in (12)-(13) in the way that Lebeaux's approach does. The present proposal denies the first of the two assumptions in the previous paragraph; instead, Adjunct Adding is (intrinsically) ordered before Move Alpha. We now examine both this disagreement and Lebeaux's second assumption.

Lebeaux (1988: 150-51; 1990: 35) argues that since the two operations Adjoin Alpha and Move Alpha are defined over different domains—the former an inter-PM operation—the latter an intra-PM operation—it is natural to suppose that no ordering holds between them. I agree—if, by ordering, one means extrinsic ordering. No particular sense attaches to an extrinsic ordering of rules with different domains, I believe. Lebeaux suggests that, because no such ordering exists and both the inputs and outputs of Adjoin Alpha are PMs, the intra-PM operation can operate both before and after the inter-PM operation.

Move Alpha, however, is not simply an intra-PM operation. It is also the essential content of the mapping between D-structure and S-structure. If Move Alpha precedes Adjoin Alpha, then we are creating adjuncts in S-structures, not D-structures. Lebeaux's Adjoin Alpha, evidently, is not defined as part of the mapping from D-structure to S-structure. It is not at all clear what the restrictions on possible S-structure adjuncts would be such that we end up with just the structures we do under Lebeaux's proposal.[22] Lebeaux, it should be recalled, simply adverts to "general principles, interpretive or otherwise." (Lebeaux 1988: 148; 1990: 33) Notice that he cannot appeal to well-formedness conditions on base PMs, because the adjuncts in question are being added to S-structures. If there are general structural well-formedness conditions on S-structure PMs to appeal to, then their results are, apparently, exactly the same as the results of those which apply to D-structure PMs as outlined above. It might be suggested that this is due to some sort of Structure Preservation Principle; perhaps, but the question would be what sort and why it should apply to Adjoin Alpha, an apparently sui generis rule. The fundamental problem here is that Lebeaux has no theory of adjuncts, no principled proposal for why the structures are what they are and not something else.

As Lebeaux (1988: 151; 1990: 35) says, Adjoin Alpha "is simply an operation joining phrase markers." From this he concludes that pre- and post-Move-Alpha PMs are available for adjunct placement, as noted. However, because well-formed PMs are licensed **as well-formed PMs** at D-structure, this conclusion does not follow. As we saw in Chapter 3 with respect to CCC, for the output of a "joining" of PMs to itself be a PM, it must meet the well-formedness conditions on PMs; these conditions are the conditions that define the base not S-structures. We therefore reject Lebeaux's first assumption in that there is—and must be—an intrinsic ordering of Adjunct Adding before Move Alpha.

Consider now the second crucial assumption, about Condition C. This, it seems, is entirely empirically driven: if there were no data such as those in (12)-(13), there would be no reason to propose it. Theoretically, it seems to have little or no obvious rationale—why, for example, only Condition C—and Lebeaux offers no theoretical argument in its favor (but see Lebeaux 1988: 205 n.3; 1990: 76 n. 10, both for a counterexample to the proposal and some brief theoretical speculation). It is only in concert with this ad hoc stipulation that the rejected first assumption delivers the empirical goods.

But, they do deliver; the present account does not. The present account offers a theory of adjuncts (and adjunction, for that matter) embedded within a larger theory of PMs, a theory that presumes it is possible and desirable to attempt a principled account of the structure of adjuncts; but it offers nothing with respect to the antire-contruction facts. Lebeaux offers no theory of adjuncts; but, given two otherwise unmotivated assumptions, he can account for the data. Or can he?

Recall the further data from Speas (1990: 51-52 (59)-(62)), repeated here.

(16) **Temporal location vs. locative**
  a. In Ben_i's office, he_i is an absolute dictator.
  b. *In Ben_i's office, he_i lay on his desk.

(17) **Rationale vs. benefactive**
  a. For $Mary_i$'s valor, she_i was awarded a purple heart.
  b. *For $Mary_i$'s brother, she_i was given some old clothes.

(18) **Temporal vs. locative**
  a. On $Rosa_i$'s birthday, she_i took it easy.
  b. *On $Rosa_i$'s lawn, she_i took it easy.

(19) **Temporal vs. instrumental**
a. With $John_i$'s novel finished, he_i began to write a book of poetry.
b. *With $John_i$'s computer, he_i began to write a book of poetry.

Speas concluded from these data that there are two kinds of adjuncts, those added in the derivation (presumably by Adjoin Alpha) and those always present. This conclusion is forced on her because the different adjuncts in (16)-(19) do not pattern together with respect to the antireconstruction phenomenon. If all adjuncts are added derivationally, they should all show the antireconstruction phenomenon.

However, there is a problem for Speas. Despite her calling the adjuncts not added in the derivation "theta-marked adjuncts," it is still not possible that they should be present in underived D-structures. The impossibility of adjuncts in such structures within the pristine (i.e., pre-extended base) MPST has been argued above, and acknowledged by Speas. Giving them a new name does not eliminate the problem.

Another conclusion is possible given the data in (16)-(19). Lebeaux's Generalization (repeated here) is wrong. These data, in fact, counterexemplify the generalization.

(14) *Lebeaux's Generalization:*
Coreference is OK if the R-expression is in a fronted adjunct (the relative clause and the *near*-phrase [in (12) and (13)]), but is not OK if the R-expression is in a fronted argument.

Let us examine the (polemical) position we now find ourselves in. The current theory, to reiterate, cannot account for the antireconstruction facts in (12)-(13), but it does offer significant insight into the structural properties of adjuncts within the general framework of the MPST. Now, it appears that the data in (12)-(13) may be more artifactual that factual; at the very least, the approach which predicts (12)-(13) makes a wrong prediction with respect to (16)-(19). The apparent empirical advantage of Lebeaux's approach has disappeared.[23] The attempt by Speas to save the account of (12)-(13) in the face of her data (16)-(19) led her to "discover" two kinds of adjuncts, a discovery incompatible with her version of the MPST.

In sum, given the MPST approach to adjuncts and the data in (12)-(19), Lebeaux's account of the data in (12)-(13) cannot be correct. Until and unless his account is embedded in a theory of adjuncts comparable to the MPST-based approach, a theory that must **also**—because of the claim it makes with respect to (12)-(13)—account for the counterexamples in (16)-(19), we can reject the antireconstruction data as telling. We can instead accept a theory—our MPST-based theory of adjuncts—which does not account for the counterexamples, for the simple reason that it makes no claim which they can counterexemplify.[24] We give up an approach that makes one correct and one incorrect empirical prediction, perhaps embedded in an incoherent theory, in favor of a theory that makes neither empirical prediction. It is sometimes better to be silent than to either assert falsehoods or be incoherent. We may have to take an apparent step backwards in order to take two steps forward.[25]

This concludes the exposition of the theories of adjunction and adjuncts in the MPST. We turn to a recap and to some general conclusions.

6.0

This chapter has done several things in the course of elaborating theories of adjuncts and adjunction. With respect to adjunction, we have done the following. The rule of C-adjunction has been rejected. A number of suggestions in May (1985) and Chomsky (1986a) on adjunction have been both reformalized and criticized, although the "primary theorem" and its corrollaries may have been put on more solid ground. The nature of adjunction structures has been given a theoretical basis and explication.

Turning to adjuncts, we have done the following. The proposals of Lebeaux (1988, 1990) and Speas (1990) on adjuncts have been examined and revised, some parts rejected, but the "leading ideas" retained. Further, it should be clear that "matters of execution" matter, as there has been some substantive disagreement with Lebeaux and Speas, due, essentially, to the way in which the theory of adjuncts was explicitly worked out.

Adjuncts, like coordination, augment the set of base structures, creating a set of "extended base structures," subject to the constraints of the MPST. We now briefly examine the nature of the extended base.

6.1

Coordination joins PMs by allowing them to share a node which bears the same label. A crucial identity, recall, was **type label identity.** Adjuncts add a new node, but that node bears an already present label.[26] There is **token label identity** here. There is, then, a sort of complementarity to these combining operations.[27] Indeed, within the MPST these two operations exhaust the ways of combining PMs. CCC are formed by sharing a node. Adjuncts are attached by sharing a label. The MPST, recall, both separates nodes from labels and begins with the assumption that syntactic structures just are constructions built from these elements. The MPST is the theory of permissable collocations of nodes and labels (viz., PMs). So, the range of operations available for joining such MPST-licensed collocations to form a new such collocation comes down to two: (1) join at a node or (2) join at a label. Once more, the formal character of the MPST offers explanatory insight into substantive linguistic phenomena.

Each of these operations "add nothing new," though, as we have seen, they do so in different, complementary ways. The reason PM combining operations do not add anything wholly new (e.g., conjunction words with attendent nodes and labels; adjunct and host's mothers with labels identical to neither daughter) is that the resulting structures would violate the MPST. There is a simple (algebraic) idea here: combined PMs are also PMs, subject to the well-formedness conditions on PMs. It has proved very powerful.[28]

5

Islands as Noncanonical Phrase Structure

0.0

This chapter is somewhat different from the previous four. Those chapters were essentially *theory construction.* They laid out the assumptions and architecture of the approach and attempted to demonstrate that following the internal logic of the theory leads to linguistically interesting results. This chapter is more along the lines of *theory elaboration.* I assume the theory as so far discussed, add a bit more to it internally, and integrate it with some ideas from other investigations. On account of this difference, the inquiry here is less central to the theory, though not the less interesting, perhaps. It has the form of a demonstration case: it suggests how to use the theory with other existing ideas in ways that can shed light on outstanding problems. If this particular elaboration ultimately fails (and there are serious empirical questions, see note 10), at least it shows a way to think with the theory. The theory itself is only directly impugned if no such elaborations are possible or promising—a difficult conclusion to reach at this early stage.

The chapter offers an analysis of perhaps the most studied phenomenon in syntax of the last twenty-five years: Islands—constituents out of which extraction is blocked. I propose an approach to Islands that is rather different from those that have been most common in the syntax literature. In keeping with what has gone before in this book, I locate the specialness of Islands in their phrase structure, arguing that the MPST affords particular insight into this "specialness."

A similar idea was independently suggested some years ago by Janet Fodor (1983: 202), within a rather different set of assumptions: "What I propose is that a marked syntactic configuration tends to act as an island, and that the strength of the island is roughly proportional to the degree of markedeness of the construction. . . . (The general suggestion here obviously bears a close resemblance to the Freezing Principle of Wexler & Culicover, 1980. . . .)"

My proposal is that Islands are, in a sense that will be made precise, *Noncanonical Phrase Structure* (NCPS, hereafter), and that the fact that such configurations are **Islands** is, as alluded to by Fodor, relatable to Learnability through the Freezing Principle. Further, the notion of NCPS within the MPST will require analysis and clarification of the distinction between **Core** and **Periphery** in (Government & Binding) syntactic theory.

0.1

Stepping back a bit, there are two questions that could immediately be asked about Islands. One is, *what* are they? The other is, *why* are they?

The first question admits basically of two sorts of answers: as we might say, an extensional and an intensional, where the former sort is a list of the members of a set of structures which are Islands (it is popular to view Ross 1967 in this way—see, e.g., van Riemsdijk & Williams 1986: 32—but this is a canard that ignores Ross's discussion (1967: section 6.4.3) of "(maximal) strips"), and the latter sort is a characteristic function for such a set (perhaps as envisioned by Bounding Theory in its various forms).

The second question seems to be less often asked. To answer it, we want to know how it comes to be that this set of structures—whatever it is, however we identify it—is a set of **Islands—and not something else.** To answer this second question, then, necessarily engages in explanation in a way that answering the first need not. However, the answer I give to the **first** question is ineliminably tied to an answer to the second. That is—once more—the MPST-based approach is explanatory in ways that other proposals have not been.

I do not directly discuss alternative approaches. This is because they do not in general share the explanatory goals of my account, so, strictly, they are not in competition. The main goal of other approaches seems to be improved observational or descriptive adequacy: more extensive and principled data coverage. If one prefers the explanatory goals of this inquiry, then one accepts the challenge of reanalyzing facts and phenomena that have been discussed with other goals but which do not appear to fit within the present account. In other words, accepting the goals of this approach as more desirable entails that successful approaches with other goals provide only problems, not alternatives.

0.2

The chapter is organized as follows. Section 1 presents some familiar data types and proposes, with minimal discussion or justification, some structures for these examples. It should be noted that some of the structures proposed are not licensed by the MPST as so far developed. Section 2 discusses two general theoretical underpinnings for my proposal. The first is from the Learnability Theory of Wexler & Culicover (1980), specifically what they call (1980: 120) *characteristic structures. NCPS is noncharacteristic structure.* The second is the distinction between Core and Periphery and draws on an analysis by Fodor (1989). Section 3 is the heart of the proposal. To anticipate, there are no rules in Core MPST, while the Periphery has rules. *NCPS is rule-licensed phrase structure.* Section 3 discusses the rules involved, including explicit phrase structure rules that license the otherwise unlicensed structures proposed in Section 1. Section 4 is a general conclusion. The Appendix discusses the Coordinate Structure Constraint (CSC) and WH-Islands.

1.0

The data types we are concerned with are Complex Noun Phrases (CNPs)—both relative clause (1) and noun-complement (2) types—Subjects (3), and adjuncts (4). The proposal does not cover WH-Islands or the CSC, which are discussed in the Appendix. Some familiar example types are given in (1)-(4). Sections 1.1-1.3 provide structures for (1)-(4).

(1) a. Kim met a child who read *If I ran the zoo.*
 b. *Which book did Kim meet a child who read?

(2) a. Pat mentioned Dale's belief that you saw Robin.
 b. *Who did Pat mention Dale's belief that you saw?
 c. Pat mentioned that Dale believes that you saw Robin?
 d. Who did Pat mention that Dale believes that you saw?

(3) a. That Kim ate the oysters surprised most of the guests.

b. *What did that Kim ate surprise most of the guests?
c. It surprised most of the guests that Kim ate the oysters.
d. What did it surprise most of the guests that Kim ate?
e. Sentences about the present king of France terrified Lee.
f. *Who did sentences about terrify Lee?
g. Lee heard sentences about the present king of France.
h. Who did Lee hear sentences about?

(4) a. Terry was bothered because Lou explained *Barriers.*
b. *What was Terry bothered because Lou explained?
(cf. Manzini 1992: 3 (18))

1.1

There is some subtlety in the analysis of CNPs. Weisler (1980) presents the data in (5)-(7) in arguing for a categorial distinction between, respectively, relative clauses with and without either overt complementizers or relative pronouns. The set in (5) demonstrates that free relatives can be modified only by relative clauses with complementizers or relative pronouns; that in (6) shows stacking of relative clauses, demonstrating both that only those with complementizers or relative pronouns stack and that relative clauses without complementizers or relative pronouns must precede those with complementizers or relative pronouns ((6b) & (6c)); (6d) does not appear in Weisler 1980); (7) shows that the two sorts of relative clauses do not easily conjoin (the judgments are from Weisler 1980; I am skeptical of these data, and note that Weisler only gives (7b) & (7d) ? versus acceptable).

(5) a. I will read whatever you recommend that Bill wrote.
b. I bought whatever you sold that my wife thought we could afford.
c. *I will read whatever you recommend Bill wrote.

d. *I bought whatever you sold my wife thought we could afford.

(6) a. The book that Bill bought that Max wrote was boring.
b. The book Bill bought that Max wrote was boring.
c. *The book that Bill bought Max wrote was boring.
d. *The book Bill bought Max wrote was boring.

(7) a. The book that John read and that Bill wrote is boring.
b. ?The book John read and that Bill wrote is boring.
c. A moose that Mary shot and that Sue stuffed is in the corner.
d. ?A moose Mary shot and that Sue stuffed is in the corner.

Weisler (1980) actually distinguishes the two sorts of relative clauses in two ways. One is categorial: relative clauses with complementizers or relative pronouns are S′; those without are simply S. The other is structural but not categorial: the S′ relative clauses are sisters (and daughters) of N″; the S relatives are sisters of N′ (and daughters of N″). It is this second distinction I want to maintain, although in slightly altered form. Relative clauses with complementizers or relative pronouns will be sisters (and daughters) of N′;[1] those without will be sisters of N and daughters of N′ (in all of what follows, I ignore the so-called "DP hypothesis," but mean to take no stand on it). All are CPs.

(8) a.
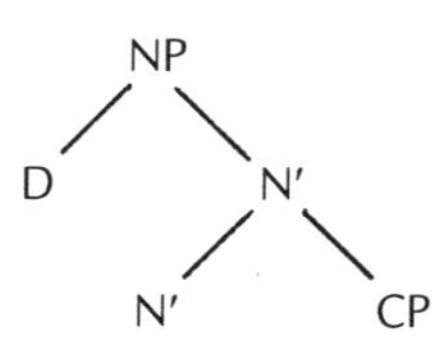

b.
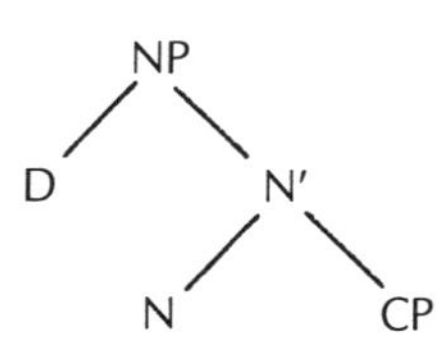

Noun complement CNPs independently require structures identical to (8b).

(9)

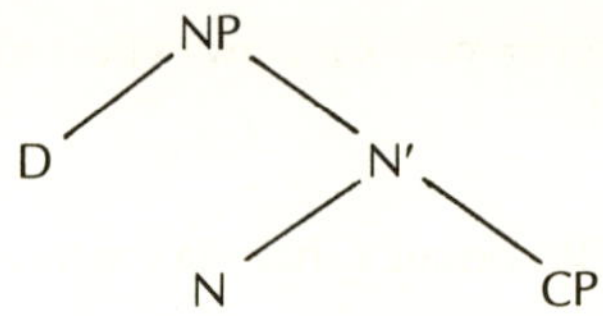

These non-MPST-licensed structures are discussed in Section 3.

1.2

There are two main points to make about the structure for subjects. First, all subjects originate within VP. Second, Sentential Subjects are CP not NP. Both are results of the MPST. Sentential subjects cannot be NPs because an ill-formed Projection Chain would result. The particular structure in (10a) is discussed in Section 3.

(10) a.

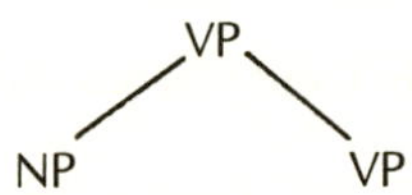

b.

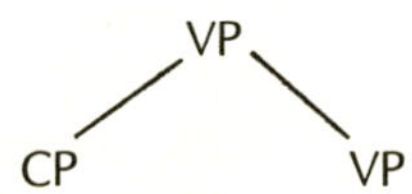

1.3

The structure for adjuncts is no surprise, given the results of Chapter 4.

(11)

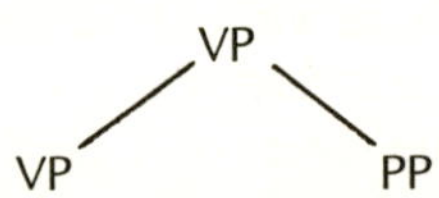

The structures proposed in this section are, as noted, discussed in Section 3. Before these particular structural proposals can be motivated, however, the overall theoretical proposal must be outlined and justified.

2.0

We turn now to theoretical motivations for my approach to Islands. The first subsection (and motivation) deals with Learnability. The second subsection (and motivation) involves Core versus Periphery.

2.1

As part of their proof of the learnability of an (essentially) *Aspects*-style transformational grammar from input of "Degree 2" (having only structures with no more than two embedded clauses), Wexler & Culicover (1980: 119–20) require something they call the **Freezing Principle** (FP, hereafter), for which they provide the following explication (1980: 119):

(12) **Definition:** If the immediate structure of a node in a phrase marker is nonbase, that node is **frozen.**

(13) **Freezing Principle** (FP): If a node *A* of a phrase marker is frozen, no node dominated by *A* may be analyzed by a transformation.

They go on to explain the significance of the FP (1980: 120):" we may think of the base grammar as providing *characteristic structures* of the language. Transformations sometimes distort these structures, but only these characteristic structures may be affected by transformations. . . . The freezing principle leads to a very important property of the learning system, namely the ability to learn grammar from the exposure to relatively simple sentences. The crucial property of FP is that **only base structures may be used to fit transformations**" [bold added].

My proposal—much as Fodor's (1983) was—is that something very much like the FP is behind the existence of Islands.[2] If learnability considerations justify (something like) the FP, then the fact that **Islands** are NCPS—that is, "nonbase" in a sense made precise below—is exactly what we should expect. Simply put, Islands are non(canonical) base structures and only (canonical) base structures (= *characteristic structures*) "may be used to fit transformations."

Having seen that, given something like the FP, the existence of NCPS leads ineluctably to Islands, we now must analyze "noncanonical phrase structure." That is, we need an independent (of Islands) characterization of NCPS within our MPST that will enable us to pick out the sorts of structures given in (8)–(10). We turn to this task.

2.2

I suggest that all NCPS is "Periphery" not "Core grammar." Fodor (1989) has pulled together and analyzed various remarks by Chomsky on the distinction between Core and Periphery. She notes that, together, these remarks form a set of "Discontinuity Assumptions," by which Fodor means that Chomsky's view is that "there are discontinuities with respect to the sorts of formal system that underlie the core and periphery. . . . there is discontinuity with respect to how much of the final system is innately supplied. . . . there is discontinuity with respect to how what is not innate is acquired" (Fodor 1989: 131).

For our purposes, the crucial sort of discontinuity is the first, formal, kind. According to this assumption, the Periphery may contain rules, whereas the Core is not a rule system. As Fodor observes, Chomsky has allowed that, for example, a rule of S′-deletion might be a rule of the Periphery (this is independent of whether the suggestion itself has merit, because the point is just that "rules are not forbidden in the periphery, as they are in the core" (Fodor 1989: 131)).

My proposal is that the structures for Islands are explicitly licensed by specific (base-extension) rules. We have already seen that adjuncts are licensed by the base-extending rule of Adjunct Adding. It remains to show how CNPs and Subjects are also rule licensed. Inspection of (10), repeated here, shows that Subjects have adjunct phrase structure. This is justified in Section 3, but note that, if it is correct, then Subjects cannot be present in unextended base structures under the MPST.

(10) a.

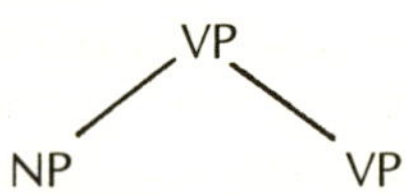

b.

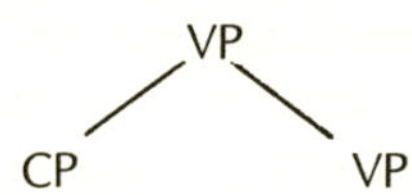

This suggestion (or result)—that Subjects are Periphery not Core—may strike some as a *reductio* of the entire proposal. However, it is worth noting in this regard, following Fodor (1989: 132), that, for example, T. Roeper has proposed that in English, at least, Passive is in the Periphery, and that, to repeat, S′-bar deletion was also in the Periphery. **Being in** the Periphery does not entail a peripheral **role,** it seems.

Fodor actually argues that methodologically the discontinuity position is inherently less desirable than the alternative assumption of continuity between Core and Periphery. I shall not rehearse or evaluate her arguments here, but I do want to highlight one, because I believe that my proposal goes some distance to reconcile Fodor's methodological point with the suggestion of formal discontinuity. So, Fodor (1989: 131, italics added): "the continuity assumption offers fewer degrees of freedom, with the result that success in the characterization of the class of human languages would be more convincing, and even failure would be more informative. Specifically, continuity renounces a wide range of otherwise available choices—choices about where the dividing line between core and periphery falls, *and about how the systems on either side differ from each other.*"

Now, my proposal for specific rules—by definition part of the Periphery—is going to be one that is, nonetheless, constrained by a property of the Core. This, then, goes some way in clarifying the relation between the two systems, which clarification the emphasised material in the above quote points out is required of discontinuous theories and theorists.

In particular—and this is one of the central claims of the analysis—the possible base extending rules, although **not required by** the MPST, are **consistent with** and **constrained by** it, just because they serve to extend the base. And it is the structures **required by** the MPST—the unextended base—that form the "base structures" relevant to the FP.

We have, in a sense, only a single theoretical motivation, although it is one with two components which, outside of the MPST analysis of Islands, have never before been brought together. The first component is from Learnability theory, and the second component comes from an analysis of the Core grammar versus Periphery distinction. Given the MPST, we can characterize the Periphery so that the structures licensed therein are just those which (our interpretation of) the FP also picks out. Thus, if the structures suggested in (8)-(10) are defensible as rule licensed in the MPST, we can derive their Island status. We return, therefore, to the structures in (8)-(10).

3.0

In this section I first discuss the structures for Subjects. Then I turn to rules for the structures for CNPs.

3.1.0

The discussion of the structures for Subjects ((10a), repeated here) has two parts.

(10) a. b.

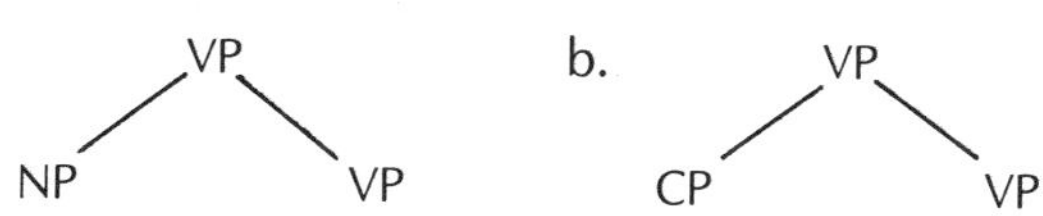

On the one hand, there is a positive discussion, which argues for the structure given in (10a). On the other, there is a negative discussion, which argues against an alternative proposal by Speas (1990). I begin with this latter discussion.

3.1.1

Speas (1990: 101–9) suggests that the proper structure for Subjects is not the "adjunct" structure given in (10a) (and advocated in Kuroda 1988 and Sportiche 1988, among others), but rather one in which the subject is a sister to a nonmaximal member of the V Projection Chain, as in (10′).

(10′)

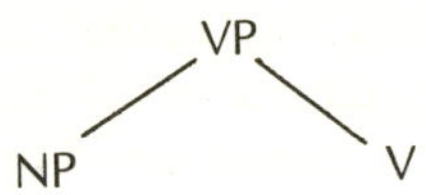

These are the two choices available which are in keeping with one of the guiding premises of the MPST, viz., the Lexical Clause Hypothesis (LCH, hereafter), in which "all of the arguments of the predicate are in some sense internal to a projection of the predicate." (Speas 1990: 102) Given this premise and, in addition, that her elaboration of the MPST does not allow for adjunct structures, it is no surprise that Speas does not embrace a structure such as that in (10a) but rather opts for the alternative (10′); her choice is forced by the theory.

Speas does not rest content with the theory, however. She argues (1990: 106–8) that, although traditional movement and deletion constituency tests show that the mother of the subject position in the LCH is a maximal projection, they do not show that the subject position's sister is also a maximal projection. Thus, she is able to argue that such considerations are at worst neutral with respect to her proposed structure for Subjects. The crucial move is to assume that, in an example such as (14) (Speas 1990: 107 (176a)), both *John* and *arrested* are coindexed with empty positions in the empty V Projection Chain of the subordinate clause (the empty V position is the head of this Chain). Essential here is the idea that an NP trace (of *John*) is present in subject position of the embedded V Projection Chain, preserving the full clausal nature of this lower (V Projection) Chain (there is, she argues, independent need for "deletion of material which includes NP traces . . ."). A similar analysis is given of VP movement.

(14) Mary was arrested before John was ———.

I would suggest, however, that her argument shows no more than that the facts are neutral—that is, the empirical results may be consistent with either structure.

Speas (1990: 109) also takes on data involving pleonastic subjects; that is, data indicating that all sentences must have syntactic subjects regardless of the thematic absence of a subject. These are important because they illustrate that "the subject requirement cannot be a thematic requirement." This is somewhat embarrassing for the LCH, because, as just quoted, it requires that "all arguments of a predicate are in some sense internal to a projection of the predicate." Once more, Speas follows where theory leads and bites the unavoidable bullet: "[t]here is no requirement that all verbs have a subject in underlying structure." Instead, she claims, following H. Borer, that there is a requirement that (in English) "agreement indexing between INFL and its specifier position is obligatory." Presumably, this agreement requires that [Spec, IP] be nonempty at S-structure, even when the position is nonthematic; thus, pleonastics are required (in English). The LCH is saved and all underlying subjects are daughters but not sisters of V^{max} because some verbs have no such underlying subjects. Apparently, then, pleonastic subjects are simply licensed outside the V Projection Chain, in the Specifier of IP position, perhaps underlyingly.[3]

3.1.2

The alternative structure in (10a), repeated here, is no longer ruled out under the MPST, given the base extending rule of Adjunct Adding discussed in Chapter 4.

(10) a.

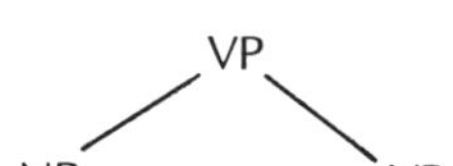

We thus are not immediately forced by theoretical considerations into the structure Speas advocates. And, as already noted, the deletion and movement facts do not obviously favor one structure over the other.

The pleonastic subjects facts are somewhat more interesting. We are free, of course, simply to take over the suggestions made by

Speas. However, unlike Speas, we can accept an alternative she is forced to reject. Under that alternative, sentences have subjects due to a requirement that *syntactic predicates* must be *saturated* (Rothstein 1985: 7; see Speas 1990: 99ff.).[4] All syntactic predicates, on this view, are maximal projections; some maximal projections (V^{max}, A^{max}, and P^{max}) are always predicates. Speas (1990: 100 (161a)) rejects the contention that predicates must be maximal projections. In example (15), she labels a constituent consisting of *Mary* and *intelligent* with AP, while *intelligent* itself instantiates a node simply bearing the label A. This, again, follows from her theory.

(15) We consider Mary intelligent.

The theory developed here, however, does not require this labelling. First, we are not committed to a single label on a given node (see Chapter 1 Section 2.4), so there is no a priori reason that the node *intelligent* instantiates cannot be labelled both A and AP. Further, our theory allows for adjunct structures, so there is no bar to a node labelled AP directly dominating another node labelled AP. Hence, it is open, in principle, for us to accept the maximal projection condition on predicates.

Speas's version of the MPST and Rothstein's approach to predicates force positions on their adherents; this is generally a good thing for a theory to do. Our version of the MPST, however, does not force us into Speas's rejection of the maximal projection condition on predicates; nor are we forced into accepting it. Our theory, then, is somewhat weaker here than the alternatives. Are there reasons to take one or the other position?

Speas (1990: 128–38) reviews a range of evidence that converges to strongly suggest "that the underlying structure of English is hierarchically organized in such a way that the subject is structurally superior to the objects and is outside of a maximal constituent of VP." (Speas 1990: 138) This is an interesting conclusion, and one that seems hard to combine with her statement about the LCH, quoted previously, that "all of the arguments of the predicate are in some sense internal to a projection of the predicate."[5] Of course, if we adopt the adjunct structure of (10a), then these two statements fit together nicely, and we see exactly what "in some sense" comes to: in the terms of Chapter 4, Section 3.1.1, the subject is not c-dominated by the category VP, though it is l-dominated by VP; that is, Subjects have adjunct phrase structure. This "in some sense" is significant;

Subjects are arguments of their predicates, but, as the evidence Speas reviews indicate, they are not just arguments. The adjunct structure, with the analysis of adjuncts developed in Chapter 4, reconciles these opposing tendencies in the analysis of subjects.

The question of whether all predicates are maximal projections has not been addressed, however. If there is some conceptual reason to suppose that Subjects have the adjunct structure proposed in (10a), as has just been suggested, that still leaves open the question of examples such as (15). Whether these should also be given an adjunct structure depends, I suggest, on the status of an example such as (16b).

(16) a. We consider sentences about the king of France tiresome.
b. ??Who do you consider sentences about tiresome?

If the Island effect in (16b) is robust, then we have evidence for the adjunct structure and the maximal projection status of the node instantiated by *tiresome* (*intelligent*). At least, we have such evidence under the current theory of Islands. A theory-internal reason for choosing a structure does not make the present proposal a less attractive one, given that the alternatives—Speas, Rothstein—posit their structures for theory-internal reasons. There are further empirical issues and questions here, as well, but I do not pursue them.

3.1.3

To sum up this subsection, we can have the adjunct structure for Subjects because our version of the MPST has a theory of adjuncts. The adjunct structure seems to simultaneously account for both the fact that Subjects are arguments of their predicates (when they are not pleonastic) and for the facts indicating that Subjects differ from other arguments. Speas cannot have the adjunct structure because no allowance is made in her version of the MPST for adjuncts and she rejects the Rothstein assumption of maximal projection status of all predicates. A Rothsteinian LCH approach requires the adjunct structure because it assumes predicates must be maximal projections and predicates must be saturated.

I suggest that combining our version of the MPST with the Rothstein approach to predicates yields the proper sort of theory, one in which the constraints of the phrase structure component define a space which can accomodate the separate requirements of a theory of predicates and predication. This allows us to see how it is possible to classify Subjects as part of the Periphery. It is the **Saturation Requirement** of the theory of predicates and predication that forces the presence of a Subject, not the lexical requirements which the MPST translates into structure. But once a Subject is required, the MPST-driven LCH requires that this structure be integrated into the verb(predicate)-headed Projection Chain (if the Subject is thematic). And our theory of adjuncts provides the means for so integrating the Subject PM. In other words, formally Subjects really are adjuncts, added to the predicate-headed PM by the rule of Adjunct Adding as part of the formation of the extended base. Notice that even though the Saturation Requirement may be Core, it itself does not license structure. The licensing of the structure which the Saturation Requirement makes necessary is done by Adjunct Adding, which makes it Periphery.

We turn now to CNPs, the analysis of which requires further elaboration of the the notion "extended base" by means of the introduction of phrase structure rules.

3.2

The structures given for CNPs in (8), repeated here, involve a category label, N′, that is not projected under the MPST.

(8) a.

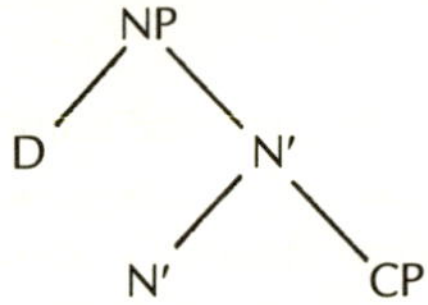

b.

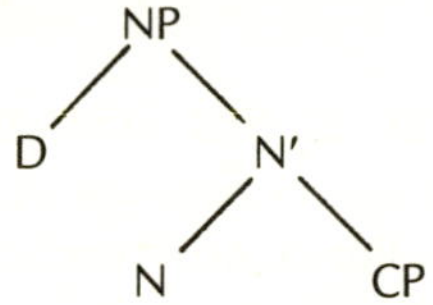

My proposal for licensing these structures is the following. Phrase structure rules can license a theoretically potent, distinguished intermediate label on nodes. That is, the MPST eschews phrase structure rules, but the overall theory of grammar need not. This is, in a sense, just a corollary of the position that the Core does not contain rules, while the Periphery does (or may). In the particular case of licensing phrase structure in the base, the Core is the MPST, hence its rulelessness. The Periphery, if it is to both license such phrase structure and do it by rule (as it may or must), virtually by definition contains some sort of "phrase structure rule." I suggest the following universal phrase structure rule schemata for phrase structure rules (the rules are to be understood as node admissibility conditions (McCawley 1968), not as string-to-string rewrite rules, which does not make them any the less rules).

(17) a. X → . . . X′ . . .
b. X′ → . . . X . . .

The intended interpretation of the variable X is such that it ranges over any member of a Projection Chain (viz., the Maximal Projection, the Minimal Projection, an intermediate link, although not the new distinguished label X′).[6] Notice that X in the right-hand side of (17b) cannot be XP (the Maximal Projection), because, if it were, X′ would also have to be XP, and it is not—it is defined as a distinct label—and labels do not change. It would have to be XP because it would meet the definition for Maximal Projection, and that condition holds for the structures licensed by the explicit phrase structure rules, structures which are part of the extended base. By parity of reasoning, the value of X on the left-hand side of (17a) cannot be the Minimal Projection, because then X′ would also have to be X^0, and—again—it is not. It is therefore the case that this label is an "intermediate" one, not because this is encoded in the label itself—there is no positive content to the label other than "distinctiveness"—but because it cannot directly dominate the Maximal Projection nor be directly dominated by the Minimal Projection in a Projection Chain. We have not, then, reintroduced a contentful notion of "bar level" into the theory; we have, instead, simply introduced a notation of "bar level," essentially on account of its familiarity, although a different notation is, of course, perfectly acceptable.

The idea behind (17) is that UG makes available for grammars of particular languages the possibility of incorporating a theoretically potent intermediate node label in any category, but it is not required that any be chosen. The MPST does not enjoin such intermediate labels, it simply does not itself license them.

Phrase structure rules conforming to (17) and licensing the structures in (8) is given in (18).

(18) a. NP → . . . N′ . . .
b. N′ → . . . N . . .

The analysis of examples such as (1a), (2a) (repeated here) and (19) goes as follows.

(1) a. Kim met a child who read *If I ran the zoo.*

(2) a. Pat mentioned Dale's belief that you saw Robin.

(19) A child I saw was reading *If I ran the zoo.*

Relative clauses with relative pronouns (complementizers), (1a), stack, as we saw from (6) (repeated here).

(6) a. The book that Bill bought that Max wrote was boring.
b. The book Bill bought that Max wrote was boring.
c. *The book that Bill bought Max wrote was boring.
d. *The book Bill bought Max wrote was boring.

This is an argument for their having adjunct structure; indeed, there is little dispute about their status as adjuncts (see, for example, Lebeaux 1988: 148ff.; 1990: 32ff.). As they are adjuncts and stack, they must, within the MPST, involve both (1) a label distinct from the "elsewhere label" of the Projection Chain and also (2) the rule of Adjunct Adding. The first requirement, the distinct label, is licensed by (18). A node bearing the N label, such as that instantiating *child,* can be on the right-hand side of a rule that has a node bearing N′ on its left-hand side.[7] The rule of Adjunct Adding, which heretofore had been limited to adjoining to the Maximal Projection due to the nature of the Projection Chain and the lack of distinct intermediate labels, can now adjoin to the node labelled N′. The arguments in Chapter 4 that showed the impossibility under the MPST of adjunction to anything other than the Maximal Projection do not go through with respect to this distinguished intermediate label—as is desirable.[8]

An example such as (19), a relative clause without a relative pronoun (complementizer) presents a different problem. Even though these seem to be adjuncts in some sense, they do not stack and they must precede relative clauses with relative pronouns (complementizers), as shown in (6). In the absence of some independent account of these facts, they cannot have adjunct structure. Therefore, the suggestion is that these relative clauses are not the product of Adjunct Adding; rather, they are licensed by the phrase structure rule (18). They are not added to an already existing PM, as structural adjuncts are, but they are licensed by explicit rule, hence part of the Periphery, the extended base. This may profit from some more discussion.

The extended base is the result of two different kinds of rules: the "generalized transformations" for CCC and adjuncts which join well-formed PMs, and the PSRs which license nodes with a distinguished intermediate label. These are formally distinct sorts of rules. It seems *prima facie* unlikely that they should form a natural class. Natural classes, however, are discovered theoretically. Given our theory—the MPST—these two sorts of rule share the crucial property of licensing structure that is not otherwise available.[9] This property is crucial because what the analysis of Core versus Periphery tells us is that Core Grammar is ruleless, while the Periphery may have rules. Thus, our theoretical categorization in terms of a property (licensing extended base structures) that cuts across formal rule-type categorization converges with an independent analysis of a taxonomy of the syntactic component. In this way, our MPST-based analysis gives principled content to the Core versus Periphery distinction, perhaps for the first time.

Returning to relative clauses without relative pronouns (complementizers), we can account both for the fact that such relative clauses are "in some sense" adjuncts—they are not licensed by MPST projection of argument structure—and for the structural differences between these relative clauses and those with relative pronouns (complementizers). We can now account for examples (1a) and (19) and for the facts in (6).

Noun complements such as (2a) are surely not adjuncts. There is no question of their being the product of Adjunct Adding. There is a question as to why they too should be licensed by rule (18). An obvious alternative is simply to have the mother of the complement clause and the noun be labelled simply N. This suggests that noun complement clauses are licensed within the MPST projection theory, rather than by explicit rule. Theory internal reasons can be advanced for rejecting this proposal.

First, there is the arguably question-begging fact that this alternative loses the analysis of Islands being advanced, for no compelling reason and with no obvious advantage. Second, one can follow a noun complement clause with a restrictive relative clause with a relative pronoun (*Dale's belief that you saw Robin which I accepted*), and under our analysis (8a), this requires the presence of an N′.

Still, the suggestion that complement clauses are Periphery may not seem entirely unproblematic. Complement clauses, after all, are supposed to be **complements,** so it may seem that structure for them would have to be projected from the lexicon under the MPST. In other words, if an advantage of the proposal with respect to relative clauses without relative pronouns (complementizers) is that it means such clauses are not licensed by MPST licensed projection, then a disadvantage may be that it entails exactly the same thing with respect to complement clauses. However, Grimshaw (1990: 73-80) has demonstrated that "sentential complements to nouns are never arguments." This conclusion is based on two pieces of evidence: first, that such complements are never obligatory and, second, that they "never behave in any respect like complex event nominals" (Grimshaw 1990: 78) (discussion of this latter notion would, unfortunately, take us too far from our project and into Grimshaw's to be practical here). Because they are neither arguments nor adjuncts, we are left to wonder what they are and how to integrate them into a PM. A theory which incorporates the possibility of phrase structure rules in accord with (17) allows us to answer such questions with structure that is neither argument projection nor adjunct addition, yet remains severely circumscribed with respect to the analytic options it makes available. In this way, noun complement clauses and relative clauses without relative pronouns or complementizers form a structural natural class in the MPST.

This ends the discussion of the specific structures proposed for Island constituents. Those in (9), for adjuncts, have already been justified in Chapter 4. Those in (8) for Subjects and (10) for CNPs, I have argued, can be integrated into the MPST as well. To do so, however, we have had to add to the MPST (1) the theory of predicates and predication for Subjects and (2) phrase structure rule schema for CNPs. Still, there is little cost to these additions. Something, after all, must presumably be said about the subject-predicate relation, and a theory of that relation is a logical place to look for such a something. Furthermore, although the MPST does not license PSRs, neither does it proscribe them, and indeed, it serves to severly constrain the range of possible PSRs as discussed previously and in 4.1 below. I thus conclude that we can accept the proposed analysis and turn to some more general issues.

4.0

This chapter has attempted rather more than the previous ones. A number of further proposals within the MPST-based theory have been advanced, basic ideas from other areas of research have been drawn on, and an approach to Islands that essentially flies in the face of over twenty years of work has been presented. I review these in turn.

4.1

Explicit phrase structure rules have been suggested to augment the MPST. The proposal is for a pair of universal schemata for an "intermediate" level node label. It was shown that any such distinct label, however it is annotated, would necessarily be "intermediate," given adherence to the MPST, and thus no reintroduction of primitive "bar levels," and concomitantly the rest of X-Bar theory, had been advanced. Such rules allow for structure that is neither projected from the lexicon in accordance with the MPST nor added to a basic PM by means of Adjunct Adding (or CCC formation), and exactly such structure, it was argued, is needed for noun complement clauses and relative clauses without relative pronouns (complementizers). I also suggested that explicit phrase structure rules are expectable if there is a Core versus Periphery distinction in the licensing of base structures based on the fact that the Core is ruleless while the Periphery may contain rules.

It was also argued that the structure for Subjects is provided by the rule of Adjunct Adding. This means that Subjects are not projected due to the MPST, and so are not present in the unextended base structure. Instead, they are positioned due to a combination of MPST thematic requirements (VP internal if thematic, in [Spec,IP] if pleonastic) and (something like) the **Saturation Requirement** on predicates (Rothstein 1985). Since in the predication theory predicates must be maximal projections, combining this analysis with the MPST makes (thematic) Subjects both sisters and daughters of a maximal projection, an impossibility in Speas's analysis. Our result, that Subject structure is adjunct structure, captures the status of subjects as both (external) arguments and also as distinguished from other (internal) arguments.

In addition to the specific structures proposed, theoretical motivation for the approach was developed out of analyses from other domains, to which we now turn.

4.2

The argument of the chapter is underpinned by an appeal to Learnability theory and to the analysis of Core versus Periphery in grammar. Without these concepts, there would be no reason at all to entertain the proposal.

From Learnability theory, we adopted the (idea behind the) Freezing Principle. The crucial notion here is that, for a grammar to be acquirable from primary linguistic data that is not overly complex, only a set of *characteristic structures* is available as input to transformations. Our reliance is vulnerable on more than one front. It might be shown that a better Learnability theory requires nothing like the FP; that is, that acquisition is possible based on a set of appropriately uncomplex primary linguistic data with no such restriction. Or, it might be shown that something like the FP is needed, but that the set of structures taken as basic should not be identified with the unextended base structures projected by the MPST. These are real possiblities and worries.

Nonetheless, it is good to keep in mind the advantages of the present proposal. We **can** give a specific content—what I have called *noncanonical phrase structure*—to the idea of *characteristic structures* given the MPST and the extended base. This is yet another convergence of the MPST with an independently motivated analysis, one that was obviously not in the minds of the promulgators of the FP, barring clairvoyance. Second, and perhaps more important, the proposal provides explanatory insight into the **existence** of Islands. As noted earlier, other research on Islands does not do this. Here, the fact that Islands exist is the result of the architecture of the syntactic component (the MPST licensed base, the extended base, transformations) and the requirements of the acquisition theory. Islands arise **inevitably** from the interaction of a restricted theory of the base with Learnability theory.[10]

This leads us into the Core versus Periphery distinction. Fodor's (1989) analysis isolated both the central place of rules in the distinction and the need to clarify just how the two sides can differ. Our proposal to extend the base by means of rules places restrictions on what the rules can do, because the output is still in the base and thus must still fall under the MPST, and so puts both specific content into and constraints on the Periphery. A minimalist approach to extending the minimalist phrase structure theory provides the basis for bifurcating the primary linguistic data along the Learnability-motivated distinction between *characteristic structures* versus *others* line; I find this quite striking.

4.3

At least as striking, no doubt, has been the complete lack of discussion of Subjacency, Bounding nodes, Barriers, and the like. Implicitly then, the chapter has been an argument that this entire line of research has been misguided.[11] If the kind of proposal I am making is on the right track (even if the specifics are not entirely correct), then Bounding Theory is otiose. Islands need not be the accidental product of arbitrary definitions and stipulations about "Bounding" or "Blocking Categories"; it is possible, I suggest, to ask more from—and find more in—our inquiry than this. We can attempt to tie Islands to the fundamental problem of generative grammar, the acquisition problem; we can attempt to reach explanatory adequacy.

The attempt at explanatory adequacy, flowing as it does from the MPST, seems to me most compelling. Consider a possible alternative: (1) a Learnability theory that is plausible on its own terms but does not involve anything like the FP, and so has nothing to say about Islands; (2) an approach to Islands that gives, say, a simple recursive definition of *Bounding Node* along with Subjacency, and so has no particular relation either to the acquisition problem or to other parts of syntactic theory (e.g., the theory of the base component). This seems to me a virtually best case scenerio for the direction of most current research: we end up with subtheories which we feel individually pleased with, but there are no evident connections between them—due, apparently, to a belief that none need be sought.

Compare such an approach to the one outlined in this chapter. It seems to me a strong argument in favor of the present approach that it makes the connections it does. Even if our Learnability theory and the account of Islands were observationally less adequate than the alternatives previously suggested, the advantage in terms of explanatory adequacy could, in my view, lead one to prefer the present account. This is no doubt to large degree a matter of taste, but I think the task of adjusting a theory with explanatory force toward better empirical coverage is to be preferred to—and perhaps is even simpler than—the task of reconstructing an empirically better theory so that it has an explanatory structure.[12]

5.0

Once again, we have seen convergence between the MPST and other inquiries. In this case, the architecture of the MPST (with the minimal addition of PSRs) brings together an understanding of the Learnability-inspired notion of characteristic structures with an analysis of Core versus Periphery in syntax. Although this is not the formal and substantive convergence we have seen before—hardly surprising, since we have moved from theory construction to elaboration—it is nonetheless quite striking. Our MPST, constructed largely on grounds of internal coherence and simplicity in the face of some very general explanatory desiderata (What is a PM? Why (C-)command? How can PMs combine?) not only sheds explanatory light on an all too often overlooked question (Why *Islands*?), but also does so by unexpectedly bringing together otherwise unrelated findings from Learnability theory and the architecture of GB theory.

Appendix: The CSC and WH-Islands

A.0

We have not discussed either the Coordinate Structure Constraint (CSC) or WH-Islands. These present different problems for the theory just outlined. We begin with the CSC, then move to WH-Islands.

A.1.0

The CSC places CCC within the Islands. Our theory should also categorize CCC as Islands, because they are rule-licensed extended base structures. A number of questions and problems remain, however.

A.1.1

One problem is that Goodall (1987: 64–77) offers an account of the CSC within his version of the 3-D theory. This is a problem because there is no "account" of other Islands within our theory: the theory is the account, so having a further analysis of their ill-formedness is somewhat odd, presumably redundant.

But, as Goodall notes, an example such as (A1) (his 169a), is ill-formed because one of its input sentences is itself ill-formed; viz.,

(A3) (see Goodall's 170). In our terms, (A3) is not a string that the MPST would license.

(A1) *What did Mary cook the pie and Jane eat?

(A2) Jane ate what

(A3) Mary cooked the pie what

Goodall also observes that the well-formed (A4) and (A5) (his 171) cannot be the inputs for (A1) due to problems in "linearization."

(A4) Mary cooked the pie.

(A5) Jane ate what.

In our terms, the problem is that we have here coordination at the full sentence level; that is, there are no other conjoinable categories in the terms of the construction in Chapter 3. Suppose, then, that Goodall's theory-internal, technical "linearization" problem alluded to can be understood as a theory-internal, technical issue in the interpretation of coordination of full sentences. If this is so, then we are still faced with the puzzle that the CSC seems to have an analysis distinct from the theory of noncanonical phrase structure.

In general, we should be uneasy with this sort of redundancy. The problem is one of killing one bird with two stones, we might say.

A.1.2

A further fact about the CSC is the existence of "across-the-board" (ATB) exceptions to it. So, for example, we have (A6), (Goodall's (176)).

(A6) Which film did the critics hate and the audience love?

As Goodall points out, the inputs to such an example (A7) & (A8), are themselves well-formed (see his (178a) & (178b)). He argues that the well-formedness of (A6) follows in his version of the 3-D theory.

(A7) The critics hated which film.

(A8) The audience loved which film.

A problem for our theory is that, despite the well-formedness of (A7) & (A8), extraction from a noncanonical structure should be ill-formed. Because our theory should not be ruling out the ill-formed extractions in the independent way suggested in A.1.1, it should also not be licensing the ATB exceptions in the way Goodall advocates. As noted, it should not allow them at all.

It is worth pointing out that the sort of coordination we see in (A9)—presumably the source of (A6)—is nonconstituent coordination, and we have not argued how, or whether, our approach to CCC should analyze such examples. It therefore may not count directly against the theory that it cannot account for (A6); nevertheless it cannot, of course, count in its favor.

(A9) The critics hated and the audience loved which film.

A.1.3

Finally, we can raise the problem of data such as (A10) & (A11), from Lakoff (1986, his (10) & (11)) and Goldsmith (1985, his (5)), respectively.

(A10) a. What kind of herbs can you eat and not get cancer?
b. What forms of cancer can you eat herbs and not get?

(A11) How many counterexamples can the coordinate structure constraint sustain and still be considered empirically correct?

The cited works contain numerous other violations of the CSC of various forms and complexity. The authors suggest (although their proposals are not the same) that there is no formal syntactic CSC, but rather that there are semantic constraints on extraction from CCC. In the face of their data, it is difficult to convincingly argue otherwise. To do so requires that the syntactically ill-formed examples they give be judged acceptable for other reasons, yet still, presumably, be classified as ungrammatical. This is not an incoherent position, because the notions *(un)acceptable* and *(un)grammatical* are distinct, but it does require a certain fondness for bullet biting.

A.1.4

A mouthful of bullets may be the best we can do. Perhaps the entirely unelaborated and unexplicated recasting of the linearization problem is not viable (Goodall himself is short on details about how his suggestion is to work), and so no independent account of the CSC is actually available. In that case, the extended base theory nonredundantly rules out all extraction from CCC. Apparent exceptions must be just that: either from nonconstituent coordination that is not analyzed in the theory of CCC in Chapter 3, or acceptable but ungrammatical strings made palatable for the sorts of semantic cum pragmatic reasons probed by Lakoff and Goldsmith.

Even though this is not particularly strong, it should be recalled that, except for Pesetsky's (1982) Path Theory, nothing very general has been offered in the syntax literature with respect to the CSC. It is usually just ignored in the discussion of Islands in, for example, bounding theoretic terms. It is thus a strength of the present proposal that it brings the CSC back into the discussion; it is maybe a weakness that it seems to add relatively little to that discussion. Still, new questions and problems do arise, and this is no a bad thing in itself.

A.2.0

WH-Islands are not noncanonical phrase structure, they are not rule licensed, they are not extended base. They therefore should not be Islands. I argue that they are not Islands within the theory of Chomsky 1986a (*Barriers*) either. There is therefore nothing to choose between at least these two approaches to Islands on this score. Further, it is of some significance that these otherwise quite divergent approaches should agree on this point. I argue also that, within the *Barriers* framework, WH-Islands can be analyzed as Relativized Minimality (Rizzi 1990) violations. I then conclude that a Relativized Minimality analysis is available to us, without invoking *Barriers* assumptions.

A.2.1

Chomsky (1986a: 36) explains (A12) (his 77a) in the following way: "In [(A12)] *what* moves from the position of t_i, adjoining to the lower

VP. Still assuming that adjunction to IP is barred for *wh*-movement, the next step is movement to the matrix VP, crossing CP, which inherits barrierhood from the non-L-marked IP. Therefore, one barrier is involved, and a weak Subjacency violation results."

(A12) *What$_i$ did you wonder [to whom]$_j$ John gave t_i t_j

However, instead of adjoining to the matrix VP in the second step, it is also possible to adjoin to the Specifier of the lower CP; that is, adjoin to (the node dominating) the phrase [*to whom*]. This is a nonargument position, and the label it bears is that of a maximal projection; hence such an adjunction is licensed (Chomsky 1986a: 6 (6)). Further, no barriers intervene between this position and that of the trace left by adjunction to the lower VP. From this position, crossing the embedded CP creates no Subjacency violation because the CP cannot be a barrier for its Specifier by inheritance from IP, as IP does not dominate [Spec, CP].

There is no way to avoid this result short of abandoning one of the following from *Barriers:* (1) the theory of adjunction or (2) the notions of blocking category-barrier. But each of these is both fundamental to and independently required in the framework of Chomsky (1986a). Giving up either is tantamount to rejection of *Barriers.*

Alternatively, we can accept the result and give up WH-Islands as Islands. Chomsky (1986a: 37) notes the well-known variability of the WH-Island effect; using our result, we might seek to explain this variability. As there is no longer a general syntactic violation, what we will have is some congeries of factors that lead to the observed variation. Should we not wish to lose the venerable WH-Island generalization, we might try Relativized Minimality.

A.2.2

Rizzi (1990: 7, his (15)) offers (A13) as an "intervention constraint" for types of government.

(A13) X α-governs Y only if there is no Z such that
(1) Z is a typical potential α-governor of Y
(2) Z c-commands Y & does not c-command X

The intent is that, for example, only typical antecedent governors can intervene in a putative antecedent government relation; other sorts of governors should be irrelevant, regardless of their structural positions.

WH-Islands under *Barriers*—either the Chomsky (1986a) analysis or the alternative just sketched—violate Relativized Minimality with respect to antecedent government in various ways. In (A12), repeated here with a filled-out structure, the trace (t_i) left by adjunction (to either embedded or matrix VP) and the phrase [*to whom*]$_j$ form a pair that violate Relativized Minimality with respect to the original premovement D-structure positions.[13]

(A12) *What$_i$ did you wonder [to whom]$_j$ John gave t_i t_j

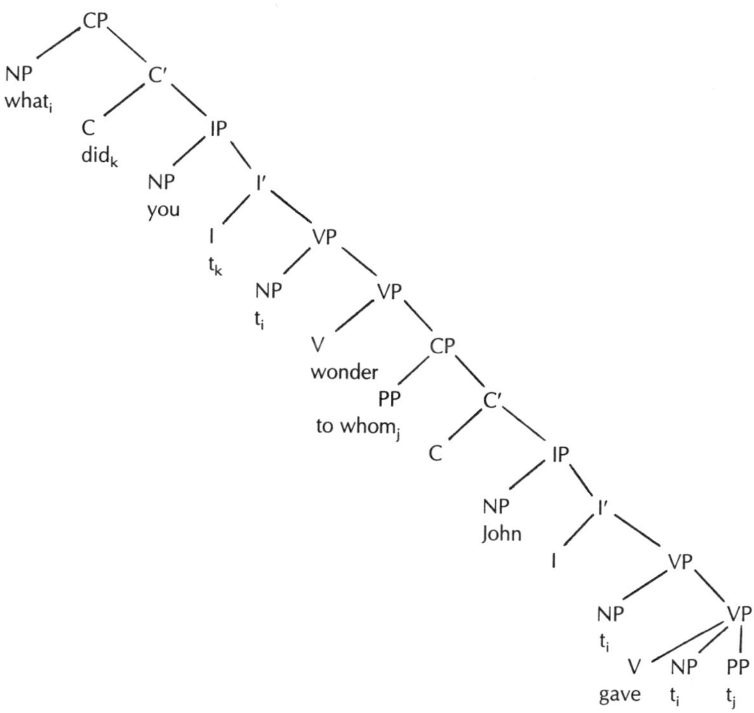

On this account, WH-Islands fail with respect to antecedent government, which amounts to a failure of binding, because antecedent government is defined in terms of being coindexed with a C-commander. This disunifies the account of Islands, as WH-Islands do not come under bounding theory. We might say that, under this analysis, a WH-Island is not an Island, it just acts like one.

A.2.3

We could adopt the movement-adjunction analysis from Chomsky (1986a), which leads to the Relativized Minimality violation just outlined. Although this sort of adjunction looks somewhat suspect after Chapter 4, nothing in our theory either requires such an approach or disallows it. We should also note that syntactic movement adjunction is largely without any theory, the stipulations in Chomsky (1986a) notwithstanding. Moreover, much of the motivation for it—the anlaysis of Islands—is gone in our theory.

For these reasons, it is heartening to note that, should we wish to do without the movement-adjunction analysis, we still have a Relativized Minimality violation. If *what*$_i$ from (A12) is in the matrix (Spec, CP), then [*to whom*]$_j$ intervenes between *what*$_i$ and t_i, creating a violation.[14] In other words, without Barrier / Bounding theory or the movement-adjunction analysis, we can rule out WH-Islands as Relativized Minimality violations.[15]

A.3

WH-Islands cannot be Islands on our account. I have suggested that they are actually Relativized Minimality violations, thus not truly Islands. We have also seen that a current version of Bounding Theory cannot account for WH-Islands and must also, in all likelihood, use a Relativized Minimality, hence Binding theoretic, approach.

The CSC should fall under our account of Islands. Our problem was twofold: (1) there already is a 3-D analysis of the CSC, and (2) there are licit extractions from CCC (the ATB and the Lakoff and Goldsmith data). I suggested that the independent analysis might in fact fail, at least in our version of the theory (Goodall is not explicit on how his proposal works), and that therefore we are left with only the second problem. I ventured that these facts are either from nonstandard CCC that our theory does not analyze or are acceptable but ungrammatical. Although the theory "brings the CSC back in" and raises some new questions, this is evidently the least pleasing and convincing part of our argument. This is why it has been treated in a separate appendix.

CONCLUSION

0.0

There are three topics in this conclusion. First, I discuss some residual conceptual issues with respect to the relations between coordinate and adjunct structures. Second, I take up Chomsky's (1993) recent "minimalist" program. Finally, I review the work as a whole.

0.1

In Section 1, I address such questions concerning the relations between adjunct and coordinate structures as the following. Why do the two generalized transformations line up the way they do—that is, why is coordination the joining at a node and adjunct adding joining at a label (and not the other way round)? Because it is clear that well-formed phrase markers need not be fully sentential, must coordinate structures be formed from fully sentential phrase markers? If so, why are coordinate structures different from adjunct structures in this way? Or, to put it differently, understanding the two generalized transformations as functions, do they have exactly the same domain? Further, can we explain any categorial restrictions on possible adjuncts that might hold; that is, if not every category can be—or have—an adjunct, why should this be so?

0.2

Section 2 compares Chomsky's "minimalist" program with the MPST. Specifically, the discussion focusses on Chomsky's treatment of the interrelated issues of D-structure, X-Bar theory, and adjunct(ion)s. To anticipate, I argue that Chomsky's proposals are inferior to the theory developed herein, in part, at least, because Chomsky moves directly from conceptual considerations to analytical concerns, with essentially no stop at the "mid-level" of theory construction such as the MPST represents.

0.3

Section 3 reviews the theory and findings, stressing the formal and substantive vectors of the inquiry. Emphasis is placed on the integrated nature of the work, on how the various parts interlock and offer mutual support.

1.0

It may have been noted that, even though coordination and Adjunct Adding are the two sorts of generalized transformations that the MPST allows, they do not appear to be entirely parallel. Coordinate structures are analyzed as always arising from the combining (of subparts) of fully sentential phrase markers, while Adjunct Adding applies (in principle) to any well-formed phrase markers. Is there some theoretical account of this difference, or should the difference exist at all?

To analyze this problem, we must step back a bit. We must start with the theoretical facts, as it were. With an aim of joining phrase markers, we have seen that joining can be at a node or at a label, stemming from the two primitive building blocks of phrase markers, nodes and labels. Given this (formal) result, we can ask what (substantive) properties the product of each joining must have.

1.1

If we join at a label, we create a new member of a Projection Chain, and the nonhead daughter of this new member must be integrated into the Chain.[1] Because arguments are not placed by generalized transformation but rather are licensed in unextended base structures, the new member of the Projection Chain cannot be an argument. However, as it *is* a member of the Chain, it must be related to the Head of the Chain. Therefore, the result of label joining will be an adjunct, a nonargument modifier of a Head, because there is nothing else it could be.

Suppose we join at a node. In general, nodes are labelled, with a single label. In the general case, then, joining at a node will be possible only when the two nodes have the same label (this is the derivation of the Law of Coordination of Likes in Chapter 3). As the shared node already exists, there is no new member of a Projection Chain here. Thus, instead of requiring a new relation to a Head, arising only as a result of the operation, node joining draws on already licensed relata. And, given that, in general, the label as well as the node will be shared, the joined sub-PMs will generally bear the same relations in their respective containing PMs. Which is just to say that they will be coordinate.

1.2

But what of the differing domains of the two operations? Unextended D-structures, recall, are the structuralization of theta-grid requirements, of the "argument-of" relation. This full set, then, is the set which forms the domain for Adjunct Adding; if it does not also form the domain for coordination, we want to know why this latter is restricted to the subset of fully sentential phrase markers. Adjunct Adding places nonargument modifiers of a head. Coordinating need not involve nonarguments, although it can give rise to apparent violations of the theta criterion (in the sense that a predicate can theta license "too many" arguments if these latter are coordinated). Because D-structures represent the "argument-of" relation, no D-structure can lack an argument-taking element, viz., a predicate of some sort. Further, no D-structure can represent incomplete theta-grid requirements. These two facts mean, respectively, that there can be no D-structures for argument categories without their predicates (e.g., just a referential NP) or for predicate categories missing an argument (e.g., subjectless VPs which theta mark their subjects). Thus, the theory says there can be no referential NP adjuncts or subjectless VP adjuncts, as there will be no such D-structure PMs for Adjunct Adding to operate on. So, the theory appears to give us some reason to prefer the view that "bare NP adverbials" are really PPs (see McCawley 1988a: 587; and Emonds 1987) not NPs (see Larson 1985a) and to tell us why adjuncts are sentential or PPs.[2] Unfortunately, things are not quite so straightforward, as a return to our question about the differing domains of the operations reveals.

So, *do* Adjunct Adding and coordination have different domains or not? Actually, no, they do not, although they appear to. Adjunct Adding appears to operate on any two full PMs, coordination on sentential (sub-)PMs. But, in fact, each joining can occur anywhere within a PM; that is, the locus of joining in Adjunct Adding need not be a root node any more than it need be the label associated with the root node in coordination. Any sub-PM of a PM can be the locus of joining with either operation. But now we have lost the apparent explanation for the limitations on adjuncts suggested at the end of the previous paragraph, as well as any account of the differences between the two operations.

The resolution lies in something already discussed: that joining at a label requires integration of a new link into an existing Projection Chain, while joining at a node does not. For label joining, only elements that are both capable of functioning as a modifier and do not themselves require licensing by some other head are possible candidates. This means that, if we attempted to proceed as we do with coordination, in terms of operations on sub-PMs of sentential PMs, we would end up with either elements that cannot be modifiers or elements that were "doubly licensed" (e.g., both an argument of one head and a modifier of another), and so we have an ill-formed structure in either case. Conversely, just because joining at a node will not require a new licensing condition, it will allow for the full range of categories, hence the operation on any sub-PM of a sentential PM, not just on "freestanding" PMs. Thus, we can explain the apparent difference in the domain of the two operations and do so based squarely in our theory; it is a result of the interaction of nodes, labels, the nature of D-stuctures, and the licensing of links in a Projection Chain. We turn now to Chomsky's "Minimalist Program."

2.0

Chomsky's (1993) "A Minimalist Program for Linguistic Theory" (hereafter MP) suggests some rather radical changes in the organization of a transformational generative grammar. As noted in 0.2, I shall focus on the topics of D-structure, X-Bar Theory, and adjunct(ion)s, although to begin I shall also lay out a bit of the general program.

2.1

The position adumbrated in MP is one that perhaps no one could have anticipated: a unistratal but derivational syntax. Generative syntax had previously seen the other three possible combinations of crossing multi/unistratalism with (non)derivationalism: multistratal and derivational (all previous transformational grammar, as well as early Relational Grammar, or RG); multistratal and nonderivational (current RG); and unistratal and nonderivational (LFG, G/HPSG). If it does nothing else, then, MP should once and for all make clear that these are two completely independent dimensions for theory construction in syntax.

The theoretical architecture is determined by "virtual conceptual necessity" in that there must be two "interfaces" of the linguistic system with nonlinguistic systems. One will be in the realm of pronunciation, the other in the realm of thought (broadly speaking). Thus, the linguistic system *must* provide representations of Phonetic

Form (PF) and Logical Form (LF), but any other representations are, from a conceptual standpoint, strictly unnecessary. The task MP sets, then, is to realize such a system, one in which there are only PF and the one syntactic stratum, LF. In particular, there is no D-structure and no S-structure. (see MP: 2–5) I shall give further details only when and as they are needed for our discussion.

2.2

Within MP "[t]he concepts of X-bar theory are . . . fundamental." (MP: 6) The content of X-Bar Theory is given in two sets of schemata, reproduced here as (1) and (2) (MP: 21, 23 (18) & (20)), where the former accounts for, in our terms, a Projection Chain, and the latter for adjunct(ion)s.

(1) a. X
b. $[_{X'}$ X]
c. $[_{X''}[_{X'}$ X]]

(2) a. $[_{X}$ Y X]
b. $[_{XP}$ YP XP]

The status in MP of (1) and (2), and X-Bar Theory more generally, is not particularly clear. The schemata in (1) and (2) are simply stipulated to hold, with no (theoretical) discussion. It is not clear whether they are freestanding statements stipulated to constrain a derivation, or inductively arrived at generalizations about derivations, or a result of some (umentioned) independent (theoretical or virtual conceptual) consideration. Note in this regard, however, the repeated claim that X-Bar concepts are "fundamental" (MP: 6, 10), which might suggest that no investigation or explanation, theoretical or conceptual, is needed or desired. What discussion there is of X-Bar consists essentially of a repeated statement to the effect that items are selected from the lexicon and projected into syntax with an X-Bar structure (MP: 6, 21) and the single statement that "GT [a generalized transformation, see below Section 2.4] and move α must form structures satisfying X-bar theory, now including [(2)]." (MP: 24) This last is unfortunately unclear in a familiar way: we do not know whether the rules are directly (stipulated to be) constrained by (1) and (2) themselves or are constrained by other (unmentioned) considerations which result in satisfying (1) or (2).[3] Neither alternative, it should be noted, is particularly desirable.

We can constrast the attitude toward X-Bar Theory in MP with that in our MPST. This might seem somewhat unfair, in that the MPST is, after all, explicitly about phrase structure and X-Bar Theory, although MP is concerned with other issues of overall grammar architecture. With this caveat in mind, some comparison can still be instructive, I believe.

The work of Speas (1990) on which we have built aims both to derive from other considerations such content of traditional X-Bar Theory as is needed for language and also to theoretically motivate X-Bar(like) structures. The central idea, as we have stressed, is that there is a structuralization of theta requirements of lexical items such that a lexical item projects (i.e., licenses) all and only the structure needed to represent the satisfaction of those requirements syntactically, where such satisfaction takes place within a constituent headed by the lexical item in question (viz., its Projection Chain). In the pristine version of Speas (1990), there are no distinct labels at different levels in a Projection Chain; instead, there are definitions for Minimal and Maximal Projection in terms of hierarchical position in a Chain. One main goal of such work has been exactly to do away with explicit statements such as those in (1) and (2), and this has been done with some success, it seems.

A crucial question now arises. How much of this theoretical investigation of X-Bar could be reconstructed within MP? More specifically, how much of the MPST account relies crucially on the existence of D-structure as the stratum which is the structuralization of lexical requirements? Insofar as any of the theoretical content relies on there being a "pure representation of the argument-of relations," prospects for the reconstructive project look bad. And if that project fails, and if there is no endogenous theoretical inquiry into X-Bar Theory within MP, then to that extent, at least, we might prefer our MPST to MP. Let us turn, then, more directly to D-structure.

2.3.0

An obvious contrast between MP and MPST is that the former dispenses with D-structure. The crucial property of D-structure is that it is the interface between the lexicon and the syntax (or, more generally, "the computational system" in MP). Three sorts of considerations are raised against D-structure in MP (20–21). These are given in (3), and we discuss each in turn.

(3) a. Problems of the interface with the lexicon
b. Redundant conditions on D-structure
c. Empirical problems

2.3.1

In a theory with D-structure (e.g., our MPST), it is suggested that "an array of items from the lexicon" is selected and that these items must "Satisfy" (as the operation is dubbed) X-Bar Theory "all-at-once" (MP: 20). But, it is objected, we do not know what an "array" is, other than it is not a *set,* because "different arrangements of lexical items will yield different expressions." (MP: 20) Evidently, the intent here is that, for example, we should think it incorrect if a single set of lexical items, say that in (4a), were to undergo Satisfy for the D-structures for both (4b) and (4c), because these last two are, obviously, "different expressions."

(4) a. {Kim, Pat, kiss}
b. Kim kissed Pat.
c. Pat kissed Kim.

The difficulty here lies, I think, in the way in which Satisfy is conceptualized in MP. Satisfy "selects an array of items from the lexicon and presents it in a format satisfying the conditions of X-bar Theory." (MP: 20) The problem here arises, I believe, from assuming that there *are* some "conditions of X-bar Theory" somehow independent of the specification of well-formed D-structures, including lexically instantiated terminal nodes. The MPST has definitions for Projection Chain and for which labelled nodes are Minimal & Maximal Projections, but no "conditions of X-bar Theory" (viz., (1) and (2)) in the sense of MP. This may not be entirely clear, and the issue is of some importance, so I elaborate.

As explained in Chapter 1, Section 3.1, in our version of the MPST, we have supposed that lexical items are specified as bearing syntactic category labels of the X^0 ("lexical") level and they instantiate terminal nodes which they are categorially identical to (or, perhaps, nondistinct from). The items themselves do not "satisfy" any further syntactic conditions. Rather, we assume that a lexical item projects, that is, licenses, further structure as follows. A fully labelled PM is taken as given, and if a lexical item instantiates a terminal of that PM, then if that terminal heads a Projection Chain of just the number of links necessary to satisfy the requirements of the instantiating lexical item and if the constituent defined by that Projection Chain also contains categories satisfying whatever requirements the Chain's instantiated head has (say, an NP sister to a V instantiated by an obligatorily transitive verb), then the sub-PM headed by that instantiated terminal and rooted in its Maximal Projection is licensed. The question here is whether a selected set of lexical items can instantiate the terminals of a given PM.[4] On this conception, I see no problem in saying that the set in (4a) is selected to instantiate the PMs of both (4b) and (4c). There is an issue only because of the problem discussed in Section 2.2: the status of X-Bar conditions in MP.

The objection in (3a), then, is a nonobjection to our MPST. It depends crucually on the status of X-Bar theory. X-Bar seems to be a set of freefloating stipulations in MP, while the major goal of the MPST tradition is precisely to theoretically analyze away the special status of X-Bar conditions.

2.3.2

Two principles are objected to under (3b): the Projection Principle and the Theta-Criterion. The objection is that at LF they "have no independent significance" and are required of D-structure only so that this latter stratum will have "basic properties of LF" (MP: 20). The idea here is that for something to *be* LF—the interface with the nonlinguistic conceptual system—it would just have to have the properties which the Projection Principle and Theta criterion stipulate. So, there is no need to state these principles as holding of LF. But, if there is D-structure—a distinct stratum which is the interface of the syntax with the lexicon—then the two principles are needed "to make the picture coherent." (MP: 20) This is certainly true, given the assumed architecture. So, if one does not assume this architecture, then one (likely) can do without the principles. And, this architecture dependence means that the principles should not be a part of a "minimalist" approach which tries to stick to "virtual conceptual necessity" and nothing more. "These principles are therefore dubious on conceptual grounds. . . . " (MP: 20)

This is fine, as far as it goes. However, some nonconceptual reason to eliminate (or retain) D-structure must still be given. There is recognition of this: "[i]f the empirical consequences [of D-structure] can be explained in some other way" then D-structure and the principles can be eliminated (MP: 20). But, there is a lacuna here. It is claimed that D-structure is suspect on *conceptual* grounds. It is recognized that further reasons to reject (or accept) D-structure are required. In order to find such reasons there is an immediate jump to *empirical* issues. That there could be *theoretical* grounds for maintaining D-structure (or anything else, for that matter) is simply not recognized. But it is exactly on theoretical grounds that the MPST makes its argument for the utility of D-structure, as we shall see. First, however, we turn to the empirical questions.

2.3.3

The general empirical difficulty is with "expressions interpretable at LF but not in their D-Structure positions." (MP: 21) The only specific instance given is that of *tough* constructions, as in (5). The point is the familiar one that, within the assumptions of Chomsky (1981) and later GB work, there is no coherent analysis of (5).

(5) Kim is easy to please.

Equally familiar, however, is the fact that given a set of assumptions (e.g., D-structure, Case Theory, A vs. A′ Movement/Binding, Theta Theory) and a false entailment of that set (e.g., no *tough* constructions), all one may conclude is that *at least one* member of the set must be false. In this particular case, one cannot simply conclude that it must be D-structure that is to be rejected. It is open to the advocate of D-structure to propose some other alteration(s) in the set which would solve the empirical problem.

It has, therefore, not been shown that "[w]ithin anything like the [Chomsky 1981] framework, then, we are driven to a version of generalized transformations [in the place of D-structure and Satisfy]" (MP: 21); or, rather, much depends on what we are willing to call *anything like.* Surely on its most natural reading, which allows for some degree of variation in the set of assumptions, the assertion is just that, a mere assertion. We need to be shown that *all* sets of assumptions which could be termed *anything like* Chomsky (1981) and which include D-structure necessarily cannot analyze *tough* constructions. This has not been attempted, let alone done, and given the vagueness of *anything like,* among other problems, I doubt it could be achieved. We might also note that, even though it is true that the "special assumptions underlying the postulation of D-Structure . . . lacked independent conceptual support" (MP: 21), the same can surely be said for other members of the set of assumptions from Chomsky (1981), including those carried over into MP. That is, it has never been conceptual considerations which have motivated for example, Case Theory, Chains, or A vs. A′ Binding (or their progeny). Rather, these proposals are analysis driven and theory internal. So, conceptual considerations alone cannot favor maintaining (any of) these unchanged over keeping D-structure.

It is also of some interest that no analysis of the *tough* construction is offered in MP. So, even if it cannot be analyzed within the assumptions of Chomsky (1981), we have no concrete evidence that it can be done in the MP. At the very least, I believe, it needs to be shown that the subject (e.g., *Kim* in (5)) and the object trace of the embedded predicate form a Chain for purposes of Theta discharge/interpretation. And this would seem to require that the empty operator assumed to occupy the specifier position of the embedded CP be invisible or eliminated. These are murky, technical questions which, however, the MP advocate is obligated to address.

To sum up, examples such as (5) are indeed impossible within the set of assumptions from Chomsky (1981). This does not, however, require that D-structure be the assumption dropped or changed. Other members of the set have no more independent conceptual support than does D-structure. It is open to the D-structure advocate to alter the set in some other way in order to account for (5) (and, we hope, other phenomena). This has not been done. But, there has also been no analysis of (5) given in MP. I conclude, therefore, that currently (5) has been shown to count against the *particular* set of assumptions of Chomsky (1981), but for no other set.

2.3.4

We return now to the issue of possible *theoretical* justification for D-structure, despite the conceptual considerations against it.

Syntax is, in the first instance, the structuralization of information required by lexical items. It is therefore necessary that there be canonical syntactic representations of the different kinds of information required by lexical items—as it might be: head, specifier, complement, adjunct. To canonically represent such information, syntax needs to be a systematically organized set of principles. However, once such a system is in place, it is possible that noncanonical structuralizations may also arise from internal interactions of parts of the system. It is also possible, however, that such noncanonical structuralizations do not arise. This much, at least, is uncontroversial, I believe.

Now, it is a striking fact about languages that, so far as we know, all of them do show such noncanonical structuralizations. We might wonder about this. We might also wish our theoretical architecture to help us to understand this fact. At the very least, we might prefer our linguistic theory not to lead us to expect the facts to be otherwise—if, that is, we still have explanatory adequacy (Chomsky 1965: 26, 36, 46) as our major goal.

Let us now suppose that linguistic theory (UG) mandates multiple syntactic strata. It would be natural, though admittedly not inevitable, were one singled out for the required canonical structuralization of lexically mandated information. If so, then any other strata would necessarily be noncanonical structuralizations. We might further subdivide the canonical stratum into two stages, one with all and only the required information, the other with optional information. Such an architecture should seem familiar, being basically our MPST with the extended base. In such an architecture, noncanonical structuralizations are unsurprising. Were there a language with only canonical structuralizations, this would be surprising, as resources provided for all grammars would be unexploited; and worse: the multiple stata, mandated by linguistic theory (UG), would be redundant. It would arguably be "costly," in such an architecture, to have only canonical structuralizations.

Such an architecture embodies two ideas. One is that the different statuses—canonical versus non-canonical, required versus optional—are *natural kinds* and should, therefore, be explicitly represented as kinds in the grammar. The second idea is that these are fundamental properties of grammars, not ones in which we expect to see cross-linguistic variation.

Consider now an alternative architecture, one in which there is necessarily only one syntactic representation—say, MP. In such an architecture, should there be noncanonical structuralizations, they must be realized in the single representation, along with the canonical. But in such an architecture noncanonical structuralizations should seem odd and surprising. Given the architecture with only one representation and the requirement of canonical structuralization, the most natural meshing would have just these. There is no natural locus for noncanonical structuralizations; they might exist, but they should be rare, because the grammar is forced to overlay them on the single representation. In this architecture, it should be "less costly" to have only canonical structuralizations. Further, the different kinds noted previously are run together in the syntax. If indeed (either of) the distinctions pointed out earlier (canonical versus noncanonical, required versus optional) are fundamental ones and the architecture does not explicitly and transparently represent this state of affairs, then so much the worse for the architecture.

The point here should be clear. It is not that one cannot in principle manage analyses in an architecture of the second sort. It is, rather, that with such an architecture we should expect to see many—or at least *some*—languages that only have canonical structuralizations. But we do not. And the architecture makes this seem to be an odd and accidental fact, rather than something fundamental. This is a crucial issue when it comes to explanatory adequacy; as Chomsky (1965: 36) put it "[a] theory of grammar may be descriptively adequate and yet leave unexpressed major features that are defining properties of natural language and that distinguish natural languages from arbitrary symbolic systems."

The claim I would make, then, is that an architecture of the first sort—our MPST—more accurately models and represents the kinds in, and some fundamental aspects of, language than does an architecture of the second sort—the MP. MPST in this respect approaches explanatory adequacy, whereas MP does not. This is not a conceptual argument nor is it a straightforwardly empirical one in the sense of being based on detailed analyses of linguistic phenomena. It is, of course, empirical in that it adverts to some very general facts about languages. But, given that the facts are so general and, I believe, so fundamental and that the way of accounting for them is architectural, it is appropriate, I think, to say that this is a *theoretical* argument, distinct from, and situated between, the conceptual and the analytically empirical.

We turn now to adjunct(ion)s.

2.4.0

As noted above, adjunct(ion)s are licensed in MP by means of the schemata in (2), repeated here.

(2) a. $[_X$ Y X]
  b. $[_{XP}$ YP XP]

As well as these two schemata, we need the two rules also alluded to previously, GT and move α. The first is a generalized transformation which, essentially and nontechnically, "pastes" together two PMs. These PMs are those which arise from heads which are selected from the lexicon and projected into syntax in accordance with X-Bar structure (MP: 6, 21). GT effects the selection and projection, thus eliminating D-structure and Satisfy: "[a]t each point in the derivation, then, we have a structure Σ, which we may think of as a set of phrase markers." (MP: 22) GT is the inter-PM operation. Move α is the familiar intra-PM operation, leaving a trace and forming a Chain. GT places adjuncts, move α does adjunctions. Notice, though, that each of these opeations also does other things. That is, GT places not just adjuncts but everything that is drawn from the lexicon, and move α does not only adjunctions, but also substitutions. So, at least in terms of the rules, the argument-adjunct(ion) asymmetry is not formally recognized as a distinction of *kinds* in MP. Three further points should be noted.

1. The possibility of either adjoining to or moving X′ is explicitly "put aside" in a note (MP: 45, n. 15).
2. Lebeaux's Generalization (repeated here) is apparently endorsed: "Leabeaux's analysis . . . therefore could be carried over." (MP: 37)

(5) *Lebeaux's Generalization:*
Coreference is OK if the R-expression is in a fronted adjunct, but is not OK if the R-expression is in a fronted argument.

3. Adjunct(ion)s "need not extend" their host PMs, unlike substitutions. "Extension" is a (stipulated) condition that a rule's output PM contain the input host PM as a proper subpart (MP: 22–23).

We now take up this approach, both discussing it on its own terms and comparing it to our MPST.

2.4.1

Although there is no discussion of this issue, the two parts of X-Bar theory in MP (repeated here) seem not to be on a par.

(1) a. X
b. $[_{X'}$ X]
c. $[_{X''}[_{X'}$ X]]

(2) a. $[_{X}$ Y X]
b. $[_{XP}$ YP XP]

Only (1) is indicated when head selection and projection are mentioned (MP: 21). (2) appears to function only to constrain the outputs of the two rules, as (1) also does (MP: 23). But if indeed only (1) is relevant for head selection and projection, while both (1) and (2) constrain rule outputs, this should be explicitly stated and discussed. Why should there be such a distinction within MP? What, if anything, does it explain, or what, if anything, explains it? If this is meant to architecturally reconstruct the argument-adjunct asymmetry, some discussion is surely in order.

More generally, we can return to our original questions about the staus of (1) and (2): Why should (1) or (2) hold of the rule outputs at all? At several places (MP: 22, 23, 24) it is said that they do hold, but there is not only no elaboration but also our familiar ambiguity. For example, "GT and move α must form structures satisfying X-bar theory, now including [(2)]." (MP: 24) How are we to understand this *must*? Is X-bar somehow independently required? If so, how? Or do (1) and (2) themselves constrain the outputs? But then why these statements?

2.4.2

We can contrast this situation with that in our MPST, as developed in Chapter 4. Adjuncts are placed by our generalized transformation, Adjunct Adding. This is part of forming the extended base. There must be such an extended base because (1) only base structures are constrained by the remnants of X-Bar theory, but (2) base structures are, in the first instance, structuralizations only of Theta-grid requirements, and (3) adjuncts are definitionally not part of Theta-grid requirements, yet (4) an adjunct must be part of the Projection Chain of some head, so (5) to accomodate adjuncts, there must be some representation that both falls under X-Bar Theory (hence, is a base structure) and is not the representation of Theta-grid requirements (hence, is not a base structure). The extended base resolves the apparent contradiction. Our theory allowed us to deduce the X-Bar structure for adjuncts, and allowed adjuncts only to the XP level (this was extended to the X' level in Chapter 5, where the extended base was further analyzed and a distinguished intermediate level tentatively (re)introduced).

Both the MPST and MP seem to make a distinction between structure projected by a head and other structure. In the MP, however, the form of both is stipulated by X-Bar schemata—those in (1) & (2). In our MPST, there are no such schemata. Rather, we have the principle that heads project, the definitions of Maximal and Minimal Projection, the requirements that (1) D-structure be the structuralization of Theta-grid requirements and (2) all Theta-grid requirements of a head be satisfied within its Maximal Projection (extended to include other, nonrequired, semantic relations for adjuncts) from which we deduce the form of each structure. The distinction between the two sorts of structure is fundamental to the MPST and shapes its architecture. The distinction plays no such crucial role in the MP, and recognizing it requires an encoding by means of a number of unexplicated, arbitrary stipulations.

2.4.3

The exclusion of X′ from consideration, along with the limitation of adjunct(ion)s to (2)—wherein only X^0 level items adjoin to X^0 and only XP level items to XP is not without effects. Specifically, ambiguity of output is avoided (see, e.g., MP: 23, where this is tacitly invoked).[5] That is, the only level that can have sisters of different levels is X^0: its sister can be of either the X^0 or XP level. In the former case, the mother must also be of the X^0 level; in the latter it must be of the X′ level. X′ and XP can each only have a sister of the XP level, and in each case the mother must also be of the XP level. But, if adjunct(ion)s to X′ and level mismatches between adjoiner and host are allowed, then there is indeterminacy as to the identity of the label on the mother of the adjunction structure.[6]

As we have noted, if there is no adjoining to X′ in the MPST, this would be for the principled reason that there is no X′. If, on the other hand, we allow for X′, it is because we accept the analysis of the extended base, Core versus Periphery, and rule licensed structure from Chapter 5; and again, we have a principled basis for our result. In the latter case, as discussed, the theory allows for—indeed cannot prevent—adjunctions to X′. Again, the MPST has principled accounts where the MP is obscure, unexplicated, or stipulative.

2.4.4

We have argued in Chapter 4 that Lebeaux's Generalization is false, and so an approach which predicts it cannot be correct. The MPST does not predict Lebeaux's Generalization. The MP apparently does, though the matter is somewhat unclear, given the modal nature of the claim made ("Lebeaux's analysis . . . *could* be carried over").

2.4.5

"Extension" distinguishes adjunctions from substitutions, and reconstructs some empirical results of the strict cycle and rules out "raising to a complement position" (MP: 23). All discussion of extension, and such motivation for it as is given, is entirely in terms of its empirical consequences. There is no indication that there might be anything within the architecture of the theory, or in its choice of primitives, that would suggest this condition. Were the facts otherwise, apparently, the theory could as easily and naturally accomodate them. Nor is there any but an empirical basis given for why extension holds only of substitutions and not of adjunctions.

We have distinguished substitutions from adjunctions in the MPST, as well, in Chapter 5. There it was suggested that the distinguishing characteristic is structure (= label) preservation versus structure creation, that is, movement to an existing position versus movement to a nonexisting position (or, in the case of adjuncts, structure creating joining versus the nonstructure creating joining of coordination). There is no new ad hoc condition here; it is really no more (and no less) than the explicit recognition of the essential difference between the two sorts of operations. And, of course, because the MPST is derivational and multistratal, it can retain the strict cycle condition.

This concludes the discussion of MP. We turn to a summary of this discussion and comparison.

2.5

We have examined the MP on the home turf of our MPST: the interrelations of X-Bar Theory, D-structure, and adjunct(ion)s. Perhaps not surprisingly, MP has not done well in the comparison. As noted at the start of the discussion, MP is not primarily about such matters, while the MPST is. Still, even on its own terms, without comparison to our

MPST, MP is often unclear or stipulative in these areas. I conclude that for now, someone concerned with such issues has two options: first, opt for the MPST and out of MP, or, second, take the MPST and this discussion as setting part of the research agenda for MP—the tasks within MP are to meet the criticisms and to reconstruct whatever is of worth in the MPST approach. I have no objection to either option.

3.0

We have come a rather large conceptual distance in relatively few pages. I began by suggesting that the phrase structure theory to be proposed contained only elements that any phrase structure theory would have and that therefore disagreement would be, as we might say, monotonic. We have ended up with both an approach to Islands that rejects most of what has been thought and written on the subject in the last twenty-five years and a lengthy disputation with Chomsky's (1993) Minimalist Program. How did this happen?

In this section, I (re)trace this path. I review the chapters that have gone before, stressing their connection to the general theoretical project, both in its formal and substantive aspects.

3.1

The first chapter proposed the general framework: a formalization of PMs that reduced them simply to hierarchical structures, organized by means of a single primitive relation, immediate/direct dominance; and a substantive "X-Bar-like" (though barely) theory of phrase structure, reduced (following Speas 1990) to a single principle of projection from the lexicon, with defined Maximal and Minimal Projections. These two parts converge in that the substantive portion assumes a formal relation of dominance (the reflexive, transitive closure of direct dominance), and no other formal relation. We also leave formally open such issues as multiple labelling of nodes, multiple motherhood, and discontinuous constituency, arguing that any restrictions that might exist should be the result of substantive theory.

The argument against a formal precedence primitive comes directly from the assumed conceptions of the concepts category and structure: word class and immediate constituent node, respectively. This argument provided the means to explain the dominance-precedence asymmetry with respect to parameterization of relations and predicates which they respectively mediate. Dominance is universal, the formal, primitive basis for a *syntactic kind,* the X-Bar "module"—in our terms, base structures. Precedence is parochial, based in *formatives,* is the basis for no syntactic kind, no module—hence the parameterization.

Thus, we have the two vectors of the MPST theory: formal minimal PMs, and substantive minimal "X-bar"; the subsequent chapters tend to extend along one or the other of these.

3.2

The account of C-command pursues the formal inquiry. C-command is reconceived, following Richardson & Chametzky (1985), from the point of view of the commandee and found to be a generalization of the sister relation and thus has no specifically linguistic content. This conception of C-command is available to other inquiries that do not accept the MPST, of course, but it does not so readily flow from them. This is because other theories often include some sort of primitive precedence relation, and thus do not need (yet) another relation (and family of relations) with which to relate nodes not in a dominance relation. Other approaches can (and should) appropriate the conception, but they do not motivate it.

Once the crucial shift to the "commandee's viewpoint" takes place, further insight into command relations is possible. For example, C-command is the basic command relation, all other command relations being supersets of C-command.

3.3

Chapters 3 and 4 turn to the substantive portion of the theory. Together they develop the idea of the "extended base." The analyses of CCC and adjuncts enlarge the set of PMs, but do so within the constraints of the MPST. That is, since the enlarged set is a set of PMs, its members must meet the conditions on membership in that set, viz., the conditions on base representations in the MPST.

Note, also, that if the theory of well-formed PMs is the theory of base structures (D-structure), defined as structuralizations of Theta-grid requirements, then if there are to be adjuncts or CCC, there **must** be some way to enlarge the set of PMs. Given the MPST approach to D-structures, either there are no structural realizations of non-Theta-grid required relations or there is an extended base.

PMs are constructed from two sets, nodes and labels, and one relation, (direct) domination. To expand the set of such PMs, we "join" two PMs. That is, we integrate them in terms of dominance by means of sharing either a node or a label. These two ways of joining—the only two available to us—turn out to analyze CCC (node joining) and adjuncts (label joining). We have also seen, in Section 1 of this Conclusion, that the operations analyze what they do nonarbitrarily. Once the MPST architecture is set, adjuncts and CCC could not be other than joining PMs at a label and a node, respectively.

The turn in these chapters is to the substantive, but there is a formal component to it. The problem we are posing—and proposing to solve—is how could the original set of PMs be expanded in a principled way. In the case of CCC, the fact that PMs can be construed as sets of (labelled) nodes is crucial, because the analysis is essentially set union. With adjuncts, it is crucial that more than one node can bear a single label—recall that this label identity is token identity, cashed out in terms of the lexical index (a substantive notion, to be sure). Our use of node-label pairs also allows us to define l-domination and c-domination, thus clarifying some obscurities in the May / Chomsky approach to adjunction (though we ultimately reject that approach).

Finally, there is a difference between the means of licensing the original set of PMs and the extensions. The former come under the single principle Project Alpha; the latter are rule licensed. In our terms, this is a substantive difference, not a formal one.

3.4

Chapter 5 pursues implications of the idea of the "extended base," furthering the substantive inquiry. A new rule type is introduced, phrase structure rules, along with the possibility of theoretically potent "intermediate labels." By pushing the distinction between *rule-licensed* versus *non-rule-licensed* structures, an analysis is made available for *characteristic structures* in the sense of the Learnability Theory of Wexler & Culicover (1980) in terms of the Core versus Periphery concepts of GB theory.[7] The resources of the MPST-driven extended base theory allow us to adopt relatively common structures for Subjects, Adjuncts, and CNPs that, in combination with the analysis of characteristic structures and Core versus Periphery, suggests an **explanation** for the fact that these structures are *Islands.*

The advantage of this theory is that it brings these structures together; it finds in them a natural class. If we want to know **why** *these* structures, and *not others,* are Islands, and **why** they are *Islands,* and not something else, we need such a theory. Further, the analysis made available of characteristic structures and Core versus Periphery is in itself something of an advance, I believe.

An evident disadvantage is that the theory is unidimensional. Other approaches to Islands, though unexplanatory, tend to have several interacting factors which determine grammaticality. This gives them a decided observational advantage: they cover more data. Given, too, that the data elicit gradient judgments from informants, unidimensionality is not clearly a desirable feature for a theory.

3.5

The components of the theory of structures proposed and developed here are quite tightly interconnected. The account of Islands is driven by the distinction between unextended and extended base structures analyzed as non-rule-licensed versus rule-licensed structure. That distinction arises in the analyses of coordination and adjuncts, which are structures that the pristine MPST cannot license. In our accounts of these structures, crucial use is made of both the formal and substantive portions of the pristine MPST. Our reanalysis and rejection of the May and Chomsky approach to adjunction flows directly from MPST's account of the relation between nodes and labels. The analysis of C-command is somewhat more hermetic, as it is purely formal. Nonetheless, a formal aspect of our MPST motivates the existence of C-command, because without C-command the MPST has no straightforward formal way to pick out nodes not in the dominance relation for further linguistic relations. I have engaged Chomsky's (1993) Minimalist Program because it directly denies the crucial premise of the MPST architecture: the existence of a distinct D-structure stratum that is the interface of syntax and the lexicon.

4.0

Our inquiry has first developed a minimal phrase structure theory and then pushed this theory along its formal and substantive vectors. I have sought to extend and elaborate the theory along both lines in order to see what insights might be implicit in the theory while minimizing additional "modules" or "principles." I think the results are surprisingly rich, and I hope the project may lead others to pause and examine more closely the resources they already have at hand before they set off prospecting for imagined treasures elsewhere.

NOTES

Introduction

1. Chomsky (1994), Kayne (1994), and Williams (1994) appeared after this work was drafted, but I address them in work in progress.

1. Minimal Phrase Structure

1. This is meant as an untendentious observation, even a truism. Those who find it problematic may be assuming particular **conceptions** of the **concepts** category and structure (see, e.g., Dworkin 1977: 134-36, on **conception** versus **concept**). Thus, the concept category might, on a given conception, include, for example, "direct object," and the concept structure on such a conception might include "relational network." 'Structuralist' conceptions such as "word class" (e.g., N, V, NP, VP) and "immediate constituent" (and their theoretical progeny) occupy no privileged place *a priori,* although they are the conceptions with which I shall work in this essay, and the argument against precedence developed in Section 2 of the text depends crucially on these conceptions.

2. I should point out that Speas (1990) also has a theory of the relation of category to structure, one that I do not adopt as fully as I do her theory of categories. See Section 3.1.

3. The work of Hale on Warlpiri is an apparent exception that proves the rule. In Hale (1981), a parameter is proposed that divides languages into two types: W* (e.g., Warlpiri) and X-Bar (e.g., English)—basically, the former lack all hierarchical structure. But Hale (1983) repudiates this suggestion, rejecting the parameterization.

4. This conclusion is not one which the authors I examine draw themselves, nor do I know whether they would endorse it.

5. I should note, however, that in later chapters more "apparatus" is proposed, though, I argue, it is apparatus that flows naturally—and minimally—from the theory.

6. The claim that the view of trees which incorporates lexical items as distinct nodes is incorrect is meant to apply to notions of tree (or phrase marker) in linguistics, not more generally in formal

language theory. It is not clear that there would be much sense to the latter claim. I thank Christopher Culy for help here.

7. Lasnik & Kupin (1977) revise the notion of PM found in Chomsky (1955/1985), defining what they call a *Reduced PM* (RPM). Under this conception, an (R)PM is a set of strings, where each string is drawn from the equivalent phrase structure derivations of a terminal string. This is then a distinct sort of object from our PMs. See Chametzky (1987a: Introduction) for discussion.

8. It appears that (7a) & (7b) are redundant. As noted in Section 2.3 in the text, Higginbotham's (1983) revision of these axioms obviates what he sees as the need for a stipulation of a unique root, thus eliminating any redundancy that may exist.

9. As Christopher Culy has pointed out to me, the claim in the text is too strong as it stands. Specifically, one could define a notion "head of" that would be entirely nonlinguistic, such as, for example, "leftmost daughter." But the point in the text that any such notion would have to "pan out empirically" is still valid. Regardless of how it is defined, "head of" just is a substantive notion, and which definition we accept depends on what results it gives us analytically. So, the contrast with dominance remains, I believe.

10. It is perhaps worth noting that the status of dominance as a syntactic primitive is not undermined by its having a rationale outside of syntax; quite the contrary, in fact.

11. Strictly, the text is inaccurate because, evidently, lexical items do "partake of" word class category labels. But, lexical entries for lexical items contain information of various types—phonological, morphological, syntactic, semantic—and these sorts of information are, on the one hand, on an equal footing in the sense that none is "more essential" than any other and, on the other, in principle are present or absent independently of one another (see Sadock 1991 for development of consequences of these aspects of lexical entries). For our purposes, the importance of these facts is the following. A lexical item is not ineliminably syntactic—it is not "built up" from the basic notions of syntax—and, indeed, a lexical entry may have no syntactic information in it all (see Chapter 3, for example) and still be a lexical entry. And, if an item falls under "the physics of speech" and "the human mouth" it can do so only insofar as it is a phonological/phonetically interpreted element, not on account of the syntactic portion of its entry. Thus, PRO, a lexical item with a lexical entry containing syntactic information, has no phonetic interpretation, and so could not be subject to "the physics of speech" and "the

human mouth." So, though lexical items do "partake of" the word class category vocabulary, they do so only (1) partially (just a small portion of the vocabulary, the Minimal Category level, is used), (2) inessentially (there need not be such information in an entry), and (3) irrelevantly (with respect to "the physics of speech" and "the human mouth").

12. It is somewhat unclear whether we should take over McCawley's third axiom, repeated here as (i), which we have not discussed, because McCawley himself (1982: 99, n. 9) has to violate it in his analysis of right-node-raising; hence the issue here, again, may be an empirical rather than a formal one.

(i) For every $x_1 \in N$, there is at most one $x_2 \in N$ such that x_2 directly dominates x_1 (that is, the tree has no loops).

See Chapter 2, note 5 for more discussion and a reason to retain this axiom.

13. Branching is not required by the construction as given. It is discussed in Section 1.0 of Chapter 2.

14. Eilfort (1986) suggests a possible empirical restriction on discontinuity. Yngve (1960), as discussed by Ojeda (1987: 260-61), provides a formal restriction within a phrase structure rule grammar. Interestingly, the two restrictions are the same.

15. It is perhaps of interest that branching structures are used and studied in other sciences, particularly systematics in biology, and that the notion of left-to-right order—precedence—plays no role in the general formal theory of such "cladograms," as they are sometimes called. See Hull (1989: 150-53, 173-74), Platnick (1977; 1979), Platnick & Cameron (1977), and, for helpful discussion of cladistics, phenetics, and taxonomy, Sober (1988) and Hull (1988).

16. It might be objected that "adjunct" is not a structural term but rather a functional one, so it is out of place in this discussion. But, under the sort of theory provided by Speas (1990) and adopted here, D-structure just is the "structuralization" of the "theta grid" requirements of heads. Because adjuncts are definitionally not required (by the "theta grid"), it follows that they cannot be part of this "structuralization." See Chapter 4 for extensive discussion.

17. According to Speas (1990: 57), the point missed by Pullum is the following: "The goal is not to formulate any set of rules which will correctly describe the linguistic structures of any language.

Rather, the goal is to formulate a theory of what principles a person actually knows when they know a human language. The claim embodied by X-bar theory is that the human langauge faculty does not include phrase structure rules." As this argument is orthognal to what I shall have to say, I take no position on it.

18. Speas (1990: 35) notes the convergence with respect to the eliminability of bar levels.

19. Here is a way to save a version of the Kornai & Pullum point. In a standard GB theoretical architecture, there can be no such syntactic thing as a "phonetically null category." Therefore, if there are to be syntactic "empty categories" at all, they must be of the sort Kornai & Pullum discuss. There can be no "phonetically null empty categories" in GB syntax because the fact that some lexical item has no phonetic interpretation is not the sort of information that the syntax can have access to—at least, it can no more have access to this information than to any other phonetic or phonological information. So, if "phonetically null" is a way to distinguish subcategory kinds in syntax, so too should be, say, "monosyllabic" or "contains a nasal." If "phonetically null" elements are to be distinguished and referred to in syntax, this must be done using the vocabulary of syntax. Perhaps this can be done; but it has not been attempted, to my knowledge.

2. The Explanation of C-command

1. It is worth noting that within Lasnik & Kupin's (1977) formalization of a "restrictive" transformational theory, there can be no nonbranching domination, because in that framework each member of such a pair dominates the other. It follows that for Lasnik & Kupin there can be no substantive, analytic point that depends on asymmetric nonbranching domination—because there is no such relation. The empirical claim that this entails is that no grammar will require such an asymmetric relation. See Kupin (1978) for discussion. Our theory perhaps cannot claim to be as explanatory in this regard, because for us nonbranching domination does not exist for reasons of substantive linguistic theory. The formal but nonstipulative nature of the result is an advantage of the Lasnik & Kupin formalization, but as noted in Chapter 1, note 7, the objects called PMs in the two approaches are quite different. This makes straightforward comparisons difficult. See Chametzky (1987a: Introduction) and Chametzky & Richardson (1985) for some discussion.

2. A *factorization* is simply an exhaustive, nonoverlapping

constituent analysis of a PM, as familiar from the structural descriptions in transformations in the Standard Theory. Thus, strictly, "complete factorization" is redundant, as an incomplete constituent analysis is not a factorization.

3. As R/C note (340), if there is nonbranching domination then there may be no unique minimal factorization. Instead, there can be a set of "minimal factorizations" in the sense that these factorizations have equal cardinalities and all other factorizations have greater cardinalities.

So, the more general way to define the C-commanders for a node G is to take the union of all the "minimal factorizations" for G in the preceding sense. All members of this union C-command G. When there is no nonbranching domination, then there is only one member of the "minimal factorizations" set, and so this reduces to the version in the text. In the more general case, daughters in a nonbranching domination relation are in the set of C-commanders, so C-command is not strictly equivalent to (1). The only significance of this, in my view, is that it further suggests that there is no nonbranching domination.

4. Our diagram (3) could, for example, just as easily be the representation of the managerial structure of a corporation or the representation of phylogenetic relationships among species as the representation of the syntactic structure of a sentence.

5. A technical question arise with regard to multiple motherhood and "looping." The issue concerns cases in which a node dominates its own mother, hence also its sister(s). Because sisters are definitionally C-commanders on our view and also, definitionally, nodes in a dominance relation are not in the C-command relation, we have a contradiction. In graphs without loops, sisterhood and dominance will be mutually exclusive, but with loops they need not be. Thus our approach to C-command holds only in graphs without loops, a less than totally general setting, but not, I think, much the worse for that. A problem does arise, however, given McCawley's allowance for loops, noted in note 12 in Chapter 1. We now have reason to resist his analysis and maintain his axiom (7c). My thanks to Christopher Culy for alerting me to this potential problem.

6. Kayne (1981: 130) offers a geometric cum pictorial attempt at intuitive clarification of his idea. However, it is of minimal helpfulness, I find.

7. Since we are here concerned with comparing the merits of the Barker & Pullum versus R/C approaches, it seems pointless to

discuss arguments which Barker & Pullum themselves do not take as supportive of their position.

8. Condition (2) is evidently just an example of the fact that the general theory of grammar can decide among analytic choices when the facts under analysis do not force a choice. This is one of the things a theory of grammar is for.

9. It should be recalled that the other researchers discussed in Chapter 1 also do not assume the standard Exclusivity Condition, although they do still claim to have (some sort of) precedence primitive. Thus, elimination of Exclusivity is independent of, although of course it follows from, elimination of precedence as a formal primitive.

10. My thanks to Christopher Culy for help with the formal statement here.

11. There are actual as well as hypothetical concerns here. On Chomsky's (1986a: 4-5) analysis of wh-movment, this operation results in a structure in which the binder is immediately dominated by an intermediate member of the C Projection Chain and is sister to C. Thus, this structure would not be licensed by a rule fitting the schema given by Gazdar and described by Fodor in the quotes in the text. The relation of binder to gap in such a structure is not C-command but rather M-command. It is hard to see how a GPSG-type theory, which does not explicitly use command predicates, would capture this generalization. The obvious response, of course, is to deny the analysis—as, indeed, GPSG analyses do.

3. Coordination

1. We can formalize (something like—see below) our procedure as follows. First, we partition set D with respect to the first members of its ordered pairs; call this set P.

$$P = \{X \subseteq D\text{: } (x, y), (x',y') \in X \leftrightarrow x = x'\}$$

If (5a) in the text is our D, then P is

P_5 = {{(S,V/drank), (S,N/sodas), (S,V/ate), (S,N/donuts)},
{(VP,V/drank), (VP,N/sodas), (VP,V/ate), (VP,N/donuts)},
{(NP,N/sodas), (NP,N/donuts)},
{(V/drank,V/drank), (V/ate,V/ate)},
{(N/sodas,N/sodas), (N/donuts,N/donuts)}}

We next form a set C which has as its members only those members of P which include all the second elements of members of D:

$$C = \{X \in P: (\forall: (x, y) \in D)((\exists: (x', y') \in X)(y = y'))\}$$

Given P_5, our C is then

$$C_{P5} = \{\{(S,V/drank), (S,N/sodas), (S,V/ate), (S,N/donuts)\}, \{(VP,V/drank), (VP,N/sodas), (VP,V/ate), (VP,N/donuts)\}\}$$

Finally, we can form the set of conjoinable categories—CC; the set of first elements of members of members of C:

$$CC = \{x: (x, y) \in X \,\&\, X \in C\}$$

In the example, this gives us what we want:

$$CC_{CP5} = \{S, VP\}$$

The formalization does not follow the text in that the sets P and C are not the same as sets F and I. In hopes of easing comprehension, the text simplifies the construction. I do not intend to suggest that this formalization provides any further insight into the nature of the syntax of CCC.

2. I assume, but do not argue, that any failure of different "sentence types" (Sadock & Zwicky 1985) to conjoin has a nonsyntactic explanation.

3. Recall that conjuncts stand in no precedence relation to one another in Goodall's version of the 3-D analysis. Hence, there must be some sort of "linearization procedure" to meet the demands of "the physics of speech." This need obviously carries over into the present version of the 3-D theory.

4. Notice that this account predicts (i), because the two instances of **herself** should be collapsed under union.

(i) *$Sue_{\{i\}}$ considers $herself_{\{i\}}$ and $herself_{\{i\}}$ lucky.

5. This device will extend to examples of split antecedents, (i), as well. See Chametzky (1987a: 138–40, 155, 183) for discussion.

(i) $Kim_{\{i\}}$ told $Pat_{\{j\}}$ $they_{\{i,j\}}$ should leave.

6. Under current assumptions, semantic interpretation is not done off of D-structure. Therefore, the fact that (20a) and (20b)—essentially the D-structures—are anomolous does not matter. See Goodall (1987: 55-57) for argument and results.

7. The definition will also cover split antecedent cases as in note 5, while the standard definition will not.

8. Should the reflexives be coindexed with **Sue,** then interpretive principle (23) would rule out the example. Thus, it would be syntactically well-formed, but it is impossible to understand **himself** as a variable bound to **Sue.** In general, I think that gender and number (mis)matches should be analyzed interpretively, not syntactically.

9. SI-1 and SI-2 in (24) stand for "semantic interpretation 1" and "semantic interpretation 2," respectively.

10. Partee & Rooth (1983) first drew attention to this aspect of disjunction. According to these authors and to Larson, CCC with **and** do not have the "wide-scope" reading. Thus, (i) (Partee and Rooth's (21); Larson's (92)) is not supposed to have the reading represented in (ii) (Larson's (93)).

(i) Bill hopes that someone will hire a maid and a cook.

(ii) Bill hopes (∃x [hire (x, a maid)]) and
Bill hopes (∃y [hire (y, a cook)])

However, there seems to be some difference in judgments with respect to these examples. Some speakers do, apparently, get the supposedly unavailable reading. I shall not discuss this question further.

11. Chametzky (1987a: Chapter 3) discusses Larson (1985a) at length, pointing out both theoretical and empirical errors in the analysis.

4. Adjuncts & Adjunction

1. Speas does not draw either of these conclusions from her facts.

2. This is still true on the view put forward in Chomsky (1986b: 86-92), in which there is only "s(emantic-selection)" and no "c(ategorial)-selection" in the listed properties of lexical items. On this view, s-selection of a semantic category implies the "canonical structural realization" of that category (CSR(C)) as well. This termi-

nology is misleading in that it is not **structure** but **syntactic category** that is implied by the CSR(C); thus Chomsky (1986b: 87) takes "CSR(patient) and CSR(agent) to be NP . . . " and NP is a category (name), not a determinate piece of structure. Given this, it is still the case that heads select for syntactic categories, though indirectly, mediated by s-selection and CSRs.

3. I am endebted here to Christopher Culy.

4. William Davies has pointed out that adjunction to the root node, if necessary, would not result in a structure in which the new mother is labelled, because the root node is not selected for. In other words, since the entire PM is not a subphrase marker, the label on the root node is licensed only by projection, not by projection and selection. This asymmetry between the root node and all others may provide some indirect support for the proposed new understanding of the Projection Principle in Section 3.4, because under that understanding no new mother need be labelled, eliminating the asymmetry.

5. It might be objected that the argument in Section 2.3 of the text already shows that neither of these options, though in principle available, could satisfy the Projection Principle, hence they are unavailable in practice. Thus, the transformational component could be entirely silent with respect to what label application of the adjunction rule gives rise. However, labelling would still fail to be a theoretical kind, the more serious problem, in my view.

6. Because May does not discuss "adjuncts"—nonargument modifiers—he does not distinguish these from "adjunctions"—the results of his rule of C-adjunction. Thus, for (5) to be comparable to (6), *adjuncts* in (5) should be taken to mean either nonargument modifiers or the moved element in C-adjunction. My thanks to Christopher Culy for pointing this out to me.

7. The variable α cannot take a Category in the sense of (4i) as its value, because a dominated element can only be a labelled node. This is a consequence of May's definitions and what I take to be his assumptions, but I do not know whether it is an intended consequence.

8. Stabler (1992: 252) also reformalizes (6) in a way that meets such objections.

9. My thanks to Christopher Culy for help with the formal statements in (4′).

10. Actually, May (1985: 57-58) also suggests extending these notions to CCC. He writes (1985: 57) "we can take a conjoining node

as the intersection point of the conjoined projections." That is, he holds that the labelled node dominating the conjuncts is itself a member of both conjunct "projections" (where this last term seems to be equivalent to his 1989 "Category"). This is of particular interest to us both because it purports to be another construction that requires these conceptual revisions and because of our own analysis of CCC in Chapter 3.

As is explained in Section 6.1, there is a connection between CCC and adjuncts. They are the two ways in which PMs may be joined: CCC join at a node, adjuncts join at a label; label identity in CCC is type identity, in adjuncts, token identity. They thus do not get the same analysis, as May suggests, but rather are complementary. As May does not seem to distinguish between nodes and labelled nodes, it is not surprising that he cannot make the correct connection. Indeed, May has no analysis of CCC at all; he offers just a brief suggestion for node labelling in CCC. No reason is given for **why** they should be so labelled, other than a single, empirical observation (about lack of C-command between conjuncts, which obviously also follows on the 3-D analysis).

Further, nothing in what May writes suggests that an example such as in (i), generally thought to have a structure such (ii), would not also fall under his revisions, if CCC do. It will not work to say that, because the mother NP is a projection of (the head of) N′, it cannot also be a projection of its daughter NP, when it is exactly his suggestion with respect to CCC that a single mother is part of two distinct projections. Our approach to CCC makes a similar claim, but it does so on account of a theoretical analysis particular to CCC, so it cannot extend to (i).

(i) Kim's parents
(ii) $[_{NP}$ NP N′]

The central problem for May is that he does not have a theory either of CCC or of adjunct(ion)s. He has (re)definitions of some basic syntactic predicates and some rules that stipulate that some structures exist which meet those definitions. But there are no independent reasons for these rules to license such structures—the structures are only indirectly justified, by empirical observations; theoretically, it is just as possible that no such rules and structures be in the grammar. Once counterfactual supporting, theoretically grounded analyses of the structures of CCC and of adjuncts are developed—as in the present work—the two phenomena diverge. Particularly in the present context, May's invocation of CCC cannot be taken as independent support for his (re)definitions.

11. Notice, too, that we are still undoing the main result of the adjunction rule, even though the labelling that results from the rule having applied is now derived from a general principle, rather than stipulated.

12. Using our revisions from Section 3.1.1, we would understand (7) in the following way: "α" is a Category, "β" is a labelled node, "a segment of" is a member of (the Category), and "dominates" is l-dominates.

13. I am assuming here that labelled nodes, not Categories in the sense of 3.1.1, would be barriers. If there are cases where adjunction is to a C-adjunction structure and the second, higher, adjoiner should govern across two adjoined-to labelled nodes, then the stipulation will have to be more complex.

14. In (9′) I assume that a Category becomes a barrier just in case all its members are barriers—labelled nodes are still the basic barriers. Because no member of a labelled node can be a barrier, (9′) will apply only to Category barriers.

15. May (1985: 56–57) holds that his version of C-adjunction is "'structure-preserving' in the sense that the categorical structure imposed by X-Bar theory on D-Structure representations will remain unchanged in the course of derivation . . . " This depends on stipulating the C-adjunction rule and on the definition of "category" given in (3) in the text, because the labelled node added by the C-adjunction rule is taken to be part of the Projection Chain (May does not use this term) from which the label is copied. However, May does not give any argument for why adjunction should be "structure preserving" in his sense, and his analysis simply stipulates this outcome.

16. Actually, things are not so simple here. Because structure is licensed at D-structure only as labelled nodes that satisfy lexical requirements, it is not clear how the positions called "Specifier of CP" and "Specifier of IP" are licensed. Both of these positions are uninstantiated at D-structure (Specifier of IP is "empty" in the analysis under which all subjects originate within VP—what Speas (1990) calls the *Lexical Clause Hypothesis*—see Chapter 5) and elements of almost any category can move to these positions (see Chametzky 1985 on non-NP subjects). Several ways out of this problem suggest themselves, all based on the fact that CP and IP have functional rather than lexical heads (Fukui & Speas 1986).

The most radical way out is to deny the generalization of head projection from lexical to functional categories—there would then be no CP or IP. Less radically, one could claim that functional heads have no lexical selection requirements and so always simply give rise to a "default" structure with a(n unlabelled) Specifier position present. Or, one could posit a maximal projection XP with no lexical content, which such functional heads select. And other alternatives are imaginable. My thanks to Mercedes Gonzalez for discussion of this issue.

17. The text is perhaps somewhat misleading. It might be better to say simply that there is movement and that there are, logically, two sorts of landing sites: pre-existing positions (structure- and label-preserving substitutions) and nonexisting positions that must be integrated into the phrase marker (structure creating adjunctions).

18. Sister- and daughter-adjunction (Bach 1974: 86–87) would seem to be possibilities that would not require a new node. But, sister-adjunction was considered a subcase of substitution. More important, exactly because no new node is created, either sort of adjunction would violate the Projection Principle.

19. I note that Lebeaux's use of *"argument-of" relation* seems to pick out the same elements as Speas's use of *theta-grid* in that only adjuncts and not, say, specifiers are excluded.

20. Our two axioms in Chapter 1 (10) do not identify a particular label on the root node.

21. This might not be true on Speas's view in which labelling and structure projection are collapsed, as discussed in Chapter 1, Section 3.1, with respect to my revisions in (11′) and (14′) there. On her view, such ill-formed Projection Chains perhaps cannot arise at all.

22. Recall that I argued in Section 3 that there may be no restrictions on the distinct process of syntactic adjunction at S-structure; at most, there is the Projection Principle.

23. And the empirical motivation for Lebeaux's "Condition C everywhere" assumption has also disappeared.

24. We may be able to capture Speas's observation that "theta-marked" adjuncts are those usually analyzed as VP-internal adjuncts within our version of the MPST. In Chapter 5, Section 3.2, we propose that the theory include phrase-structure rules licensing a theoretically potent distinguished "intermediate label" (the discussion there deals with relative clauses). If this is correct, then we can have both VP-internal adjuncts—adjuncts to a node labeled with the

distinguished intermediate label—and VP (Maximal Projection) adjuncts. This still would not explain the antireconstruction facts, but it might provide the structural basis for such an explanation.

25. Speas (1991) takes up her data and the analysis of adjuncts once again. She argues here against Lebeaux's "derivational" approach and in favor of a "representational" analysis in which adjuncts are always present in a PM, not added by Adjoin Alpha. Noteworthy from our point of view are the following.

In discussing Lebeaux's analysis, Speas (1991: 244) writes "[t]he identity of the new node created by Chomsky adjunction will presumably follow from the principles of X-bar theory . . ." and "[f]inally, as adjunction constructions are not created until after DS [D-structure] in this theory, it would permit a version of X-bar theory in which every category has one and only one maximal projection at DS, and all structures in which one XP node immediately dominates another are derived structures." The first quote oddly assumes both that the rule in question would be C-adjunction and that the label on the new mother node would be determined by general principles, not by the rule itself. But it also assumes that the general principles in question, X-Bar theory, hold of strata other than D-Structure, a novel assumption, to my knowledge. Compare this to our theory, in which Adjunct Adding is simply PM joining by means of token label sharing (see Section 6.1 of the text), and X-Bar principles (viz., Project Alpha) hold because the structure is still a base structure. The second quote assumes that base structures cannot be derived structures, the common assumption we are contesting here.

Speas (1991: 249–50) tries to justify the odd behavior of adjunct structures with respect to Condition C within the "representational" approach in which an adjunct-argument distinction is not represented in the base (unlike in Lebeaux's approach). She does so by pointing out that the representational account "relies on the definition of the adjunction configuration given in May (1985)." The crucial point is the by now familiar one that we can express as "l-domination does not imply c-domination." Speas continues by noting that neither the adjunct nor the host c-dominates the other, and that it could be argued that neither truly precedes the other, because a "segment" of the host l-dominates the adjunct. Thus, she continues, PMs with adjuncts seem to require "categories bearing neither a dominance nor a precedence relation to one another." These considerations, she concludes, make adjunct structures atypical D-structures and, indeed, are how the "representational" approach makes the adjuncts "'not present at D-structure'." Since we have undermined both assumptions, Speas's reliance on May's reformulation of *dominance* and on the requirement that PMs include a precedence relation are reasons for us to doubt the "representational" approach.

Finally, Speas (1991: 252–55) offers an empirical argument for the superiority of the "representational" approach to Lebeaux's derivational analysis. The crucial fact is that a sentence such as (i) is good if *pictures* is given focus intonation, bad otherwise.

(i) Pictures of $John_i$, he_i likes.

Speas's argument relies on an analysis in which focus is a type of quantification, hence represented at LF but not at D-structure, and its LF structure is an adjunction structure. Given this LF adjunction structure, the "representational" analysis will allow the coreference in (i); if there is no focus, hence no adjunction structure, coreference is correctly disallowed. Speas's point is that on Lebeaux's analysis the focussed and unfocussed versions of (i) would have to have different D-structures because the referring expression *John* would have to be inserted after D-structure in the focussed variant to evade Condition C and be present at D-structure in the unfocussed variant. But, she objects, if D-structure "is a pure representation of GF-Theta, it is difficult to see how focus intonation could change the D-structure of a sentence" (1991: 254). The crucial fact about this argument is that it runs together adjunction—syntactic movement—with adjuncts—nonargument modifiers—using the former as evidence with respect to an analysis of the latter. Once we separate these two, Speas's datum can be seen to support our theory of adjuncts. Because the "antireconstruction" facts apparently do not obtain only (nor, recall, always) with adjuncts, but also with what at least one analysis takes to be adjunction, it is no surprise that a good theory of adjuncts—ours—does not account for these facts. Lebeaux's analysis of adjuncts automatically accounts for the antireconstruction effect, but it seems that adjunction structures not created by Adjoin Alpha may also give rise to the effect, and so Lebeaux's analysis is undermined. Our theory involving Adjunct Adding does not account for the antireconstruction effect, so it cannot be undermined—and indeed is further confirmed—by showing that the effect can arise from adjunction as well.

I conclude that Speas (1991) does not provide reasons for doubting the theory of adjuncts developed here.

26. Interestingly, the notion Category (either May's or Section 3.1.1's) might be useful with adjuncts, though I have argued it may be otiose with respect to adjunctions. The new node-label pair created with an adjunct could be seen as a member of an already existing Category, should that be useful.

27. Lebeaux (1988: 159-69; 1990: 42-55) suggests coordination as a "default" applying if Adjoin Alpha fails.

28. Adjunctions differently create "nothing new." As they are not (extended) base structures, the MPST does not hold. As argued in Section 3, this might mean that they need not have labelled mothers. And without a label, the new node is syntactically inert, as desired. This is the sense in which, although the node is new, there is really "nothing new." If there is a label, it is, of course, identical to that of the host, hence also "nothing new."

5. Islands as Noncanonical Phrase Structure

1. See, e.g., McCawley (1981) for arguments that restrictive relative clauses are adjunct sisters of N′.

2. I say "very much like" because the FP *strictu sensu* is embedded within the particular Learnability Theory of Wexler & Culicover 1980.

3. See Chapter 4, note 14, for related discussion.

4. This is an alternative to Borer's agreement indexing between INFL and its specifier. It does not suggest that nonthematic—pleonastic—subjects must be VP internal. This is still disallowed by the MPST, given its thematic requirement on VP internal arguments. Within the MPST, adopting the predication analysis has the following consequence. Pleonastic subjects are not in the adjunct structure (10a), hence are not Islands. This seems to be a good result, in that it would be bizzare to require pleonastics—single lexical items—to be Islands, given that the issue cannot, in point of fact, come up. It is of some interest that just those subjects—pleonastics—which cannot have internal syntax, hence cannot be Islands, are the subjects which cannot appear in the Island phrase structure in our MPST-based theory.

5. This quote might be reconciled with the one earlier in the paragraph by saying that subjects are external at S-structure and internal at D-structure. However, the earlier quote says "the *underlying* structure of English . . . " (italics added), so this way out seems blocked.

6. Thus, strictly, the "elsewhere case" label—that on an intermediate link—is still not directly referred to in the rule schemata, as Speas argues it cannot be, because no specific labels are directly referred to.

7. There is an issue with respect to nonbranching domination and the interpretation of PSRs here. Ordinarily, PSRs license mother-daughter configurations; that is, they encode permissable direct domination relations. However, if the MPST has no nonbranching domination, but rather has multiple labelling of nodes, then our MPST PSRs will have to license both direct and reflexive (i.e., self-)domination. Thus, both of the "local" cases of domination are PSR licensed, but the transitive, nonlocal, dominance at a distance is still not PSR licensed. Though nonstandard, I do not find this interpretation of PSRs objectionable. It is another result of trading non-branching direct dominance for multiple labels on nodes.

8. As discussed in Chapter 4, the central problem with Adjunct Adding to any but the Maximal Projection was the following. Adjunct Adding below the Maximal Projection "disappears" in the sense that the added adjunct's mother bears a label indistinguishable from all other labels on the intermediate links in the Projection Chain. Thus, it simply looks like an ill-formed unextended base structure, rather than a well-formed extended base structure. Adjunct Adding to a node bearing the new distinguished intermediate label eludes this problem because the presence of this label already indicates an extended base structure, and the phrase structure rules do not themselves license stacking with respect to nodes with this label. That is, the only way to derive a structure with consecutive nodes bearing the distinguished label would be by means of Adjunct Adding.

9. The grammars of particular languages determine whether such structures are necessary for specific analyses; languages may, presumably, differ with respect to which of the "base extenders" they employ.

10. There is an obvious empirical problem with variation with respect to Island effects, both cross-linguistically and within a language. This is one aspect of a larger issue. Our theory, unlike others, has very few degrees of analytic freedom. This is because we do not derive Islandhood from interacting stipulations, which are themselves subject to relatively unconstrained parametric variation. Thus, the theoretical strength of the proposal—that Islands result from the architecture of the syntax and the requirements of acquisition theory—may also be its empirical undoing. This is a familiar issue, of course.

11. The approach outlined here might be understood as a complete "structuralization" of the idea behind Huang's Condition on Extraction Domains (i) (the formulation is quoted from Kaplan & Zaenen 1989: 23).

(i) No element may be extracted from a domain that is not properly governed.

Kaplan & Zaenen (1989: 23) observe that "[i]ntuitively, the distinction between 'governed' and 'ungoverned' corresponds to the difference between 'argument' and 'nonargument'." They suggest that this indicates "an emerging functional perspective formulated in structural terms." Perhaps so, and perhaps the same could be said for the MPST-based approach; but, I am not sure what the significance of this observation is with respect to either the MPST-based or Huang's approach. I would say that our approach seems an improvement over Huang's theoretically, in that his "Island = not-properly governed" is just another floating stipulation, whereas our "Island = NCPS" is grounded in the MPST, Learnability, and their interaction.

12. The approach to the Core versus Periphery outlined here has the following learning advantage. The only time anything is put into the Periphery is when (1) there is positive evidence for it and (2) it cannot be analyzed within the Core.

13. This still is true under the alternative analysis with adjunction to the lower (Spec, CP) *to whom*. In both cases, I am assuming that the intermediate traces count as "typical potential antecedent-governors" for Relativized Minimality. See note 14 for the case in which they do not so count.

14. This is true if either intermediate traces are not present or do not count as "typical potential antecedent governors." Thus, whether intermediate traces count or not, there is a Relativized Minimality violation; cf. note 13.

15. An obvious question at this point is: what about an example with *whether* such as (i), which are traditionally taken as ill-formed WH-Island violations?

(i) Which election did they wonder whether the Democrats could win?

The contrast with, e.g., (ii) is evidently strong and clear.

(ii) Which election did they claim that the Democrats could win?

On the other hand, for my informants and for me, (i) seems not so bad as the CNP and Relativized Minimality violations in (iiia) and (iiib), respectively.

(iii) a. Which election did they believe the claim that the Democrats could win?
b. Which election did they wonder which party could win?

The problem for a Relativized Minimality approach is that *whether* does not seem to fit into the set of "typical potential" antecedent governors, hence should not be able to intervene in the putative relation between *which election* and its trace. I would, nonetheless, like to suggest that Relativized Minimality is at work in (i). We need to compare (i) not just with (ii) (and (iii)), but also with (iv).

(iv) Which election did they wonder if the Democrats could win?

For both my informants and me, this is much better than either (i) or (iii) (although for some, it is still not as good as (ii)). It is hard to see how the traditional approaches to WH-Islands would account for this.

I suggest that it is exactly the WH-y form of *whether* that is at work. Though it may not be a "typical potential" antecedent governor, it looks like one, unlike *if,* which does not show the Relativized Minimality effect. Whether this means (i) and the like are more in the realm of performance or processing than competence or grammar I cannot say. I can say that this suggestion seems to cast some light on the status of (i) as better than (iii) and worse than (iv) (or (ii)).

Moreover, Kayne (1991: 665-66) gives syntactic arguments that *whether* "is not a lexical complementizer, but a *wh*-phrase," unlike *if,* which he claims is a complementizer. If Kayne is correct, then, of course, *whether* really is a "typical potential" antecedent governor, unlike *if.* More generally, see Stuurman (1991) on *whether* versus *if.*

Conclusion

1. If we join at a label without a new node, then label joining collapses into node joining—or there is a nodeless label, an impos-

sibility. In this way, then, nodes and labels are not exactly on a par in phrase markers: labelless nodes are possible, but nodeless labels are not. So, for there to be a distinct operation based on label joining, there must be a new node.

2. An important issue, which I leave for further research, concerns ADJs and ADVs. Specifically, if only representations of the "argument-of" relation are available in the unextended base and this forms the primitive basis for the Adjunct Adding (the outputs of Adjunct Adding are also available for further applications), then what is the analysis of these elements? Are they placed by Adjunct Adding? If so, how do these represent the "argument-of" relation? If not, how are they placed and when? What options does the theory make available, and how acceptable do we find it/them?

3. See also (MP: 22, 23) for similar statements with respect to the rules in question, with the same unclarity.

4. As noted in Chapter 1, Section 1.2, instantiation is analyzed and a formalization is given, in Chametzky (1987a: 51f.). Although the assumptions of that theory are different from the MPST, the discussion there was intended to be general enough so that much of it could carry over into other sets of assumptions, as I believe it does.

5. Both GT and move α place a PM as a sister to a "targeted" PM (MP: 22-23).

6. Actually, the indeterminacy arises with just mismatches even without adjunction to X′, although there are more indeterminacies when the latter is admitted as well.

7. It should be noted that for Wexler & Culicover (1980) the noncharacteristic structures arise through transformational derivation. This is not true in the MPST-based account.

REFERENCES

Bach, Emmon. 1974. *Syntactic theory.* New York: Holt, Rinehart, & Winston.

Barker, Chris, & Geoffrey Pullum. 1990. "A theory of command relations." *Linguistics & philosophy* 13: 1-34.

Carlson, Greg. 1983. "Marking constituents." In *Linguistic categories,* ed. F. Heny & B. Richards, pp. 69-98. Dordrecht: Reidel.

Carrier, Jill, & Janet Randall. 1992. "The argument structure and syntactic structure of resultatives." *Linguistic inquiry* 23: 173-234.

Chametzky, Robert. 1985. "NPs or arguments." *CLS* 21, no. 1: 26-39.

———. 1987a. "Coordination and the organization of a grammar." Ph.D. dissertation, University of Chicago.

———. 1987b. "Syntax without the S." *ESCOL '86:* 71-85

——— & John Richardson. 1985. "Taking strings seriously." *University of Chicago working papers in linguistics* 1: 1-8.

Chomsky, Noam. 1955/1985. *The logical structure of linguistic theory.* Chicago: University of Chicago Press.

———. 1957. *Syntactic structures.* The Hague: Mouton.

———. 1964. *Current issues in linguistic theory.* The Hague: Mouton

———. 1965. *Aspects of the theory of syntax.* Cambridge, Mass.: MIT Press.

———. 1981. *Lectures on government and binding.* Dordrecht: Foris.

———. 1986a. *Barriers.* Cambridge, Mass.: MIT Press.

———. 1986b. *Knowledge of language.* New York: Praeger.

———. 1993. "A minimalist program for linguistic theory." In *The view from Building 20,* ed. K. Hale & S. Keyser, pp. 1-52. Cambridge, Mass.: MIT Press.

———. 1994. *Bare phrase structure.* MIT occasional papers in linguistics 5. Cambridge, Mass.: MIT Working Papers in Linguistics.

Dowty, David. 1988. "Type raising, functional composition, and nonconstituent conjunction." In *Categorial grammars and natural language structures,* ed. R. Oehrle, E. Bach, & D. Wheeler, pp. 153-98. Dordrecht: Reidel.

Dworkin, Ronald. 1977. *Taking rights seriously.* Cambridge, Mass.: Harvard University Press.

Eilfort, William. 1986. "A possible constraint on discontinuity in syntax." *University of Chicago working papers in linguistics* 2: 19-32.

Emonds, Joseph. 1976. *A transformational approach to English syntax.* Orlando, Fla.: Academic Press.

———. 1987. "The invisible category principle." *Linguistic inquiry* 18: 613-32.

Fodor, Janet. 1983. "Phrase structure parsing and the island constraints." *Lingusitics & philosophy* 6: 163-223.

———. 1989. "Learning the Periphery." In *Learnability and linguistic theory,* ed. R. Matthews & W. Demopoulos, pp. 129-54. Dordrecht: Kluwer.

——— & Charles Jones. 1987. "Connectedness, c-command, and GPSG." *ESCOL '86:* 209-20.

Fukui, Naoki, & Margaret Speas. 1986. "Specifiers and projection." *MIT working papers in linguistics* 8: 128-72.

Gazdar, Gerald. 1980. "A cross-categorial semantics for coordination." *Linguistics & philosophy,* 3: 407-9.

———. 1982. "Phrase structure grammar." In *The nature of syntactic representation,* ed. P. Jacobson & G. Pullum, 131-86. Dordrecht: Reidel.

———, Ewan Klein, Geoffrey Pullum, & Ivan Sag [GKPS]. 1985. *Generalized phrase structure grammar.* Cambridge, Mass.: Harvard University Press.

——— & Geoffrey Pullum. 1981. "Subcategorization, constituent order, and the notion 'Head.'" In *The scope of lexical rules,* ed. M. Moortgat, H. v. D. Hulst, & T. Hoekstra, pp. 107-23. Dordrecht: Foris.

Goldsmith, John. 1985. "A principled exception to the Coordinate Structure Constraint." *CLS* 21, no. 1: 133-43.

Goodall, Grant. 1987. *Parallel structures in syntax.* Cambridge: Cambridge University Press (revision of 1984 UC-San Diego Ph.D. dissertation).

Grimshaw, Jane. 1990. *Argument structure.* Cambridge, Mass.: MIT Press.

Hale, Kenneth. 1981. "On the position of Warlpiri in a typology of the base." *IULC.*

———. 1983. "Warlpiri and the grammar of non-configurational languages." *NLLT* 1: 5-47.

Heny, F. 1979. "Review of N. Chomsky, *The logical structure of linguistic theory. Synthese* 40, 317-52.

Higginbotham, James. 1983. "A Note on phrase-markers." *Revue Quebecoise de linguistique* 13: 147-65.

———. 1985. "On semantics." *Linguistic inquiry* 16: 547-93.

———. N.d. "Phrase markers." Unpublished.

———. 1989. "Elucidations of meaning." *Linguistics & philosophy* 12: 465-87.

Hornstein, Norbert. 1985-86. "Restructuring and interpretation in a T-model." *The linguistic review* 5: 301-34.

———. 1987. "Levels of meaning." In *Modularity in knowledge representation and natural-language understanding,* ed. J. Garfield, pp. 133-50. Cambridge, Mass.: MIT Press.

Huck, Geoffrey. 1985. "Exclusivity and discontinuity in phrase structure grammar." *WCCFL* 4: 92-98.

Hull, David. 1988. *Science as a Process.* Chicago: University of Chicago Press.

———. 1989. *The Metaphysics of Evolution.* Albany: State University of New York Press.

Kaplan, Ronald, & Annie Zaenen. 1989. "Long-distance dependencies, constituent structure, and functional uncertainty. In *Alternative conceptions of phrase structure,* ed. M. Baltin & A. Kroch, pp. 17-42. Chicago: University of Chicago Press.

Kayne, Richard. 1981. "Unambiguous paths." Reprinted in R. Kayne *Connectedness and Binary Branching,* pp. 129-63. Dordrecht: Foris, 1984.

———. 1991. "Romance clitics, verb movement, and PRO." *Linguistic inquiry* 22: 647-86.

———. 1994. *The antisymmetry of syntax.* Cambridge, Mass.: MIT Press.

Keenan, Edward, & Leonard Faltz. 1985. *Boolean semantics for natural language.* Dordrecht: D. Reidel.

Kornai, Andras, & Geoffrey Pullum. 1990. "The X-bar theory of phrase structure." *Language* 66: 24-50.

Kupin, Joseph. 1978. "A motivated alternative to phrase markers." *Linguistic inquiry* 9: 303-8.

Kuroda, S.-Y. 1988. "Whether we agree or not." *Linguisticae investigones* 12: 1-47.

Lakoff, George. 1986. "Frame semantic control of the Coordinate Structure Constraint." *CLS* 22, no. 2: 152-67.

Langacker, Ronald. 1969. "On pronominalization and the chain of command." In ed. D. Reibel & S. Schane, *Modern studies in English,* pp. 160-86. Englewood Cliffs N.J.: Prentice-Hall.

Larson, Richard. 1985a. "On the syntax of disjunction scope." *NLLT* 3: 217-64.

———. 1985b. "Bare-NP adverbs." *Linguistic inquiry* 16: 595-621.

Lasnik, Howard, & Joseph Kupin. 1977. "A restrictive theory of transformational grammar." *Theoretical linguistics* 4: 173-96.

Lebeaux, David. 1988. "Language acquisition and the form of the grammar." Ph.D. dissertation, University of Massachusetts, Amherst. Amherst: GLSA.

———. 1990. "The grammatical nature of the acquisition sequence: adjoin-alpha and the formation of relative clauses. In *Language processing and langauge acquisition,* ed. L. Frazier & D. de Villiers, pp. 13-82. Dordrecht: Kluwer.

Manzini, Rita. 1992. *Locality.* Cambridge, Mass.: MIT Press.

May, Robert. 1985. *Logical form.* Cambridge, Mass.: MIT Press.

———. 1989. "Bound variable anaphora." In *Mental representations,* ed. R. Kempson, pp. 85-104. Cambridge: Cambridge University Press.

McCawley, James. 1968. "Concerning the base component of a transformational grammar." *Foundations of language* 4: 243-69.

———. 1981. "The syntax and semantics of English relative clauses." *Lingua* 53: 99-149.

———. 1982. "Parentheticals and discontinuous constituent structure." *Linguistic inquiry* 13: 91-106.

———. 1983. "The syntax of some English adverbs." *CLS* 19: 263-82.

———. 1988. *The syntactic phenomena of English.* Chicago: University of Chicago Press.

———. 1988a. Adverbial NPs. *Language* 64: 583-90.

Ojeda, Almerindo, 1987. "Discontinuity, multidominance, and unbounded dependency in generalized phrase structure grammar." In *Syntax & semantics 20: discontinuous constituency,* ed. G. Huck & A. Ojeda, pp. 257-82. Orlando, Fla.: Academic Press.

Partee, Barbara & Mats Rooth. 1983. "Generalized conjunction and type ambiguity." In *Meaning, use, and interpretation of language,* ed. R. Bauerle, C. Schwarze, & A. v. Stechow, pp. 361-83. Berlin: de Gruyter.

Partee, Barbara, Alice ter Meulen, & Robert Wall. 1990. *Mathematical methods in linguistics.* Dordrecht: Kluwer.

Pesetsky, David. 1982. "Paths and categories." Ph.D. dissertation, MIT.

Platnick, Norman. 1977. "Cladograms, phylogenetic trees, and hypothesis testing." *Systematic zoology* 26: 438-42.

———. 1979. "Philosophy and the transformation of cladistics." *Systematic zoology* 28: 537-46.

——— & H. Cameron. 1977. "Cladistic methods in textual, linguistic, and phylogenetic analysis." *Systematic zoology* 26: 380-85.

Pullum, Geoffrey. 1985. "Assuming some version of the X-bar theory." *CLS* 21, no. 1: 323-53.

———. 1986. On the relations of IDC-command and government. *WCCFL 5*, 192-206.

———. 1989. "Formal linguistics meets the boojum." *NLLT* 7: 137-43.

Reinhart, Tanya. 1981. "Definite NP anaphora and C-command domains." *Linguistic inquiry* 12, 605-36.

———. 1983. *Anaphora and semantic interpretation.* Chicago: University of Chicago Press.

Richardson, John. 1982. "Constituency and sublexical syntax." *CLS* 18: 466-76.

——— & Robert Chametzky. 1985. "A string based reformulation of C-command." *NELS* 15: 332-61 (corrected version available from the authors).

van Riemsdijk, Henk, & Edwin Williams. 1981. "NP structure." *The linguistic review* 1: 171-217.

———. 1986. *Introduction to the theory of grammar.* Cambridge, Mass.: MIT Press.

Rizzi, Luigi. 1990. *Relativized minimality.* Cambridge, Mass.: MIT Press.

Ross, John. 1967. "Constraints on variables in syntax." Ph.D. dissertation, MIT. Published as *Infinite syntax!* (Hillsdale, N.J.: Erlbaum, 1986).

Rothstein, Susan. 1985. "The syntactic forms of predication." Ph.D. dissertation, MIT. Distributed by IULC.

Sadock, Jerrold. 1991. *Autolexical syntax.* Chicago: University of Chicago Press.

——— & Arnold Zwicky. 1985. "Speech act distinctions in syntax." In *Language typology and syntactic description,* volume 1. *Clause structure,* ed. T. Shopen, pp. 155-96. Cambridge: Cambridge University Press.

Sag, Ivan, Gerald Gazdar, Thomas Wasow, & Steven Weisler [SGWW]. 1985. "Coordination and how to distinguish categories." *NLLT* 3: 117-71.

Sampson, Geoffrey. 1980. *Schools of linguistics.* London: Hutchinson.

Simon, Herbert. 1962. "The architecture of complexity." Reprinted in H. Simon *The sciences of the artificial,* 2d ed., pp. 84-118. Cambridge, Mass.: MIT Press, [1981].

Sober. Elliot. 1975. *Simplicity.* Oxford: Oxford University Press.

———. 1988. *Reconstructing the past.* Cambridge, Mass.: MIT Press.

Speas, Margaret. 1990. *Phrase structure in natural language.* Dordrecht: Kluwer.

———. 1991. "Generalized transformations and the D-structure position of adjuncts." In *Syntax & semantics 25: perspectives on phrase structure: heads and licensing,* ed. S. Rothstein, pp. 241-57. Orlando, Fla.: Academic Press.

Sportiche, Dominique. 1988. "A theory of floating quantifiers and its corollaries for constituent structure." *Linguistic inquiry* 19: 425-50.

Stabler, Edward. 1992. "Implementing Government Binding theories." In *Formal grammar: theory and implementation,* ed. R. Levine, pp. 243-75. New York: Oxford University Press.

Steedman, Mark. 1989. "Constituency and coordination in a combinatory grammar." In *Alternative conceptions of phrase structure,* ed. M. Baltin & A. Kroch, pp. 201-31. Chicago: University of Chicago Press.

Stowell, Timothy. 1981. "Origins of phrase structure." Ph.D. dissertation, MIT.

———. 1982. "A formal theory of configurational phenomena." *NELS* 12: 235-57.

Stuurman, Frits. 1985. *Phrase structure theory in generative grammar.* Dordrecht: Foris.

———. 1991. "If and whether: questions and conditions." *Lingua* 83: 1-42.

Weisler, Steven. 1980. "The syntax of that-less relatives." *Linguistic inquiry* 11: 624-31.

Wexler, Kenneth, & Peter Culicover. 1980. *Formal principles of language acquisition.* Cambridge, Mass.: MIT Press.

Williams, Edwin. 1981. "Transformationless grammar." *Linguistic inquiry* 12: 645-53.

———. 1986. "A reassignment of the functions of LF." *Linguistic inquiry* 17: 265–99.

———. 1994. *Thematic structure in syntax.* Cambridge, Mass.: MIT Press.

Yngve, Victor. 1960. "A model and a hypothesis for language structure." *Proceedings of the American Philosophical Society* 104: 444–66.

SUBJECT INDEX

AUTHOR INDEX